Bermuda's Architectural Heritage

Bermuda's Architectural Heritage

St. George's

Volume Two of the Historic Buildings Book Project
Bermuda National Trust
1998

This book was set by Editorial Consulting Services, St. George's, Bermuda, and it was printed and bound by Courier Companies, Inc., Westford, MA.

©1998 Bermuda National Trust
PO Box HM 61
Hamilton HM AX
BERMUDA
tel 441 236 6483
fax 441 236 0617

Printed in the United States of America

10   9   8   7   6   5   4   3   2   1

ISBN   **0-969-3939-7-0 (paper)**
                  0-969-3939-4-6 (cloth)

Cover illustration
The Square, St. George's, Bermudas, Thomas Driver, 1823
from the Fay and Geoffrey Elliott Collection, Bermuda Archives, Hamilton, Bermuda

This book is dedicated to Margie Lloyd. Without her extraordinary
dedication to the preservation and recording of Bermuda's architecture,
neither this book nor the Architectural Heritage series
would ever have come into being.

Acknowledgements

First and foremost, I would like to thank my dedicated team of researchers. Jean Jones spent hours extracting more than 100 early wills. Cherie Neville-Gliddon, Jackie Meggs and Jennifer Lapsley pored over dozens of volumes of deeds extracting information about St. George's properties. Goldie McPhee read through several years of 1840s issues of *The Royal Gazette* capturing the flavour of military life at mid-century. Michelle Collier helped to sort out frustratingly difficult-to-trace properties in St. David's. Robin Judah's excellent contemporary photographs capture the essential elements of St. George's houses and make this book far more understandable. In the *Devonshire* volume, Andrew Trimingham set the high standard to which I aspired in this successor; his contagious passion and enthusiasm for Bermudian architecture was inspiring. This book greatly benefitted from the editing skills of David L. White, who transformed my American prose into the Queen's English. John Adams, Karla Hayward and the staff of the Bermuda Archives have been consistently helpful and pointed me in the direction of much new material. The book looks as elegant as it does because of the labours of Tracy Astwood.

I am grateful to Dr. Marley Brown III for introducing me to Bermuda and for his continued support of my work. I thank Ed Chapell for teaching me how to better "read" old houses. I very much appreciate Dr. Edward Harris' commitment to preserving Bermuda's architectural heritage and largely depended upon his scholarship in my discussion of St. George's forts. Our research was helped by the many St. George's property owners who generously shared their deeds with us: the two Janet Outerbridges, Rita Rothwell, Donna Bell, Nea Stack, Clyde Basden, Ross Smith, Clifford Rowe, Robert Trew, Gavin and Sylvia Shorto, Frederick Dowling, Delaey Robinson, Heman and Anthony Richardson, Lucinda O'Brien, William Frith, Elystan Haycock, Dr. William (Peter) Outerbridge, Dr. Raymond Spurling, Senator Noela Haycock, Leonard Furbert, Dixon Spurling, Elizabeth Dowling, Sandy and Hugh Lowenstein, Steven Masters, Judy Perry, Lois Perinchief, the Whayman family, the Wor. Henry Hayward and the Corporation of St. George's, the White Horse Syndicate, the Bank of Bermuda, TESS Ltd., the Bank of N. T. Butterfield and the Bermuda Government. For their intellectual and practical support, my thanks go to: Jack Arnell, G. Daniel Blagg, Terry Bowers, Peter Clark, Stephen Copeland, Robert Duffy, Fay and Geoffrey Elliott, Vanese Flood, Dace Ground, Dr. and Mrs. Hollis Hallett, Joseph and Patricia Jarvis, Alison Outerbridge, Amanda Outerbridge, Ann Spurling and the St. George's Historical Society, David Zuill and William Zuill — you know what you did. I thank the many archaeologists and volunteers with whom I have dug over the past six years, who helped to unearth St. George's history. For her careful editing and for putting up with my long hours and cluttered study, I am immensely grateful to my wife, Anna.

Michael Jarvis
October 1997

Contributors

Writer and Researcher:	Michael Jarvis
Captions and Sidebars:	Andrew Trimingham
Project Managers:	Margie Lloyd
	Dace McCoy Ground
Photographer:	Robin Judah
Archival Photography:	Michael Jarvis
	Ann Spurling
Sidebar Illustrations:	Steven Conway
Maps:	Barbara Finsness
Computer Graphics:	Heather Harvey
Editor:	David L. White, OBE
Design and Layout:	Tracy Astwood
Layout Consultant:	Charles Barclay
Historic Consultation:	William S. Zuill, MBE
	Connie Dey
Indexer:	Sheck Cho

Research Assistance:	Margie Lloyd
	Jean Jones
	Cherie Neville-Glidden
	Jackie Meggs
	Jennifer Lapsley
	Goldie McPhee
	Cathe Bedard
	Michelle Collier
	Peggy Berk

Our thanks to Bacardi International Limited for their generous sponsorship of this series, and especially for the support they have given for this volume.

Contents

Foreword

It was just over ten years ago that I first heard of the Town of St. George. My informant was Dr. Edward Harris, Director of the Bermuda Maritime Museum, who appeared to be truly shocked at my lack of knowledge of this historic original capital of Bermuda. He described St. George's to me during his first visit to Williamsburg in the spring of 1987, the same occasion when we discussed the possibility of a dig at the Henry Tucker House. Not long after his visit I mentioned my interest in the Tucker House excavation to a Williamsburg colleague familiar with the island. He explained that I would very likely be disappointed because "Bermuda has very little soil to speak of".

Despite this warning I persisted in my plans and anticipated my first field season. I did my best to imagine what St. George's must be like. As we all do about places unknown to us except through the imagination, I formed a picture of St. George's but when I first set eyes on the town that summer, I immediately realised how much my imagination had let me down. My mental image of St. George's had been a composite of the many "colonial" towns I had known either as a visitor or through the eyes of the archaeologist; towns such as Portsmouth, New Hampshire, Newport, Rhode Island, Annapolis, Maryland, Charleston, South Carolina, and of course, Williamsburg, Virginia.

I had some vague sense of a well-preserved place with narrow lanes and a lot of red brick. As it turned out, the first part of my image was correct, the latter was not. St. George's looked nothing like any colonial town in North America that I knew, and it turned out to have a history and architectural character unmatched by these other places. Thankfully, it also turned out to have soil after all, soil which has proven to be every bit as valuable as any deposit excavated in Jamestown or Williamsburg, or any other colonial-period settlement in North America. There is a very important reason for this. As the reader will learn from this book, St. George's is the oldest, continuously occupied settlement within the English New World, having begun its life as Bermuda's capital in 1612. It has also been, until the publication of this extraordinary guide to the architecture of the Parish by the Bermuda National Trust, one of the least understood and appreciated early English towns in the New World.

Some places where the English settled early in the 17th century have enjoyed a long-standing antiquarian interest in the built environment. Individual acts of building preservation have been documented as early as the late 17th century in Salem and Boston. By the beginning of this century, preservationist organisations were active in New England and Virginia, and the 1920s and 1930s witnessed serious efforts to save or restore the important buildings of Charleston, Annapolis, and other former capitals of Britain's North American colonies. In Virginia's colonial capital, Williamsburg, restoration architects recruited by John D. Rockefeller Jr. began reconstructing and refurbishing the town beginning in the late 1920s.

St. George's never experienced such conscious or comprehensive actions of preservation as these other early English New World towns but important efforts were made beginning in the 1930s to ensure that historically significant buildings in the town would be saved. The Bermuda Historical Monuments Trust was established in 1937 by Hereward Watlington and others and began soon thereafter to acquire buildings and artifacts, including such significant St. George's buildings as the President Henry Tucker House, the Old Rectory, Bridge House and the Globe Hotel. In 1950, an act of Bermuda's Parliamant established the St. George's Preservation Authority in recognition of the architectural importance of the town.

These steps certainly helped to maintain the historic character of St. George's, but important, too, is the fact that the town has largely avoided the excesses of gentrification, a process of redevelopment that often results in the preservation of historic facades at the expense of community. What makes for much of the charm of St. George's is the absence of the artificial and studied appearance of carefully manicured historic district architecture. But the uniqueness of St. George's as an historic treasure cannot be assured without some measure of vigilance and commitment to a preservation ethic on the part of the Corporation and the town's residents.

This thoroughly researched and beautifully illustrated review of the buildings and people of the Parish of St. George's comes at a most opportune time. Plans are now being prepared and decisions are being made that will essentially determine what the Town of St. George will look and feel like in the years to come. All of us who care about this special place can take comfort in the knowledge that, after reading this second volume in the Bermuda National Trust's Historic Buildings Book Project, there should be no question in anyone's mind about the international significance of St. George's architectural heritage and its largely untapped archaeological potential. More important, this book comes just when it is needed to realise the great promise of the town for a carefully crafted programme of heritage and cultural tourism. Following through on this promise will require cooperation among many organisations and individuals, and a sustained dedication to balancing economic development with the stewardship of St. George's unique physical heritage. Used appropriately, this impressive volume can guide the way.

Dr. Marley Brown III
Colonial Williamsburg
October 1997

Introduction

This volume is the second in the Bermuda National Trust's Architectural Heritage series. It covers the Town and Parish of St. George's. Because of the unique nature of St. George's we believe that it will be the longest and most comprehensive.

The first book, about Devonshire, took three years from start to finish. At that rate the parishes would not have been completed until far into the next millenium, so we looked for ways of accelerating the process. We were extremely fortunate that Michael Jarvis, a doctoral candidate at the College of William and Mary in Virginia, was available to research and write this book.

Michael first became interested in St. George's in 1991 when he visited Bermuda on an archaeological expedition with the Colonial Williamsburg Foundation, and has been absorbing information about the town and parish, people and property ever since. So he now has an unrivalled knowledge of St. George's. We realised that if we did not act quickly he would be a fully fledged Doctor of History, probably with an academic position, and might never be available to the Trust. With the help of our sponsors, Bacardi International Limited, the Trust employed him during the summer of 1996 to research this book and during the spring and early summer of 1997 to write it. Much of the rest of the project was carried out by volunteers, as all the work on the Devonshire volume had been. A number of research assistants helped to extract information from the numerous available documents, Robin Judah took a wonderful series of photographs, Andrew Trimingham wrote the captions and many of the sidebars, David L. White edited, and many others, listed in the credits, helped.

We have tried to produce a book which fulfills many functions, from being of interest to the most casual visitor to being a detailed reference book for the serious historian. One of the primary purposes of the series is to foster appreciation of Bermuda's wonderful architectural heritage. So we have tried to ensure that discussion of architectural features in this volume is not lost among the historical information. Inevitably we have had to make compromises. The most obvious is the lack of detailed foot or source notes. The author's notes would have produced two heavy tomes, so we decided that we could not publish them at this time. Details about specific properties will be available on request from the Bermuda National Trust (at minimum cost) and, eventually, from the Bermuda Archives and other academic establishments. A Note on Research (see Appendices) explains the method of research and gives general sources.

One aspect of the book may puzzle the Bermudian reader. Some building names used in the text are unfamiliar. This is because many St. George's buildings have never had a name, being either known by the name of the business occupying them at the time, or the current owner or occupier. But owners and occupiers change, and businesses come and go. So rather than give properties what may be ephemeral titles, we have given them the name of the original builder or the earliest owner we can identify. We hope that these "old names" will come to be accepted.

The third volume in the series will be about Somerset: the basic research for it has been done, and the photographs have been taken. A group of researchers is now working under Linda Abend and Diana Chudleigh on a combined Hamilton Parish and Smith's volume, and the plan is that one about Paget will follow thereafter.

Margaret Lloyd
October 1997

How To Use This Book

In this book each chapter has a theme, and within the theme discussion of the buildings tends to be in date order. The text therefore jumps from one part of St. George's to another, rather than following the pattern of a simple guide book where the reader can walk up the street, book in hand, reading about each building in turn. To help the reader make the best use of this book we have therefore provided an index, appendices with lists of buildings, and maps.

THE CENTRAL AREA OF ST. GEORGE'S
Appendix II is a complete list of all the buildings within the 1708 town boundary. It also includes some just outside the town boundary which are mentioned in the text and are on the foldout map of the central area. The list gives for each building the street address, the name of the building, current owner or occupier and a date, or range of dates.

We believe a reader interested in a particular building on this map will probably fall into one of three categories.

1) The reader knows the name and location of a building and wants to learn more about it:
Look in the index. This will lead to all the information in the book about the building (including text, photographs and their captions, sidebars and appendices).

2) The reader knows the name of a building (perhaps from reading the book) and wants to go and see it:
First look in Appendix II to get the street address of the building. Then look at the foldout map, find the street and follow the map. All street numbers are marked on the map. Occasionally it may be difficult to tell which number belongs to which street, but this problem is caused by the layout of St. George's and nothing can be done except to use common sense and see whether the description fits the site.

3) The reader, standing in a street and looking at a building, wants to know about that building:
First look for a sign giving the name of the building, or ask a passer-by its name. If unsuccessful, try to establish the street address from the foldout map. Then look in Appendix II for that street address: the name of the building is given in the same entry. Once the name of the building is known the index can be consulted.

THE REST OF ST. GEORGE'S ISLAND, SMITH'S ISLAND AND ST. DAVID'S ISLAND
Appendix III lists the buildings on St. George's Island (other than those listed in Appendix II), Smith's Island and St. David's Island of which details (often with pictures or photographs) are included in the book. The map to use in conjunction with this list is on the reverse side of the foldout map. It is copied from one of the maps drawn by Lieutenant Savage in 1898, and all the buildings in Appendices II and III are marked on it, those built after 1898 having been added.

It has not been possible to mark on the maps all the fortifications mentioned in the text and the reader is recommended to refer to "Bermuda Forts, 1612-1957", by Dr. Edward C. Harris, pub. 1997. This is a comprehensive treatment of Bermuda's forts by the acknowledged expert.

READERS ARE ASKED TO RESPECT THE PRIVACY OF OWNERS AND OCCUPIERS AT ALL TIMES

CHAPTER ONE

St. George's: Town and Parish
An Historical Overview from 1609-1997

An unusual pencil sketch of St. George's drawn in about 1853 by Mary Letitia Houghton Mondelet. An exaggerated Fort George looms above the town. St. David's, Castle Harbour and parts of Tucker's Town can be seen in the background. (Courtesy St. George's Historical Society Collection: Bermuda Archives, Hamilton, Bermuda.)

Founded in 1612, the Town of St. George has the distinction of being the oldest inhabited English settlement and the second permanent town founded by English colonists in the New World. Jamestown, Virginia, was settled five years earlier, but four devastating fires, economic decline and the ravages of several wars led to its abandonment by the end of the 17th century.

Today Jamestown exists only as an archaeological site maintained by the US National Park Service, while St. George's is a living town, after nearly 400 years of continuous occupation. Since its founding the town has changed with the times, thriving and expanding in periods of prosperity and languishing in times of want. Frontier town, colonial capital, commercial cen-

tre, international entrepôt, military outpost, naval base, St. George's has played many roles in its long history. The St. George's of today resembles a patchwork quilt of buildings, streets, parks, squares and monuments, reflecting its long and varied past and the changing roles it has played in Bermuda's history.

This book will help readers to learn and appreciate the history of St. George's Town and Parish through their buildings and architecture.

Bermuda's colonisation and the beginning of St. George's history are one and the same. Even before the arrival of the first permanent settlers, St. George's Island was the temporary home of Sir George Somers, Sir Thomas Gates and other

survivors of the wreck of the *Sea Venture*. Their sojourn led to the colonisation of Bermuda. In June of 1609 the *Sea Venture* left Plymouth, England, as the flagship of a fleet of nine vessels bound for the struggling new colony of Virginia, loaded with settlers and supplies. En route, the fleet was struck by a hurricane. It sank one ship and badly damaged the *Sea Venture* which started to leak dangerously. During the tempest Admiral Sir George Somers was in command of the battered ship while Sir Thomas Gates oversaw the pumping and bailing. Just when all seemed lost, Somers sighted Bermuda and was able to navigate within half a mile of the shore of St. George's. The *Sea Venture* caught between two reefs. She stayed afloat for four days, allowing the crew to sal-

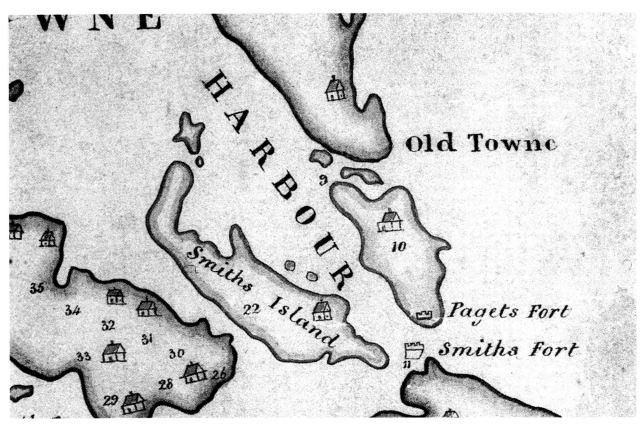

Detail from Gabriel Mathias' 1739 copy of Richard Norwood's 1663 map marking the "Old Towne" at the southeast tip of St. George's Island. ("Map of Summer Islands called Bermudas", Bermuda Archives Collection, Hamilton, Bermuda.)

vage most of her food, rigging, sails and timber. On July 28 the crew and all 150 passengers stepped ashore at St. Catherine's Bay on St. George's Island and gave thanks for their miraculous rescue from the sea.

For the next ten months, St. George's Island was home to most of the ship's company. Within days, they set to work building houses, which they thatched with palmetto leaves. In August, Sir George Somers "squared" a garden near Buildings Bay in which he planted muskmelons, peas, onions, radishes, lettuce and English kitchen herbs. The Admiral was not much of a gardener. In the heat of the summer the plants sprouted within ten days, but they "came to no proof nor thrived". Governor Gates' garden fared little better. He planted vines, lemons, oranges, sugar cane and other plants which had been intended for Virginia, but the island's wild hogs broke through his fence and rooted them up.

The exact location of the *Sea Venture* camp is unknown. One theory is that it was located where the

Town of St. George was later established. Bermuda's first Governor, Richard Moore, might have made use of an already cleared site for his capital. Alternatively, the castaways' settlement could have been situated at the easternmost tip of St. George's Island. Richard Norwood's 1663 survey labels this area "Old Towne", although there were then no buildings left standing on the site.

The settlers lived on the wild hogs and fish abundant on the island. They ate the hearts of palmetto trees which, when roasted, tasted like fried melons or, when stewed, like cabbages. They also ate prickly pears, both raw and baked, and drank a concoction of boiled cedar berries which was allowed to ferment for a few days. The "common people", or passengers, dug wells and pits around the camp to obtain water. Probably several were continually employed by Gates to boil seawater to produce salt for preserving pork and fish for the ocean voyage to Virginia.

In May 1610, Sir Thomas Gates' replacement vessel, the *Deliverance*,

was completed, as was the smaller *Patience,* perhaps built on the shores of the future Hamilton Parish. The passengers reluctantly left the paradise they had found for a far less secure future in Virginia. The company left behind seven graves and two deserters, Christopher Carter and Robert Waters, who maintained England's claim to this new land. After a short journey the *Sea Venture's* survivors reached Virginia, a year overdue.

Sir George Somers returned to Bermuda in the *Patience* in November 1610 to obtain food for the starving Virginia colony, and found the two deserters "alive and lusty". Tragedy struck and Somers died suddenly on St. George's Island, apparently after eating spoiled meat. His nephew Matthew buried the Admiral's heart and entrails at a site traditionally placed in present day Somers Garden. He secretly conveyed the rest of the body back to England.

Christopher Carter was joined by Edward Chard and Edward Waters before the *Patience* departed, and for the next two years they cleared land,

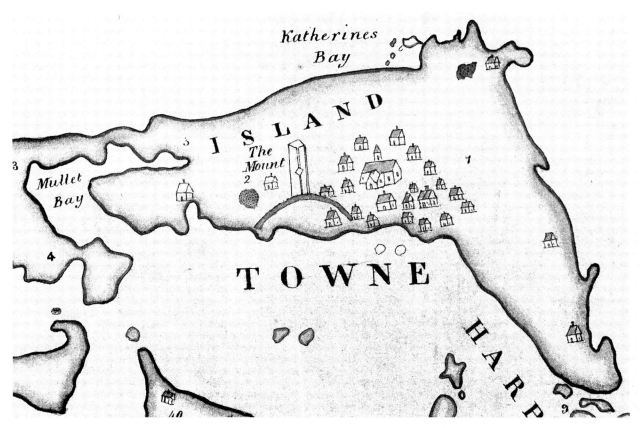

Detail from Gabriel Mathias' 1739 copy of Richard Norwood's 1663 map showing the Town of St. George. ("Map of Summer Islands called Bermudas", Bermuda Archives Collection, Hamilton, Bermuda.)

erected houses and planted a variety of crops.

The permanent settlement of St. George's began in August 1612 with the arrival of the *Plough*, bearing a governor, a minister, and 60 adventurous souls. In the next three years nearly 600 more would follow, and they would all live on St. George's Island.

Bermuda's first Governor, Richard Moore, founded the Town of St. George when, according to Governor Nathaniel Butler's account, he put the settlers to work building "cabbins of Palmitoe leaves . . . in that valley wher nowe standes the prime town of the ilands". Moore built a palmetto thatched church, a house for himself, a wharf and "a certaine slope bridge... for the easie shoreinges of goodes", a watchtower called The Mount on Fort George Hill, and laid the foundations for several forts to guard the entrances to St. George's and Castle Harbours (see chapter 2).

The Parade, perhaps modelled on the "bawn-and-green" layout of early 17th century Irish plantations, was at the heart of Moore's town; it remains so four centuries later, now called the King's Square or Market Square. When Richard Moore departed at the end of his three year term, St. George's was heavily populated and the colony was well on its way towards stability and permanence.

In 1615 the Somers Island Company took over the administration of the colony from the Virginia Company which had first sponsored Moore's efforts. The next two Governors, Daniel Tucker and Nathaniel Butler, effected changes which had a lasting impact on both the Town of St. George and the colony as a whole.

Soon after Governor Daniel Tucker's arrival in May 1616, the Islands of Bermuda were surveyed and divided between Company lands and private 25-acre shares allotted for development by individual investors. St. George's Parish, along with a number of small islands, was designated public land, set aside for the use of the Somers Island Company and its officers on the island, while the other eight tribes, or parishes, became private property. The governor tried to establish a new town near the mouth of Cas-

tle Harbour which he vaingloriously called Tucker's Town after himself, but the land was "verie meene" and few made the move from St. George's. By 1617, there were only two or three cottages of leaves at Tucker's Town, occupied by the soldiers manning Castle Island.

Thus from the beginning, land tenure and the development of St. George's differed from the rest of Bermuda. By 1616 most of St. George's Island had been deforested by settlers. This made it unsuitable for the tobacco which was increasingly being grown in Bermuda. After the private shares were surveyed, most colonists flocked to the main island and the population of the town dwindled to 150 public servants, individuals indentured to the Somers Island Company for a number of years, who happened to include the "choysest worckmen" in the colony.

Tucker put these men under the martial law he had known in Virginia, requiring them to meet at the Town Wharf in St. George's each morning at dawn and work until 9 am and then gather again at 3 pm and labour until

Captain John Smith's 1624 drawing of Warwick Fort. (Reproduced from the original engraving by The Island Press in 1983.)

sunset. They were paid in hog money which was only redeemable in the Company store.

Under Tucker's direction, they built a palisade across St. George's Island to enclose cattle sent to Bermuda by the Company and the Earl of Warwick and dug an artificial cattle pond in what is now Somers Garden. The Company servants also built several timber framed houses in the town, one of which was set aside for the minister.

When a number of blacks and Caribbean Indians were brought to Bermuda, Tucker had them plant sugar cane imported from the West Indies, but the lack of windbreaks on the deforested island made cultivation impossible. Tucker also mounted a number of cannon at the Town Wharf, Warwick Fort, The Mount and at other forts.

Tucker's successor, Nathaniel Butler (1619-1622), was Bermuda's most ambitious governor yet and he added several landmarks to St. George's which are still with us today. Butler was the principal architect of Bermuda's ring of forts, including the defensive complex on Castle Island. He completed a substantial timber framed church on the site of modern day St. Peter's Church and built the State House for the use of the island's courts and General Assembly (see chapters 2 and 3).

He also built a corn house to store grain, a shallop house for Company boats, a stout timber framed prison for criminals and a cedar framed storehouse on Ducking Stool Island just across from the Town Wharf.

Early in 1622 he erected a stone house in the town which, with the State House, he hoped might inspire the colonists to build in stone and thus spare the island's limited supply of timber. But his example was ignored and for the next 60 years almost all vernacular architecture used timber framing techniques.

Butler divided the public land on St. George's and St. David's Islands into shares, the use of which was given to the colony's governor, secretary, provost marshal, sheriff, commanders of the forts and the minister serving the capital. The western half of St. David's Island was partitioned into 40 lots of five acres each and they were awarded to the private investors of Hamilton Parish to compensate for the generally poor quality of their land for growing tobacco. When Butler left

Bermuda in 1622 the colony was flourishing and the Town of St. George could boast a population of perhaps 300 and a large number of public and private buildings.

After this auspicious beginning, the colony settled down to growing tobacco for export. Although there were villages at Port Royal and The Flatts, the Town of St. George was the principal settlement and the site of all official business. The governor, secretary and provost marshal all lived in the town, and the island's courts and Assembly met there as well. St. George's was also the site of the colony's sole prison.

In addition to its political role as capital, the town served as the main entrepôt for the colony. In November and December each year, planters brought their tobacco crop to the town for inspection and transhipment to England aboard the Somers Island Company's magazine ship which anchored in St. George's or Castle Harbour. During this time of "general division", merchants sold newly arrived goods from London, and planters settled the various debts and credits they had made during the year.

When needed, the governor convened the Assembly to raise taxes and pass new laws for better regulating the colony. During the general division, St. George's bustled with activity, and a large portion of Bermuda's population gathered there.

The rest of the year St. George's was little more than a sleepy village. Few vessels called at Bermuda during the Somers Island Company period because the London investors forbade unlicensed vessels to trade with the colony. Many of the town's 17th century inhabitants farmed the surrounding public lands, while others, chiefly craftsmen, laboured in their workshops to meet the domestic needs of planters living in the upper parishes.

At the end of the Somers Island Company period, St. George's had, according to the Governor, about 60 houses built of timber, averaging about three rooms. Few were of two storeys. Some were roofed with stone, some with wood, and some were thatched with palmetto leaves. In size, the town was tiny. A 1696 survey revealed the town's area to be 27½ acres, just

Detail from Gabriel Mathias' 1739 copy of Richard Norwood's 1663 map showing St. David's Island. ("Map of Summer Islands called Bermudas", Bermuda Archives Collection, Hamilton, Bermuda.)

slightly larger than one Company share.

The dissolution of the Somers Island Company in 1684 prompted great change in Bermuda. Administration of the colony passed to the Crown, which was too busy looking after Bermuda's larger and more prosperous neighbours to devote much attention to the tiny island. With the ban on trade and shipbuilding lifted, Bermudians rapidly abandoned the paltry profits of growing tobacco and took to the seas in search of commerce and plunder. For the next century the colony's economy centred on the cedar trees so vital to shipbuilding, and constructing and operating the fast and nimble sloops that made Bermuda internationally famous. St. George's changed dramatically between 1680 and 1720 as a result of this economic shift.

Aside from the State House, there is nothing left of the Company period in the town other than archaeological sites. The high demand for cedar timber, and concerns about fire, prompted the abandonment of timber framing in favour of building in stone.

Beginning in 1693, land in the town was permanently granted to its occupants, provided they replaced their wooden houses with stone ones. Free land was given to anyone willing

to erect a stone structure within a year or two of taking possession. These early 18th century grants shaped the lots and streets of the St. George's we know today, and literally set in stone the early haphazard arrangement of the 17th century town.

Governor Benjamin Bennett should be remembered as the father of St. George's. During his terms in office (1701-13, 1715-22) he issued at least 113 grants "for the Encouragement of Building and Englargeing the Towne of St. Georges". With secure legal title to their lots, St. Georgians invested their profits from trade and industry in building stone houses befitting their wealth and social status.

Water lots were among the first to be claimed. After commerce shifted from the decks of London ships to the holds of Bermudian sloops, there was a new urgent need for docking and storage facilities. This need was acutely felt in St. George's, for in the 1680s and 1690s all vessels were required to load and unload their cargo exclusively in the capital or Castle Harbour. The narrow strip of coastline on the south side of Water Street became crowded with the wharves and storehouses of Bermuda's first generation of entrepreneurial ships' captains. The old colonial capital grew into a port town of some sophistication, attract-

ing merchants, mariners and a host of craftsmen suited to the shipbuilding and ship repair industries. The town's taverns supplemented their quarterly assize booms in business with the more regular demands of sailors from visiting ships.

From the 1710s onwards, St. George's declined relative to the rest of Bermuda. After considerable petitioning, the Crown lifted the requirement to load and unload only at the capital. Thereafter, most merchants chose to do business near their residences in the western parishes, and not a few seized the opportunity to engage in a fair amount of smuggling far from the eyes of government searchers. Cheap, smuggled Dutch goods allowed these up-country merchants to undersell their competitors in St. George's, so the mercantile base of the port had seriously eroded by the middle of the 18th century. However, the courts and House of Assembly still met in St. George's and brought in business, while foreign merchants and ship captains unacquainted with the channels of the west end continued to call at the port.

In an effort to revive the town Governor William Popple convinced the Crown in 1758 to grant outright or for an annual quitrent all of the land at The Cut, Ferry Reach, and to the

Archaeology in St. George's

More land-based historical archaeology has been done in St. George's than any other parish in Bermuda. In 1973, Tucker House was the site of an archaeological excavation by David Fleming. Another dig jointly sponsored by the Bermuda National Trust and Colonial Williamsburg of Virginia in the cellar of Tucker House in 1988-90 shed much light on the daily life of the Tucker family and resulted in a museum exhibit housed where the excavation took place.

A dig at Stewart Hall in 1990-91 revealed an 18th century livestock watering trough and a mid 17th century woman's grave, as well as a wealth of ceramics which help us to reconstruct Bermuda's trade in the golden age of sail.

A 1994 excavation beneath the floor of the St. George's Historical Society kitchen uncovered a 17th century post hole from an earlier timber frame structure and yielded artifacts which will aid us in understanding how one black family made the transition from slavery to freedom in the 1840s (see chapter 5).

In 1996, two archaeological digs explored the town's ancient past. A site behind the Town Hall recovered many thousands of artifacts and found layers related to a late 17th century house which belonged to the Stone family. Testing at the Globe Hotel revealed what may be a 1760s stone quarry and early 18th century items left by the Tucker family.

Archaeological testing has also been conducted at Reeve Court (1989), Old Rectory cellar and garden (1991-1992), Bridge House (1993), Unfinished Church (1994), beneath the streets of St. George's during roadwork (1994-95) and Tucker House kitchen (1997).

Dr. Edward Harris' ongoing investigations of the parish's many fortifications have yielded significant insights into the configurations of Bermuda's defences. His surveys document all the forts of St. George's and his excavations include Fort Cunningham (1991-92), Castle Island (1993-96) and Paget Island (1997).

The value of archaeological investigation cannot be overstated. Despite the wealth of documentary sources, little is known about the town's 17th century past. While St. George's abounds in early 18th century buildings, the location and arrangement of the timber framed houses they replaced is largely unknown; diet, trade patterns, industrial activities and a host of details about the daily life of the people who lived in the capital also remain a mystery, to be explored through future excavations.

If we are to speak knowledgeably about the earliest years of St. George's, it will only be through a combination of systematic archaeological and archival research.

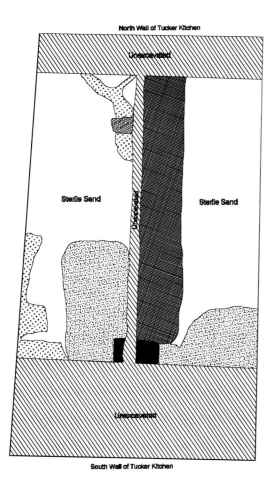

North Wall of Tucker Kitchen

Unexcavated

Sterile Sand   Sterile Sand

Unexcavated

Unexcavated

South Wall of Tucker Kitchen

Plan view of features pre-dating the Tucker House kitchen outbuilding. The trench running down the middle of the site might have originally contained a limestone wall for a structure. The two pits on either side were probably related to the construction of the house in the 1750s. They were filled with construction debris as well as numerous artifacts from the mid 18th century.

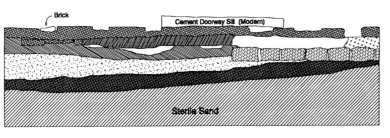

Brick

Cement Doorway Sill (Modern)

Sterile Sand

West profile of Tucker House kitchen outbuilding showing the different soil layers. Note the limestone blocks to the right which were part of the kitchen foundation and the kerb stones on top that supported joists for a wooden floor which replaced the original dirt floor.

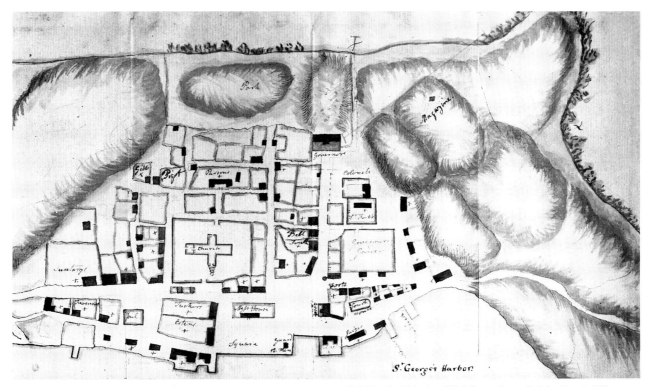

Detail of a map drawn by Bermudian Captain B. Joell around 1780 and sent to Col. Timothy Pickering, US Adjutant General of the Board of War, along with a plan to capture the town and colony. (Timothy Pickering Papers, Massachusetts Historical Society, Boston, Massachusetts.)

north of the capital on St. George's Island, as well as the whole of Tucker's Town and the eastern half of St. David's Island. This land had been let to public tenants since the 1620s; they had erected few buildings and done little to improve it. Now that secure tenure was granted, more than a score of wealthy merchants bid against each other to gain the land. Some later abused the system by clear cutting all the cedar trees and allowing the land to revert to the Crown, while others walled their tracts, cleared fields and erected substantial houses.

During the American Revolution (1776-1783) St. George's bustled with activity and at least doubled in population. Some newcomers were loyalists who, for their allegiance to the Crown, were driven from their homes in America. Many of these displaced Americans exacted revenge on their rebellious neighbours through privateering, and none was more successful than Bridger Goodrich of Bridge House (see chapter 5).

Other newcomers were British garrison troops sent from New York to guard against a potential American invasion. The arrival of these soldiers marked the beginning of a century and a half of British military presence in

St. George's. A third group came involuntarily, brought in by the loyalist privateers and Royal Navy warships stationed in Bermuda. They were French, American, Dutch and Spanish prisoners whose vessels had fallen prize. The majority were crammed into the town's two inadequate gaols, and an outbreak of deadly typhoid fever among them ensured that many would never leave Bermuda.

In the wake of the American Revolution, the whole configuration of Britain's empire in the Americas was fundamentally changed. Bermuda took on a strategic importance, linking the Canadian Maritime Provinces and the British West Indies, and became an important sentry post for monitoring the newly formed United States. The Royal Navy made the island a base and erected dockyard facilities in St. George's and Ireland Island to support the fleet.

The massive naval tanks near Murray's Anchorage, built in 1794 on the north shore of St. George's Island, were the first of many military support facilities in the parish. To protect the naval base, St. George's was girdled with fortifications.

In 1796 the arrival of four companies of British infantry and artillery

doubled the population of the town and prompted a considerable building boom. The troops stationed in St. George's lived in a considerable barracks complex built at Barrack Hill to the east of town, while their officers usually took up private accommodation in town or in sizable houses at The Cut and Ferry Reach (see chapter 8).

The impact of the garrison on the civilian population of St. George's was considerable. Commerce shifted from overseas trade with now forbidden US ports towards catering to the material and service needs of the garrison, whose expenditures subsidised the St. George's economy. Merchants who supplied the military pushed the St. George's waterfront further into the harbour through land reclamation to accommodate larger ships.

This new market softened the blow when the House of Assembly created a rival town in Hamilton in 1793 and then moved the capital of Bermuda to that town in 1815.

The Corporation of St. George's was formed in 1797 with the power to make municipal bylaws and govern within the town boundaries. It founded a market, built a new public wharf and Town Hall, cleaned up the streets, battled against straying live-

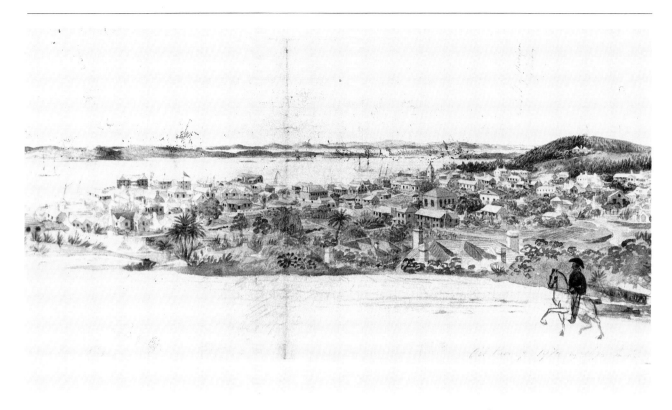

In 1824 Thomas Driver painted this watercolour sketch of St. George's from a site near the present Unfinished Church. On the far horizon is Tucker's Town and Castle Harbour with some of its islands identified by Driver. In the middle distance are St. David's and Longbird Island. (Courtesy Fay and Geoffrey Elliott Collection: Bermuda Archives, Hamilton, Bermuda.)

stock and generally improved the town. In 1793-95, and again during the War of 1812, a revival of privateering bolstered the prosperity of St. Georgian merchants and mariners.

The Town of St. George became home to a considerable free black community in the decades before the general Emancipation of 1834.

Pilot James Darrell, who was awarded his freedom by Admiral George Murray for his service in conning the 74-gun *HMS Resolution* into Murray's Anchorage, became, in 1795, the first documented black man to purchase a house in Bermuda. Former slaves freed by their masters flocked to St. George's where there were more jobs and, after 1809, a market where they could sell meat, fish and manufactured items. Baking and washing for the garrison soldiers were other lucrative jobs for ex-slaves.

In 1806, nearly 30 years before Emancipation, 147 of the 717 blacks living in the parish were free. Thus 20 percent of St. George's blacks were free, compared with just 5.4 percent for the other eight parishes. And 38 percent of the colony's free black population was living in St. George's.

By 1833 the free black population in St. George's had more than doubled. Fully 45 percent of St. George's black inhabitants was free, again the highest ratio among Bermuda's parishes.

Black St. Georgians purchased or were given no fewer than 23 houses in town before 1834, and another 13 joined the ranks of freeholders in the following two decades (see Appendix V). In addition, there were a number of former slaves who owned property in St. David's and Tucker's Town. For instance, in St. David's Thomas and Ruth Fox respectively owned 33 and 25 acres prior to 1826, and in 1846 Robert J. Packwood purchased a 65-acre tract called Underwood at Ferry Reach. More importantly, black owned houses were scattered throughout the town, rather than concentrated in one area, reflecting a marked degree of racial integration in St. George's. As pilots, bakers, masons, carpenters, grocers, butchers, tavern keepers, laundresses, fishermen, and a host of other professions, black St. Georgians made a vital contribution to the local economy.

The prosperity which stemmed from the British military presence

came at a price. Naval vessels and mail steamers returning from the West Indies brought the dreaded yellow fever which swept through the town on no fewer than eight occasions between 1796 and 1864, with fatal consequences for townspeople and garrison troops alike.

Incoming British regiments usually arrived with a contingent of camp followers, mistresses, pseudo-wives and illegitimate children who became a burden on the parish's poor rolls. A number of soldiers married local women while stationed in St. George's and then abandoned them when the regiment was posted abroad.

Murder, mayhem, riot, burglary and mutiny were committed by garrison troops, sometimes shattering the peace of St. George's and creating ill will between those living in town and those on Barrack Hill.

By far the most prosperous and turbulent period in the town's history occurred during the four years of the American Civil War. The overwhelmingly rural Confederacy needed to import cannon, rifles, gunpowder, shot and a whole range of equipment to keep its armies in the field, and the

An advertisement from Stark's Illustrated Bermuda Guide, 1902.

Northern navy imposed blockades on Southern ports to prevent these supplies from arriving. After 1861 British merchants established a lucrative trade exchanging war matériel for Confederate cotton which fetched an enormous price on the London market. Bermuda's proximity to Wilmington, North Carolina, made it the second largest transhipment centre during the war, while the convenient location of St. George's near the open ocean made it the preferred port of the sleek, speedy steamers which ran the Union blockade.

St. George's merchants made fortunes renting their wharves and storehouses to accommodate the enormous volume of goods passing through the port, while the town's grocers, tavern and inn keepers, and retailers found willing customers in the well paid sailors who manned the blockade runners. The gold and silver which flowed freely went far towards making St. Georgians overlook the pollution, overcrowding and violent crime rampant in their town.

But no one could ignore yellow fever when it appeared in late June 1864. A passenger from Nassau died of the fever shortly after his arrival and by early August it was rampant in the town. Worst hit was the newly posted Queen's Second Regiment: 307 of the 560 troops stationed at Barrack Hill and Ferry Reach caught yellow fever, and 139 died. Of a civilian population of 1,982 in St. George's, there were 662 cases and 113 deaths, which accounts for nearly half of all the civilian deaths in the entire colony in that year. The epidemic drove the blockade runners from Bermuda for nearly six months, and by the time they returned in late 1864 the Civil War was virtually over. After the forts guarding Wilmington fell in January 1865, blockade running ceased entirely and St. George's great boom quickly came to an end.

Merchant shipping continued to play a role in the town's economy in the closing decades of the 19th century, but business shifted towards exporting. Onions, Easter lilies, potatoes and other agricultural products grown in St. George's, St. David's, Tucker's Town and the eastern parishes, were shipped to US east coast cities in the twilight years of the age of sail.

The improvements in transoceanic transportation which doomed Bermuda's merchant fleet eventually ushered in a new source of prosperity in the form of tourism. In the 18th and early 19th centuries a small number of visitors came to Bermuda as invalids seeking to restore their health in Bermuda's salubrious climate. In the second half of the 19th century, passenger service was added to the mail steamers which regularly made the run between Bermuda, the West Indies and Halifax. In the 1850s and 1860s, passage to or from New York on the Bermudian sailing ship *Eliza Barss* cost just £4.

The number of visitors to Bermuda rose from 1,385 in 1885 to more than 27,000 by 1911, exceeding Bermuda's population for the first time. In 1935 visitors totalled almost 75,000. In 1930 Tucker's Town, then a backwater, was transformed by the construction of the Mid Ocean Club. Its golf course and exclusive building lots appealed to elite visitors who desired a more permanent base during their extended stays on the island.

Although the number of visitors declined sharply during the two World Wars, the airfield built by the US military in 1941-45 more than compensated for the temporary lull. Regular air service in the 1950s and 1960s brought unprecedented numbers of visitors to Bermuda, while shipping lines continued to bring tourists in the pre-war seaborne manner. Bermuda's post-war success thus arose from the sacrifice of much of St. David's Island, which now lies buried beneath the runways of Bermuda's airport (see chapter 9). Today the nearly 600,000 visitors who come to Bermuda each year represent ten times the resident population.

St. Georgians responded to the growing wave of sojourners from abroad by opening hotels, restaurants and curiosity shops. The much lamented shift of the capital from St. George's to Hamilton in 1815 was now celebrated, for the economic stagnation which had followed prompted little new building and thus preserved the town's original layout, along with a high number of 18th century structures. The Causeway, built in 1865-71, supervised by the Royal Engineers and partly financed by the British government, freed visitors from the uncomfortable and occasionally hazardous ferry which had connected St. George's to the main island, and was a great boon to the town's early tourism.

The St. George's Improvement Commission, created in 1875, widened a number of main thoroughfares to make the town more accessible. Duke of York Street, then only ten feet wide near Somers Garden, Old Maids Lane and Shinbone Alley were widened by the compulsory purchase of front lawns and the demolition of old and derelict houses fronting the streets.

In the 1890s visitors had the choice of a number of hotels, including the Globe (see chapter 5) and the Somers Inn on King's Square (see Stiles House, chapter 6).

In 1906 the St. George Hotel opened, offering luxurious modern rooms for up to 150 guests and a spectacular view of the town and harbour from Rose Hill. It has been replaced by the St. George's Club in recent years. The massive hotel towering above St. Catherine's Bay, built by the Holiday Inn in the late 1960s, was too

The cruise ship Reliance coming through The Cut in October 1935. (Courtesy St. George's Historical Society Collection: Bermuda Archives, Hamilton, Bermuda.)

ambitious for its location. It has been vacant for the past decade, a reminder of the limits to which the tourist trade can be pushed.

The influx of visitors made St. Georgians acutely aware of the town's ancient past. In 1920 the St. George's Historical Society was founded to save the Mitchell House (see chapter 5) from destruction. The museum, opened in the building in 1922, has been teaching visitors about St. George's history for the past 75 years. The Bermuda Historical Monuments Trust, precursor to the Bermuda National Trust, likewise purchased a number of historic properties in St. George's to save them from destruction. The Bermuda National Trust now owns 11 buildings in the former capital and operates two museums highlighting the history of the town in the 18th and 19th centuries. Other attractions include the State House, the many fortifications in the parish, St. David's Lighthouse, and the replica of

the *Deliverance* on Ordnance Island.

Over the past ten years, the Bermuda National Trust has sought to sift through the considerable jumble of facts, traditions, stories, remembrances and speculations attached to St. George's many buildings. Archaeology has recently proved to be an important tool for studying the town's past, and there have been no fewer than 11 sites excavated within the town. The Trust's Historic Buildings Survey created an architectural inventory of the town and recorded basic details of all buildings dating from before 1898. However, systematic documentary research in the Bermuda Archives and elsewhere (see A Note on Research) has played the most important role in understanding both the town's history as a whole and the histories of the individual buildings in the town and parish.

This volume is the product of a decade of sustained scholarly investigation. Of the more than 200 buildings

in the Town of St. George, 77 were selected for inclusion in this book for their architectural merit. Another 23 buildings outside the town on St. George's Island, 13 on St. David's Island and six in Tucker's Town were chosen for similar reasons. The research for this book has revealed that the Town of St. George has at least 65 buildings dating back to the 18th century, representing a concentrated collection of historic structures of international significance.

Although the main focus of the Bermuda National Trust's Architectural Heritage series is on the buildings themselves, considerable effort has been made in this volume to revive the long dead St. Georgians who lived in them. Thus, the tone follows the tourist handbooks of the early 20th century in their aim to entertain as much as to educate, and guide Bermudians and visitors alike through the history and buildings of St. George's, the cradle of the colony.

Lane off Turkey Hill, William Weiss. 1912. (Bermuda Archives Collection, Hamilton, Bermuda.)

Streets in St. George's

St. George's is famous for its winding and narrow alleyways and streets which evolved from the footpaths of the early 17th century.

The streets of St. George's acquired their names during three distinct phases of the town's history. In the 17th and 18th centuries, they were merely described by who lived on them. Modern day Queen Street, for instance, was the "Way or Path from John Hilton's Warf by way of Captain Mitchell's House to the Northside of the Island". Duke of York Street was the "Highway to the Ferry". Only Water Street was called by its modern name, for its proximity to the harbour. Several early avenues have disappeared; Broad Alley, for instance, once crossed what is now the lawn of Whitehall (see chapter 6) and connected with the Blockade Alley of to-day. Another path led directly from Government House (now the site of the Unfinished Church) to the Governor's Garden (Somers' Garden).

In the early 19th century, after the American Revolution, loyalists who had fled from America and native St. Georgians christened the town's main roads for members of the Royal Family: the Dukes of Kent, York, Cumberland and Clarence were commemorated with street names, as were the King and Queen. George, the Prince Regent, was overlooked. Throughout the 19th century, modern day Duke of York Street and Duke of Kent Street were known in reverse, a source of considerable confusion when researchers initially attempted to match title deeds to buildings. Late in the century, colloquial names like Shinbone Alley, Silk Alley, Old Maids Lane, Peach Alley (modern Blockade Alley) began to appear in deeds.

As St. George's became a tourist destination in the early years of the 20th century, St. Georgians bestowed quaint and unusual names on many previously unnamed byways. Printer's Alley, Turkey Hill, Needle-and-Thread Alley, Nea's Alley, Chapel Lane, Bridge Street, Blockade Alley and many more appeared on maps, driven by a desire to make the town more romantic and traditional. In the 1970s, a similar wave of street naming gave us Pieces of Eight Lane.

Until the late 1940s, the streets of St. George's were made of packed earth and limestone, called "gaol nuts" for the prisoners who laboured at breaking large rocks into the small stones. The streets have been paved since the advent of cars in the 1940s. In 1997 the Corporation of St. George's launched an ambitious project to repave the town's streets with artificial cobblestones from Wales. This treatment is entirely untraditional, but it offers a welcome alternative to asphalt and enhances the historic appearance of the town.

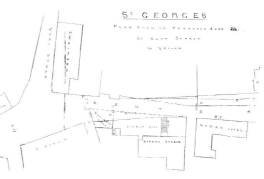

Plans for road widening in St. George's c. 1876 from the files of St. George's Corporation. The junction of Duke of York and Duke of Kent Streets is shown, but at that time the names were reversed. Somers' Garden is the blank space at top right. (Courtesy of St. George's Corporation, St. George's, Bermuda.)

CHAPTER TWO

Public Buildings

Captain John Smith's 1624 drawing of Smith's Fort and Paget Fort. (Reproduced from the original engraving by The Island Press in 1983.)

Bermuda was launched by joint stock ventures in London, backed first by the Virginia Company and then by the Somers Island Company. These backers sponsored a number of public buildings to secure their venture and to benefit the colonists. When the Somers Island Company was dissolved in 1684, the Crown inherited these public buildings and added new ones. Still others were erected by the municipal government of St. George's, chartered in 1797. Public buildings ranged from the plain and functional fortifications which guarded the colony against invasion to more ornate structures like the State House and Post Office. This chapter surveys St. George's public works, from forts built at the beginning of colonisation to more recent additions like the Police Station.

The first substantial buildings erected in Bermuda were fortifications. Of the forts constructed during the first ten years of settlement, five survive in some form today. Bermuda's first Governor, Richard Moore, felt it was pointless to clear land and plant

crops if all the colonists' hard work could be swept away by a Spanish flotilla. So as soon as temporary shelters for the people were put up in St. George's, he began to construct the island's defences. **Paget Fort** and **Smith's Fort** were among his earliest works.

In about October 1612 Moore cut a platform into the rock and mounted several cannon on the southern tip of Paget Island to guard the entrance to St. George's Harbour.

Governor Daniel Tucker spoiled Moore's fort five years later, through sheer ignorance, by deepening the platform, leaving it, according to Governor Butler, "the most vnfashionable, vncapable and vnsightlest" fort in Bermuda. In March and August 1621, Governor Nathaniel Butler enlarged Paget Fort by creating two new platforms, one on a raised redoubt, and a guardhouse. He also repaired a small tower called The Pigeon Hole, built by Moore on the northern side of Paget Island, and added a new platform; this work, perhaps also known as Peniston's Redoubt, has eluded discovery.

By the end of 1612, Governor Moore mounted a cannon, raised from the wreck of the *Sea Venture,* on Governor's Island to the south of Paget Island to guard the channel to St. George's Harbour. The following summer he cut a platform and built a redoubt which was named Smith's Fort for the Somers Island Company's first Governor, Sir Thomas Smith. Together, Paget and Smith's Forts created a crossfire. Enemy vessels attempting to attack St. George's would have to sail between ordnance firing at point-blank range. The fort was seriously weakened in 1618 when temporary Governor Miles Kendall tried to improve it but instead left it, as Butler records, "slubbred up with dangerous and unsure upperworcks of brittle stone and rubbish". Governor Butler mounted five cannon there in about March 1621 and may have corrected the mistakes made by Kendall.

Smith's and Paget Forts were the principal defence for the channel into St. George's Harbour. This defence was further improved in 1689 by Sir Robert Robinson, the first Crown-

The King's Castle on Castle Island was one of the earliest fortifications in Bermuda, built to defend Castle Roads (on the right), then the entrance to Bermuda's principal deep water harbour.

appointed Governor, who dug a line of musketry trenches to the west of Paget Fort and stretched a chain between the two islands to block the channel into St. George's Harbour. Robinson's successor, Governor Isaac Richier, used this chain to delay the escape of the suspected pirate ship *Archangel* in 1691.

During the American Revolution a battery, barracks, magazine and guardhouse were built on the rising ground behind Paget Fort. Captain Andrew Durnford expanded this new work with his Upper Paget Fort in 1791 when he deemed the earlier fort to the south not worthy of repair.

Today there is little left of Paget Fort other than the platforms cut into the rock. These platforms regularly fill with water during rough weather, which confirms Governor Butler's judgement of Tucker's 1617 work. The upper platform, or redoubt, and guardhouse have long since vanished. Upper Paget Fort has also disappeared,

replaced by its larger successor, **Fort Cunningham**. Smith's Fort is much better preserved. The lower platform is that dug by Moore in 1613, but the upper redoubt was replaced by a new masonry platform built by Durnford in 1793.

The forts at Castle Island, Brangman's Island and Goat Island at the mouth of Castle Harbour served much the same function that Paget and Smith's Forts served at the entrance to St. George's Harbour. They created a crossfire to prevent enemy vessels from invading the colony. By late 1612, Governor Moore had mounted on Castle Island a cannon from the wreck of the *Sea Venture*, "for a shewe" if a foreign vessel approached. The following June, Moore began fortifying in earnest when he put up a battery, believed to have been made of cedar, and mounted several more guns. Its completion was timely, for early in 1614 two Spanish ships attempted to land on the island, which

they thought deserted. Moore, an excellent gunner, fired two shots which persuaded the Spaniards to flee. The settlers only had a single shot left and, of the 20 people gathered, most were sick or weak and incapable of fighting. Fearing a second attack, in March 1614 Moore, again as Governor Butler recorded, pressed scores of newly arrived settlers to "make that plattforme and rayse thoes battlements, that to this daye . . . [are] called the **King's Castle**". As at Paget Fort, Moore's successor tried to improve the work but only succeeded in wasting the colonists' "labour and sweat".

Governor Nathaniel Butler made substantial improvements to the defences of Castle Harbour, which was exclusively used by the deep draught magazine ships that the Somers Island Company sent out each year to collect the annual tobacco crop. In February 1620 he began **Southampton Fort** by making a platform and mounting five cannon he had raised from the wreck

The Captain's House at the King's Castle on Castle Island is the oldest stone house surviving in Bermuda. Some restoration may have been done in the Napoleonic era, but measurements of 1811 and Governor Butler's records of 1622 are consistent with modern archaeological investigation.

of the *Warwick*, the colony's magazine ship which had sunk during a hurricane in October 1619. Additions to the fort in December 1621, made it, in Butler's opinion, "the only true peece of fortification in the whole Ilands". In March 1620 Butler replaced Moore's earlier fort, which had accidentally burnt down, with **Devonshire Redoubt**, an hexagonal tower with a lower platform, on which he mounted seven cannon. At the King's Castle, Butler cut "two newe plattformes, built a newe redoubt, made fifteene newe carriages of caeder, and mounted twenty peeces of ordnance" which had formerly lain useless. To nearby **Charles Fort**, built by Governor Moore to cover the approach to Castle Island, Butler added a corn house in July 1621. By the middle of 1620, no fewer than 29 cannon in four forts guarded the entrance to Castle Harbour.

Throughout the 17th century and for much of the 18th, the King's Castle and Southampton Fort were garrisoned by local militia. The captains of the forts enjoyed the use of common land in Tucker's Town. Many of them lived there and went to work by boat. Butler built a stone house for the captain of the Castle and his family in July 1621, and converted an older building, located near the landing place, into a guardhouse. A stone version later replaced this earlier timber frame building.

Archaeological excavations in 1993 revealed a 1620s defensive ditch dug to the north of the King's Castle to defend its approach from the landing place. Another battery was erected by 1687 on the western tip of Castle Island facing Tucker's Town.

By the 1740s the Castle Harbour defences were becoming increasingly redundant. The smaller and more manoeuvrable sloops, schooners and brigantines could land elsewhere in Bermuda. Defending Castle Harbour only countered the relatively remote threat of a large invasion, to which Bermuda was always vulnerable with most of the male populace at sea for much of the year.

There is also evidence that Castle Harbour had become unnavigable and was rarely used by mariners by 1743 when Governor Alured Popple wrote: "Castle Harbour is full of foul ground and in consequence such bad anchoring that vessels cannot ride there with any safety in bad weather, for if they should break loose, it would be a great accident indeed if they were not beat to pieces by the rocks and shoals there. Besides, there is no going from that Harbour to [St. George's Harbour], but in small boats, vessels may as well enter and clear, load and unload in the country as there."

The entrance to Castle Harbour was thus not worth the trouble to navigate, because it afforded little shelter in stormy weather. As a result, the forts were frequently neglected and almost continuously in need of repair. Even when the forts were sound, the wooden platforms, gun carriages and the cannon themselves were often unserviceable, and gunpowder and shot in short supply. During the American Revolution, Castle Island and Southampton Fort were garrisoned, but the foundering of *HMS Cerberus* in February 1783, while trying to navigate the channel leading from Castle Harbour to the open sea, confirmed the marginal value of the anchorage and led to a British Admiralty prohibition against its future use.

In the 1790s many of the Castle Island works were repaired or modified by Captain Andrew Durnford, but the whole complex was apparently abandoned two decades later in favour of guarding the approach to the newly established Naval Dockyard at the west end of Bermuda.

The decline of Castle Island in light of the changing orientation of Bermuda's defences is fortuitous in that these forts, the earliest surviving works built by the English in the New World, have remained virtually unaltered.

Southampton Fort, in particular, remains much the way Butler built it, including the crenellated curtain walls and rounded bastions. A pentagonal keep was added to the west of the

The Castle Island outhouse takes the common form of the Bermuda buttery, but it is substantially cut out of the rock. Waste disposal was accomplished through a still plainly visible short chute directly into the waters of Castle Harbour.

older fortification, probably in the late 18th century.

Castle Island, with its three extensive fortifications, is an explorer's dream; the shell of Butler's 1621 **Captain's House** stands over the upper and lower platforms of the Castle, while to the north the squat tower of Devonshire Redoubt still commands a panoramic view of Castle Roads and Castle Harbour. A subterranean dome-roofed magazine was added, probably in the 18th century. Perhaps the most striking feature of the **Landward Battery** is its most mundane, the buttery roofed privy projecting out from the north wall. Near the landing place are the remains of a late 18th century barracks, kitchen and cistern.

Charles Fort is no more; it fell into the sea in the 1960s after it lost a long battle against erosion. Pembroke Fort, erected by Governor Moore on Cooper's Island in 1614, has apparently vanished beneath the National Aeronautic and Space Administration (NASA) tracking station which covers most of the island today.

Other early fortifications in St. George's which no longer survive include: Fort St. Catherine, a tower built by Governor Moore in 1613, which has now vanished beneath later works (although the later works bear the same name); Warwick Castle, replaced by Fort William; and Rich's Mount, a watch tower built on what is now Fort George Hill as a lookout for enemy vessels in the offing and since replaced by the later fort.

The **Town Platform** in the centre of St. George's survived until the late 18th century. Governor Butler mounted eight cannon on the wharf in the town to sweep the harbour. In 1688 Governor Sir Robert Robinson boasted that he had erected "a Town Platform and several battlements, which are not only very ornamental to St. George's, but command the whole harbour" with 12 mounted cannon. The site of this fort, probably dismantled when the Town Hall and Market Wharf were constructed in the early 1800s, is buried beneath King's Square. Other later works, including batteries at Tobacco Bay, Buildings Bay and Cemetery Hill, have likewise vanished.

Some later additions to St. George's defences have fared better. The **Town Cut Battery** at the eastern tip of St. George's Island was built in about 1702 for three guns to fulfill the same role for which Moore had erected Peniston's Redoubt: to guard the Town Cut against an invasion launched in light draught ships. For, until the channel was widened and deepened early in the 20th century, only small vessels could use it. The battery was extensively rebuilt by Andrew Durnford in 1791, when he erected the blockhouse and a small guard room nearby. **Gates' Fort** is the battery's alternative name, but there is no evidence that *Sea Venture* veteran Sir Thomas Gates erected any kind of fortification in Bermuda during his short stay here.

At the western end of St. George's Island, **Burnt Point Fort** guards the approach to the old capital from the main island. Regular ferry service was established between St. George's and the main island in 1619, when the Governor appointed John Yates official ferry keeper. In return for shuttling foot passengers between the two islands, weather permitting, Yates received an annual salary equal to a pound of tobacco for every inhabitant over the age of 16. Later ferry keepers enjoyed the use of a house, 50 acres of land and a fixed salary.

Burnt Point Fort was built in 1687 and a report made in that year

The ferry at Ferry Reach c. 1871. On the left is the Martello Tower and on the right the Ferry Point Cottage. (Courtesy St. George's Historical Society Collection: Bermuda Archives, Hamilton, Bermuda.)

describes it as having nine battlements and eight mounted guns. This oval shaped fort was already in a ruinous condition in 1783 and suffered further when cannon exploded in the fort ten years later, damaging the stonework. Andrew Durnford converted it into a half-moon shaped battery with thicker front walls and reduced the number of embrasures to five.

Two more forts survive elsewhere in St. George's Parish, both of which were named for governors of Bermuda.

Fort Popple on the eastern side of St. David's Island was built in about 1737 and named for Alured Popple, who filled seven of the fort's nine gunports by taking cannon from Smith's Fort. This battery was designed to prevent the enemy landing on St. David's and launching attacks on Smith's Fort, Southampton Fort and the town. Durnford filled in three of the embrasures in 1793, before the fort was made obsolete by the construction of Fort Cunningham (see chapter 8).

Fort Bruere in Tucker's Town similarly guarded Castle Island from a flanking attack launched by enemy forces landed on the main island. Set on a hill about a mile to the west, this fort commanded the narrow peninsula of Tucker's Town and thus the landward approach to King's Castle. The fort, a small oval redoubt, was built during the American Revolution, probably during the brief tenure of Lieutenant Governor George Bruere, who succeeded his father in that office.

The first 11 forts built in Bermuda guarded the entrances to Castle and St. George's Harbours and thus the town. To these were added at least nine more in the later 17th and 18th centuries. By 1783, 80 of the colony's 145 mounted cannon defended the single parish of St. George's.

Architecturally, Bermuda's first forts break with the bastion tradition prevalent in Europe. Dr. Edward Harris, in his 1997 book *Bermuda Forts,* suggests the colony's early fortifications are best seen in the tradi-

tion of Henry VIII's earlier defences along the coast of southern England. Their builders creatively adapted their batteries to natural topography and were the first example on the island of stone used as a building material. Techniques acquired in fort building no doubt influenced later domestic building in stone. In the 19th century many of the earlier forts failed to keep pace with changes in the technology of war.

We turn now to public buildings in and around the Town of St. George.

Built between October 1620 and April 1621, the **State House** is one of the oldest standing stone structures erected by English colonists in the New World. It was rebuilt from the level of its downstairs windows in 1969 using John Smith's engraving as guidance. As the sole survivor from the town's earliest days, the State House looks strikingly different from later buildings. Its flat roof and unusual façade stand in sharp contrast to the residential buildings which

The State House resembles John Smith's 1624 drawing because the drawing was the basis of the 1969 recontruction. Recent comparisons between the early forts and Smith's drawing confirm the accuracy of Smith's work and suggest that Governor Butler supplied Smith personally with the information used for these drawings.This suggests that this is indeed a probable reconstruction of the original State House of 1620. The treatment is basic and dictated by the quality of the stone available. It is unique and seems to have had no influence at all on later architecture in the Colony.

surround it. But even when new, Bermuda's State House was unusual. Its design reflected the varied past of its architect, Bermuda's third Governor, Nathaniel Butler.

Soldier, naval captain, military architect, explorer, Nathaniel Butler was an intellectual with cosmopolitan tastes and ability. In the State House, he merged defensive architecture with the splendour of a public hall. It boldly declared the permanence of the English colonisation of Bermuda. Three years after its completion, an engraving of this building was showcased in John Smith's map of the island, at once reassuring investors and would-be settlers that Bermuda was a permanent settlement.

The appearance of the State House in the 1624 Smith engraving is reminiscent of buildings in the Mediterranean and Butler himself admits that he built it after the fashion which he had "seene in other counties in parallel with [Bermuda]". Although its original interior configuration remains a mystery, the large size of a single room measuring 22 feet by 32 feet no doubt impressed contemporaries and offered sufficient space for the courts and the general assembly, since Butler had "destinated [it] to the publick service". Its design was perhaps influenced by the Italianate style introduced into England by Inigo Jones in the 1610s. The balustrade pilasters and arched pediment surrounding the entrance, the flat roof and the decorated string course and cornice all combine to produce an elegant building which could not fail to impress visi-

tors to a colony less than ten years old.

But Butler was a soldier, and behind the decorative trappings of the State House there is a blockhouse. The State House is built on a hill which overlooked the town dock and harbour, and Smith's engraving suggests that it was surrounded by a fence or palisade. Its stone walls, bonded by a mixture of turtle oil and lime, are more than two feet thick. The narrow windows, particularly two cross-slitted ones just above the entrance, could serve as musket loops (holes from which defenders might fire) and the flat roof offered a platform for marksmen. In appearance, Butler's State House resembled forts commonly build in the Low Countries, where he had served as a soldier.

It was no accident that the colony's gunpowder was stored in this building for more than a century and a half. The State House and Warwick Fort to the north were the last line of defence in case the enemy fought their way past the forts which guarded the entrance to St. George's Harbour and landed at the town. Thankfully, the defensive role of the State House was never put to the test. To accommodate public business, later builders made several changes to Nathaniel Butler's original design. His flat roof

Captain John Smith's 1624 drawing of the State House. (Reproduced from the original engraving by The Island Press in 1983.)

A detail from Thomas Driver's 1824 painting shows the State House in the centre of the picture with a sharply peaked hip roof. (Courtesy Fay and Geoffrey Elliott Collection, Bermuda Archives, Hamilton, Bermuda.)

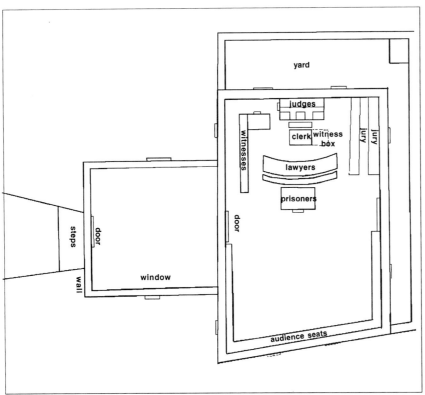

Plan of the State House in 1810 when it was in use as a Court House. (Courtesy the Corporation of St. George's.)

leaked, so a pitched one was added in the 1630s. A porch chamber was added in 1733 to regulate entry to the main chamber.

From Butler's days until the capital of Bermuda was moved to Hamilton in 1815, the building was also referred to as the Sessions House and Court House, reflecting its use by the colonial parliament and the island's legal courts. Four times a year, the people of Bermuda gathered at the Court House to hold an assize, where justice was served upon the colony's criminals and civil cases were ajudicated. Sentences were carried out at the end of the assize. Floggings took place before the Court House door, on the Town Bridge, under the gallows or in the criminal's home parish, while executions were usually performed on Gallows Island, now part of Ordnance Island, in view of the populace assembled on King's Square.

A plan of the Court House as it was laid out in 1810 gives us a rare glimpse into the State House when it was the very heart of the colony's gov-

An invitation to the 1799 Queen's Birthday Ball at the State House. (Courtesy St. George's Historical Society Collection: Bermuda Archives, Hamilton, Bermuda.)

ernment. Spectators crowded into the back of the room or sat on benches along the walls, while the justices, seated on their raised platform, passed judgement on the prisoner standing in the dock. The jury sat on two benches in the northwest corner of the room for cases tried "by country" rather than "by King".

The upstairs portion of the State House served as a magazine for storing the Colony's gunpowder. For much of the 17th century gunpowder was in short supply, but, after the House of Assembly passed an act in 1691 requiring every incoming ship to contribute money or gunpowder to the colony, the supply grew rapidly. Keeping a considerable supply of explosives in the centre of town was dangerous and on several occasions disaster was only narrowly averted.

In 1702 the chimney in Mrs. Sarah Forster's nearby house was ordered stopped up so that sparks could not ignite the gunpowder next door. Later a group of discontented privateersmen sought retribution after the colony's Vice Admiralty Court refused to condemn their prize. Luckily, the fuse which they had affixed to the gunpowder kegs was discovered and cut before this "horrid villany" could be executed. A fire in John Phillips' nearby house in October 1732 also nearly ignited the magazine, but "through God's providence" the evening was a calm one and the fire did not spread.

In 1767 Governor George Bruere persuaded the House of Assembly to sell some of the excess gunpowder and use the proceeds to build a new magazine to the north of the town. More than 100 barrels of powder were stolen from the new location by pro-American Bermudians on the night of August 14, 1775, the famous Gunpowder Plot. In the dead of night, the barrels were transported overland to Tobacco Bay where they were loaded aboard boats, ferried to waiting American vessels, and taken to Charleston for the use of the rebellious colonies. An enraged Governor Bruere gathered up what little powder remained and put it back in the old magazine in the State House, where it remained for another 40 years.

During the American Revolution, British troops from South Carolina and New York were quartered in the State House from September to December 1780. The courts and council had to convene at Chief Justice Jonathan Burch's house on east Water Street. When the soldiers departed, they left the State House it in such an "advanced state of filthiness" that the Bermuda government was required to clean and scour it before it was once again fit for occupation.

Throughout the 18th century, the State House was a place where the inhabitants of the town and colony gathered to commemorate important events. Many balls were held in the building.

The arrival of the *HMS Resolution* with Admiral George Murray, in May 1795, inaugurated the Royal Navy's use of Bermuda as a base. To commemorate the occasion, Murray and his officers held a subscription ball in the State House, "the approach of which was accommodated with a large temporary covering, handsomely illuminated".

When St. George's ceased to be the capital of Bermuda in 1815, the Assembly and courts moved to new buildings in Hamilton. John Van Norden, then Mayor of St. George's, saw an opportunity in the vacant State House. Van Norden was also the Grand Master of the town's Masonic Lodge, then lacking a permanent meeting place. He petitioned the Governor for his lodge to use the State House, and it was granted. Like earlier town grants, the wording required that a nominal rent of one peppercorn be paid on the feast of St. John the Evangelist to maintain the Crown's nominal ownership of the property. To this day the Masons deliver their token rent each year amid much pomp and ceremony.

In June 1815 the State House was briefly restored to its former role when court was held in the building, prompting the Governor to regrant it to the Masons on July 5 with the stipulation that government reserved the right that "the Honorable Courts of Justice" may "hold their sessions in the said House" if necessary in the future.

In 1969 a major renovation of the State House was launched to restore the building to its original appearance. The front porch chamber and hip roof were removed in order to return the structure to its original one room configuration. The pilasters and arch around the entrance and the string course and cornice were added to recreate the look of John Smith's 1624 engraving. The renovated building was visited by Prince Charles in October 1970 on the 350th anniversary of its construction. Although the interior retains the layout and various artifacts from the building's 19th and 20th century use as a Masonic Lodge meeting room, the exterior belongs to another era.

Captain John Smith's 1624 drawing of the 1612 Government House. (Reproduced from the original engraving by The Island Press in 1983.)

For the 203 years that St. George's was the capital of Bermuda, the colony's governor maintained an official residence in the town. The **first Government House** was built in 1612 by Richard Moore, who, according to Governor Butler, "framed a pretye handsome house contrived into the fashion of a crosse" using the remains of the timber framed church he had previously erected on one of the windswept hills surrounding the town. Moore's house stood on Water Street, behind the present Bank of Bermuda. John Smith's 1624 engraving reveals the house to be quite grand, a two and a half storey building with a porch projection, a substantial chimney in the rear and a slightly hipped roof flying two flags of St. George from its peaks. If accurately interpreted, the governor's house had one of the island's earliest hip roofs, thought to be an East Sussex innovation of the late 17th century.

Moore's house was used by his successors throughout the Somers

Island Company period. By 1685 however, the building was in poor condition. Governor Richard Cony, the last resident, complained that he and his family were "obliged to take refuge in a neighbour's house in every storm . . . [the roof] is so rotten and leaky that we eat and sleep in water". Cony's successor, Sir Robert Robinson, abandoned the house altogether and took lodging in a private house in St. George's. The ruin was sold by Act of Assembly to Samuel Harvey and others in 1693 for £83. The building was dismantled for its timber and was not rebuilt.

In 1699 the colonial government set to work building a new Government House under the direction of Governor Samuel Day. Using timber and stone cut from Crown land and workmen paid out of the colonial treasury, Day built a grand two storey house with four large rooms on each floor, capped by a double span roof, on the site of the old Company slave quarters on the northwest corner of

King's Square. In 1701 when Benjamin Bennett replaced Samuel Day as governor, Day refused to surrender the new building. Through his influential father, Sir Thomas Day, Mayor of Bristol in England, Samuel had the Board of Trade in London grant ownership of the property to him, much to Bermuda's shock and dismay. But he never enjoyed his ill-gotten house. He was arrested for debt and died in prison on Castle Island. Day's house is better known today as the Globe Hotel, which houses the Bermuda National Trust Museum.

Another 20 years passed before the colonial government started another governor's house. Governor Benjamin Bennett was quite happy living in Bridge House in the interim. In December 1721, work commenced on a **new Government House** set on the hillside to the north of the town. Captain Richard Gilbert and Major Walter Mitchell oversaw the work, completed in August 1722. John Hope was the first governor to live there and was

Detail of the 1722 Government House from a c. 1731 stylised sketch. (Bermuda National Trust Collection: Bermuda Archives, Hamilton, Bermuda.)

succeeded by an unbroken line until the capital shifted to Hamilton in 1815.

The front rooms of the house were used for balls, council meetings, offices and public functions, while the rear wing to the west housed the governor's private chambers. Outbuildings included a 16-foot by 18-foot detached kitchen built in 1724, another kitchen and several water cisterns added by 1726, and a coach house. By 1729 at least three of the rooms in the house were wainscoted. A 1731 sketch shows the new Government House set high on the hill overlooking the town, with a gate, walled garden and entry porch.

A probate inventory, taken in 1744 after the death of Governor Alured Popple, gives us a glimpse into the house at the peak of its 18th century splendour. The building's hall, parlour, study, central passage, four bed chambers and extensive library were lavishly furnished with pieces from England and Bermuda.

The front portion of this house was demolished to make way for the Unfinished Church in 1874, but the outbuildings and western wing of the house survive as the rectory for St. Peter's Church. The brick-floored coach house is of particular interest.

The construction of the 1721

Government House altered the earlier configuration of the town. The approach to the mansion, Duke of Kent Street, became a fashionable avenue and a number of houses sprang up on both sides of the road in the 1720s. The low lying green where Daniel Tucker had dug a cattle pond in 1617 was enclosed by a wall and set aside as The Governor's Park in 1722. A road once ran directly from the front door of the governor's house to the north gate of the park, but was blocked up in the 1950s after it had fallen into disrepair. A small portion of the "governor's walk" remains as part of the driveway to Banana Manor.

The Governor's Park, known today as **Somers Garden**, is one of the most historic spots in Bermuda. It is the site where Sir George Somers' heart was reputedly buried after he died in November 1610. For a decade, the grave was marked by a simple wooden cross which became "all overgrowne with bushes and rubbish". In April 1620 Governor Nathaniel Butler corrected this affront to "so noble a gentleman" by causing a tomb to be built on the site, topped with a marble tablet and inlaid brass inscription. Butler himself composed an epitaph which, although not strictly accurate, paid tribute to the dead knight:

In the Year 1611,
Noble Sr. George Somers
went hence to Heaven
Whose well trade worth, that
held him still employde
Gave him the knowledge of
the world so wide;
Hence 'twas, by Heavens
decree that to this place
He brought newe guests and
name to mutuall grace.
At last his soule and body
dying to part,
He here bequeathed his
entryles and his heart

A century later, in 1726, Governor John Hope buried his wife Charlotte in the park near the tomb. Hope granted two town lots the following year on the condition that the recipients "take care to keep in due repaire the wall, including the graves of Sir George Somers and my lady Charlotte Hope".

Somers' grave has now vanished beneath the pavement of Duke of York Street, but Charlotte Hope's grave can be seen. In the 1750s Governor William Popple was fond of playing cricket in his garden on Sunday afternoons. The 1617 cattle pond was filled in at the relatively late date of 1791, when Governor Henry Hamilton

"Post Office and Customs House, St. George's", no date but c. 1900. (Courtesy St. George's Historical Society Collection: Bermuda Archives, Hamilton, Bermuda.)

provided a new well and pump for watering cattle in place of the old pond.

After the capital was moved to Hamilton, officers from the garrison grew vegetables in the park. In the 1870s Governor Lefroy designated it a public park, as more befitting the dignity of the last resting place of the colony's founder. It was officially designated Somers Garden in 1911, three hundred years after the old knight's death.

The buildings which now house the **Post Office** and Police Station are built on the site of the colony's first gaol, a "stronge and large prison of framed cæder" erected by Governor Nathaniel Butler in 1622, and the timber framed Provost Marshal's House. Throughout the 17th and 18th centuries, the colony's prison was a place to hold accused criminals or debtors awaiting trial at the assizes, rather than a place of punishment where criminals might be sentenced for long periods. By 1700 both Butler's prison and the Provost Marshal's House were ready to "tumble down". In 1711 a new gaol with a dungeon was built on a site slightly to the east of the Police Station of today under what is now Customs House Square. By 1756, however, this new prison was in poor repair and the government drew up plans to build a two storey gaol, a 16-foot by 32-foot structure with walls three feet thick, on the site of Butler's earlier prison. In 1760 the House of Assembly passed an act authorising its construction and the work commenced.

During the American Revolution large numbers of French and American prisoners captured on privateers and prizes were crammed into this prison, as well as the older one to the north. They were shabbily treated by Governor George Bruere who considered them pirates rather than prisoners of war. Overcrowding and poor sanitation contributed to an outbreak of gaol fever (typhus), which killed many of the prisoners and spread to the garrison troops and general population. In 1800 Methodist missionary John Stephenson was incarcerated there for preaching to the colony's slaves without a licence. Tradition has it that he preached through a window

The St. George's Post Office, originally the 1760 gaol but greatly altered subsequently, has been modernised to suit changing needs and use. However the general appearance of the classically detailed arched verandah and simple railings has been carefully preserved and the impression given by the Customs House thus survives nearly intact. This might not have been the case had not the vigilant people of St. George's alerted the Bermuda National Trust to major alterations being undertaken in about 1985 without either the knowledge or the permission of the St. George's Preservation Authority. Important improvements to the plan were thus achieved before any damage was done.

"Old Guard House", Customs House Square, c.1900. The Post Office building shows clearly on the left and Duke of York Street extends to the right. (Courtesy St. George's Historical Society Collection: Bermuda Archives, Hamilton, Bermuda.)

in his prison cell to those gathered outside.

In the early 19th century attitudes towards criminal punishment changed and the sentencing of malefactors to years of hard labour became the norm. In response, in 1846 the colonial government built a new, larger prison at the foot of Rose Hill, to cope with the increased number of inmates, and the old gaol on Water Street was turned over to the Corporation of St. George's. It hired architect J.A.D. Johnson in November 1852 to convert the gaol into offices and transform the former gaunt exterior. Johnson did this by adding a verandah and arcade to the south and east sides and cutting a number of new doors and windows through the stout stone walls. When work was completed, the post office moved from James Taylor's nearby wharf at 34 Water Street to the ground floor and the officers of the Customs House occupied the upper floor. The building today remains much as it was after the 1852 conversion, following a major restoration in the mid 1980s.

The **Police Station,** just north of the Post Office, is built on the site of the 17th century Provost Marshal's House and yard and the 1711 gaol. Despite its dilapidated condition, this gaol was used in the 1770s to house prisoners and as a barracks for British troops. After the American Revolution, the building become a guardhouse, or "Main Guard", operated first by the Corporation of St. George's and later by the British military. The British War Department erected a row of storage sheds to the west in the gaol yard. By 1893 the "Old Guard House" was falling apart and St. George's Mayor Joseph Ming Hayward purchased part of the derelict building from the Royal Engineers in order to widen the street. The rest was demolished in 1911 when the Bermuda government erected the Police Station of today. The neoclassical façade of this building provides a good example of the Imperial style of colonial architecture, popular during the Edwardian period, and intended to impress Bermuda's populace.

The **Town Hall** on the King's Square was built by the Corporation of St. George's and completed less than 12 years after that body was cre-

ated. The parish vestry first proposed a building in 1765 that might serve as both a public market and assembly room, but it lacked the wherewithal to carry such a project to completion.

St. George's Police Station (1911) is one of several buildings in an Edwardian Imperial style to be built in Bermuda during the first third of the 20th century, the old King Edward VII Memorial Hospital being the last and the Somerset Police Station and (then) Post Office being the most interesting architecturally. The formal rustication of the ground floor and the classical pilasters and small pediments on the upper floor are in the grand tradition.

The Town Hall in 1902 with its original imposing form enhanced by the simplicity of typical St. George's moulding under the eaves, plain pilasters and a string course. (Taken from Stark's Illustrated Bermuda Guide, 1902.)

A detail from Thomas Driver's 1823 painting of King's Square. It shows the Town Hall, with Block House to the right. (Courtesy Fay and Geoffrey Elliott Collection: Bermuda Archives, Hamilton, Bermuda.)

The St. George's municipal government, under the leadership of its first Mayor, Andrew Durnford, resolved to build a two storey town hall with a coffee house underneath. The Corporation needed the hall as a regular place to meet, since the colonial government and parish vestry monopolised the only public meeting places in town, St. Peter's Church and the State House.

The coffee house in the 18th century was traditionally a place where merchants and ship captains gathered to do business, and thus appealed to the members of the town government, most of whom were merchants. However, before construction began on the Town Hall, the Corporation built a new Market Wharf, which spanned the inlet between the old Town Dock and Bridge Wharf.

Work commenced on the Town Hall in June 1802. A stone steeple, mounted on the southern end of the building and since demolished, was added in December 1804. The building was sufficiently complete for the Corporation to meet there for the first time in August 1805, but workmen continued over the next four years to install internal floors, doors and a staircase.

The market on the ground floor opened in September 1809, modelled after the open air markets so common in English towns and villages. A Corporation-appointed clerk regulated the market. His duties included issuing licences to vendors, renting stalls, checking weights and measures and maintaining standards of quality. The

The original St. George's Town Hall on King's Square was an early 19th century pilastered rectangular building of considerable dignity and imposing proportion which is still easily discernible behind later additions.

The design of this 1830s building off King's Square, originally a market but a tavern in this c. 1920 photograph, is austere. It is topped by a smooth hip roof and two small decorative chimneys. (Bermuda Houses, John S. Humphreys, A.I.A., 1923.)

new market was particularly popular with the free blacks and slaves living in the eastern parishes. They regularly brought vegetables, meat and fish to town.

The Corporation met in the single large room upstairs, which it occasionally rented for balls and concerts. In June 1809 Edward Goodrich contributed an "elegant chandelier of eight branches" to the Town Hall on the condition that it never be used as a "Playhouse or Sectary preaching house". Goodrich must be turning in his grave, for the upstairs room has been used as a cinema for much of this century as well as for church meetings.

By the 1830s the Corporation members had built another market to the southeast of the Town Hall, probably to distance themselves from the noise and smell. The mayor auctioned the use of the ground floor to various merchants each year to recoup the high cost of building the Market Wharf and Town Hall, but retained a small office for himself and the clerk of the market. In the 1870s a room was added on the north side of Town Hall to house St. George's first telegraph office. The lower floor was rented until 1941, home to a meat market and

hardware store early in the 20th century. The double staircase and porch chamber to the west of the Town Hall were added in the 1920s when the internal staircase was removed.

The Corporation undertook a major restoration of the building between 1945 and 1950, stopping up three doors on the east side and sweeping away a number of partitions on the ground floor to create the large room of today.

Although the theatre upstairs may resemble the stately meeting hall and ballroom envisioned by the town's early mayors, the fine cedar woodwork in the main ground floor room today is quite at odds with its original use as a market where fishmongers, butchers and bakers loudly vied for the attention of customers.

The building now housing the **Public Rest Rooms** to the southeast of the Town Hall was constructed between 1832 and 1834 as the new market house for St. George's. Its closer proximity to Market Wharf made it easier for fisherman and country traders to land their wares. By the 1840s it was open six days a week, selling everything from fresh baked bread to just-caught turtles and fish. In the 1870s the market was moved to a new,

The tavern of John S. Humphreys' 1923 photograph is still recognisable, but the relief once provided by the windows and fanlight doors is now lost to its modern use as Public Rest Rooms.

larger building to the west. Nicholas McCallan acquired the former market and converted it into a grocery store. In the 1920s and 1930s it was a tavern and restaurant. The Corporation converted the building into public rest rooms in the 1980s. The curious false chimneys or ventilation ducts protruding from the peak of the hip roof are original.

St. George's Rest Home, built in the former Government House Park, is set on a hill overlooking the parish cemetery. It was built in 1881 using a £400 gift to the parish for that purpose left by Sarah Davenport in her 1873 will, and replaced an earlier

The St. George's Rest Home is an unusual late 19th century building with a curious tower structure defining it, whose architectural significance is somewhat diminished by the later projecting additional wing.

poor house near Penno's Wharf. This 19th century institution represented a break with the past, when the parish poor lived in their own, often inadequate, houses and received weekly handouts from the parish vestry.

The poor houses of the 19th century were intended to care for the "worthy poor" of the parish, and not the newly arrived impoverished strangers who threatened to drain the parish funds. The need for distinction was particularly acute in St. George's because a large number of camp followers usually accompanied each arriving British regiment, and put a strain on local charities.

The long hip roofed building erected in 1881 was bisected by a two storey porch tower decorated on the outside with dentil moulding. The facility was designed for 24 people, 12 men and 12 women, who occupied the two wings. A shed roofed extension in the rear housed the kitchen, dining hall and sick ward and has a fine dome topped tank attached. The arched entrance to the central hall has been obscured by a 20th century addition. In 1971 the poor house was transferred from the parish vestry to the Bermuda government and redesignated a "rest home".

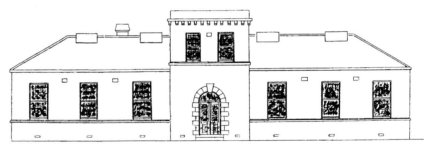

Eastern elevation of 19th century Parish Poor House from the Corporation of St. George's plans. (Courtesy the Corporation of St. George's.)

The public buildings of St. George's reflect first the Company's and later the colonial government's answer to the most fundamental needs of Bermuda: defence and administration. The forts preserved the life and property of the settlers by convincing Britain's enemies that the island was unassailable. In the State House, the colonial Assembly set policy and the courts settled differences and kept order through civil and criminal trials. The prison and Police Station aided in the administration of justice. The Government Houses in the town were home to the highest official in the colony during the two centuries that St. George's was the capital. After 1797 the Corporation of St. George's was better able to respond to the immediate and specific needs of the town than the colonial government had been in the past.

The Town Hall, market, town wharf, Customs House, and Post Office sponsored by the Corporation promoted commerce and improved the flow of information, trends which expanded the economic base of the town. The poor house was built to take care of those who did not share in that prosperity.

What remain largely invisible are the other public improvements enacted by the Corporation: building, widening and maintaining the town's roads, creating drains, legislating against pollution and harmful trades, repairing wharves and requiring safe building practices.

St. George's Walls

It is said that good fences make good neighbours. If this is so, then St. Georgians must be the best of good neighbours. Their walls and gates, though not unique in Bermuda, are certainly a defining feature of the town and add immeasurably to the distinctive differences which make St. George's so architecturally important.

Originally they must have been mere fences, stockades to keep wild pigs and domestic animals from trampling vegetable or herb gardens. By the beginning of the 18th century these fences were being superseded by stone walls and wooden gates placed between substantial gate posts. Some of these walls are quite high and reached their increased height as protection against thieves.

Bridger Goodrich topped his defensive walls at Bridge House with broken glass, a habit which was common in Bermuda into the middle of the 20th century when it was outlawed to protect the guilty. Prickly pears often served the same purpose and had to be periodically cut back to keep the alleys clear.

The sense of personal privacy that is regarded as an important part

of our rights in the 20th century barely existed in the 18th. Walls were not built to keep out prying eyes. Frequently low walls were topped with stone pillars interspersed with wooden picket fences, a charming design which allowed in both cooling breezes and chatter but still kept animals and undesirables out.

Privacy was a 19th century concept resulting from the prissiness of manners developed in the romantic era which then became the prudery of the Victorians. High blank walls to keep people from seeing into gardens which had become places of beauty and rest, rather than sources of food, began to appear.

Most of these walls were interrupted by gates, high enough to serve the purpose of their era. The gateposts supporting them were usually solid and often pretentious. As much as anything, one's status in the St. George's community was signalled by gateposts. Even the town had them, the largest and grandest of all.

CHAPTER THREE

Pillars of the Community

The public front of St. Peter's Church is entirely 19th century. The three gable ended wings, added to accommodate increasing congregations, are Anglicised with Gothic finials and arches, but rendered quite unusual by the fine, simple, classically inspired rose or bull's eye windows. The wide steps required by the advancement of the church to the south allow for dignified ceremonial. The single storey Sunday school on the right has recently had a second storey added.

Without its inhabitants, a town is merely a collection of buildings. Civil government, both colony wide and local, created order and maintained the fabric of St. George's—the roads, wells, wharves, markets and squares. But religion and social clubs were far more pervasive in daily life and played a larger role, then and now.

This chapter examines the churches and clubs of St. George's through the buildings which housed them. Their architecture differs from both civil buildings and private dwellings, reflecting the fashion of the age in which they were built and the statements they endeavoured to make to the people. These buildings are the foundations which have supported

the community of St. George's through four centuries.

A church was among the first buildings erected by the early settlers after their arrival in Bermuda. Within six months Governor Richard Moore built a framed church on one of the hills overlooking the town, but poor workmanship and high winds caused its collapse. The Governor used some of the timber to build himself a house and the remainder went to putting up "a Church of Palmitoe leaves" on the site **St. Peter's Church** occupies today.

A more substantial timber framed replacement was begun by interim Governor Miles Kendall in 1619 and was half finished when Governor Nathaniel Butler arrived that October.

Captain John Smith's 1624 drawing of Governor Nathaniel Butler's church (Reproduced from the original engraving by The Island Press in 1983.)

Butler completed the "large and handsome" church in time for Christmas services, and, the following August, the colony's first General Assembly met there to pass the first laws. In the early years the church served as a warehouse for the storage of the colony's tobacco crop as it awaited transportation to England. Throughout the

John Green's 1819 drawing of St. Peter's Church from the north, clearly shows the steeple. (Drawing in Verdmont Museum, Bermuda National Trust.)

17th century, Bermuda's courts, House of Assembly and council met in the church when the State House was occupied by other branches of the government.

According to John Smith's 1624 engraving, the church built by Kendall and Butler was a single, long room with a porch facing south. Strong wooden posts and buttresses supported the walls, upon which rested timber sills to anchor a gabled, steeply pitched thatch roof.

The church bell was hung from the branch of a cedar tree in the churchyard. The yard was later paled with a wooden fence to keep animals from wandering among the graves. From the earliest period, the cemetery was segregated: white inhabitants were buried inside the church or in the yard immediately surrounding the building; black and American and Caribbean Indian slaves, at least those who had been baptised, were interred in an adjoining graveyard to the west.

The eastern portion of the churchyard was added in 1808 when the burial ground for whites became too crowded. It was not acquired without a fight. A house on the land was occupied by widow Ann Wright. When the church vestry tried to buy the lot

from Wright in 1803, she refused to sell it because she had promised the property to her grandchildren. The Mayor, intent on getting the land, made her an offer: she would accept double the assessed value of the lot or he would get the government to commandeer the land by act of the House of Assembly. Widow Wright accepted the offer.

A terrible hurricane struck Bermuda on September 8, 1714, destroying the 1619 timber framed church, along with many other buildings. Reverend Andrew Auchinleck and his vestry elected to rebuild in stone rather than repair the damage.

The original Jacobean altar, the cedar pulpit, and a large number of timbers were salvaged from the ruins, so it can truthfully be said that the present structure has elements within it dating back to the very beginning of the colony.

About 1713 the new stone church was built by the collective effort of the whole town. Each household was required to provide help to complete the task. They were compensated with rum punch rather than wages. The design of the 1713 church was more ambitious than its predecessor. The building was of a cruciform

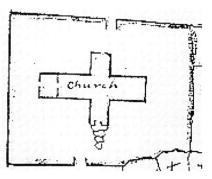

Detail from the Captain Joell spy map c. 1780. Cruciform footprint of St. Peter's Church. (Timothy Pickering Papers, Massachusetts Historical Society, Boston, Massachusetts.)

shape with the addition of a vestry room to the north and a porch to the south of the nave. Reverend Auchinleck added a wooden screen for the chancel and eight years later, a raised gallery for slaves attending services was built along the western wall, perhaps accompanied by a small entry porch on the north side of the western end.

A half century later Reverend Alexander Richardson initiated a major refurbishment of the parish church. In 1766 he removed the diamond paned casement windows installed in 1713 and replaced them with the sash variety which are present today.

St. Peter's Church and graveyard, from the only angle from which the early 18th century church can now be imagined. It was a simple gable ended rectangular church very similar to Old Devonshire Church, but considerably larger. The half-hexagon apse is an addition. The gnarled old cedar was preserved after it died in the great cedar blight in 1949-50 because it was the original belfry tree of the church.

Richardson also added a wooden steeple with a weathervane.

As the town's population expanded in the 1790s and early 1800s with the arrival of the British military and merchants from overseas, the parish church became increasingly crowded. In response, the vestry undertook a major expansion of the building in 1815.

The architect John Van Norden added two long wings to the south face of the church, on either side of the old porch, and a three sided apse onto the east end as a sanctuary and removed several interior walls. The work was done by Higgs and Richardson at a cost of £1,800.

The new wings encroached upon the south graveyard with little regard for those interred there. This nearly destroyed the addition, since several old vaults collapsed under the weight, undermining the walls. A steeple and bell tower were added to the west of the church, housing a clock purchased by Mayor John Till in Portsmouth, England, and shipped to the island. The steeple was removed in 1826 and the tower has had a flat roof since then.

The interior pews were rearranged and the vestry auctioned the right to sit in them to the parishioners for an annual rent. Competition was high for the most prestigious seats in church closest to the altar. Some people bid as much as £14 a year for their pews.

Despite the expansion, the parish church was still too crowded, thanks largely to the hundreds of garrison troops who attended services. To remedy this, the garrison chaplain usually held an early morning service for soldiers on Sunday before the regular service for the town's inhabitants. Governor Sir William Lumley arbitrarily abolished this practice in November 1819, soon after his arrival. The vestry politely petitioned the Governor to reverse his decision, objecting to the many soldiers standing in the aisles each Sunday. Their request fell on deaf ears. When the vestry attempted to take their grievance directly to the Crown, the hot-tempered Lumley came in person to their meeting, threatened arrest and reduced the vestry by dismissing most of its officers.

The battle culminated with soldiers under the Governor's orders laying siege to Mayor John Till, who barricaded himself in the Town Hall. This incident prompted the Bermuda House of Assembly to refuse any communication with Lumley, thus paralysing the colonial government. When the unpopular Lumley departed Bermuda in 1825, the rector resumed the practice of holding early services for soldiers. However, the vestry still (as recorded in their minutes of 1830) complained "[the soldiers] are not content with spitting on the floor, but actually do so on the cushions, which the pewholders provide for kneeling. Quids of tobacco were found in many of the seats last Sunday".

In April 1826, Bishop Inglis of

The interior of St. Peter's Church, Easter 1868, shows the former slave gallery and the ceiling before its beams were exposed. (Courtesy St. George's Historical Society Collection: Bermuda Archives, Hamilton, Bermuda.)

Nova Scotia dedicated the St. George's Parish Church to St. Peter the Apostle, and since then the building has been known as St. Peter's Church. During the previous two centuries, it had been known simply as the parish or town church.

A grant from Archdeacon Spencer seven years later prompted the construction of two more raised galleries for the growing number of free blacks living in St. George's. Spencer was a strong proponent of religious education for the colony's slave population and hoped the increased seating would bring more black St. Georgians to church. The pews in these galleries were likewise auctioned to the highest bidder.

A severe hurricane in September 1839 caused extensive damage to St. Peter's, which was saved only by the British garrison stabilising the ailing building. In the wake of the catastrophe the vestry initiated another expansion. In 1841 they lengthened the middle southern wing, destroying the old 1713 welcoming arms steps in

the process. The exterior of the church was decorated in the early Victorian Gothic style which was gaining popularity at the time. The vestry added arches to all the windows and supportive columns to the corners. They placed massive pinnacles upon the gable ends of the roof facing south. The 1841 renovation, as it turned out, was the last stylistic alteration to the church. St. Peter's Church today has not changed essentially in the last 150 years.

Despite this major refurbishment, the building was still considered by many to be too small and old fashioned. In 1862 the Bermuda government seriously considered razing the old building and it was only concern over disease spreading from reburials in the surrounding graveyard that saved the church from destruction.

In 1869 the parish vestry again voted to demolish the old church, a decision which was approved by the Governor. The timely granting, in 1872, of the old Government House to the vestry saved St. Peter's, for the vestry

decided it would be easier to build on a new site.

In 1874 construction began on a new place of worship and the old parish church slipped into further decay while work progressed. In 1899 the new building, now known as the Unfinished Church, was virtually finished and the bishop and vestry charitably decided not to do away with the old church. This proved to be a fortuitous decision, for financial concerns and internal disagreements permanently stalled completion of the new building.

In 1908 vital structural stabilisation was done to St. Peter's saving the church from collapse. Although a 1950 survey confirmed that the building required extensive repair, public sentiment strongly favoured preservation of the venerable old church. Under the guidance of Reverend John Stowe and Sir Stanley Spurling, the vestry launched a careful three-year restoration to preserve the church's ancient elements. The southern walls required the most attention, since their foundations still rested on open graves instead of firm bedrock. After the walls were stabilised, workmen completely replaced the decaying roof, which in some areas was held up only by the fusing of the roof slates. Beneath the 1841 extension, the original 1713 welcoming arms stairs were uncovered, as well as a number of graves.

After the restoration the original cedar box pews were reinstalled, and a number of pine ones, added in 1815 or 1841, were replaced with new cedar ones. The cedar blight of the late 1940s led to the donation of much of the timber and board used in the restoration.

As its 400th anniversary approaches, St. Peter's Church is in a good state of repair, thanks to the 1950-53 restoration. The exterior reflects early Victorian Gothic taste, but the interior houses an array of 17th and 18th century features.

In the churchyard extension, abutting Church Lane, is the **Hearse House**, built in the late 1850s. This building held the parish hearse when it was not in use. After St. Peter's graveyard was closed following a deadly yellow fever epidemic in 1853,

St. Peter's Sunday School from <u>Views</u> of <u>St. George's</u> <u>Bermuda</u> published by Robert O. Clifford, 1909. (Courtesy St. George's Historical Society Collection: Bermuda Archives, Hamilton, Bermuda.)

the government built a new cemetery on the North Shore, about a mile from the church, necessitating the use of the hearse. The Hearse House matches the early Victorian Gothic style of St. Peter's and the Sunday School. A small extension to the west was added in the 20th century.

St. Peter's Sunday School is set along Duke of York Street in front of the church. The lot on which this building stands was granted to John Zuill in 1794 as an extension of his property to the east. Reverend Richard T. Tucker purchased it from John Brownlow Tucker in 1844 to erect a Sunday school building. Since at least the early 18th century, religious education had been conducted in the church, but the vestry had finally decided to erect a separate building as a

school and function hall. The one storey school featured arched, Gothic style windows to match the post-1841 appearance of St. Peter's Church. Amid much controversy and considerable opposition, a second storey was added in 1991, complete with exterior balconies facing south and west.

At the top of Duke of Kent Street, above the old town, visitors cannot help but notice the sprawling remains of the **Unfinished Church**. This rambling Gothic ruin is all that is left of the building begun in 1874 to replace St. Peter's Church. Its simple, bold design was the brainchild of architect William Hay of the Edinburgh firm Hay and Henderson, and closely, probably deliberately, resembled the Cathedral of the Most

Holy Trinity in Hamilton. Hay's plans called for a cruciform church, crowned with a tower, whose walls were regularly buttressed and perforated with tall, arched windows. Two columns of brick pillars supported the roof internally.

Built to seat 650, the new church was substantially larger than its predecessor. Its formal design contrasted sharply with the almost haphazard evolution of St. Peter's.

Various complications thwarted the completion of the new church. First, a schism within the congregation led to the formation of the Reformed Episcopal Church, which constructed its own place of worship nearby. Then, in 1884 the Cathedral in Hamilton burnt down, and money originally earmarked for St. George's

A detail from an aerial photograph taken after 1953 shows that a surprising amount of the roof of the Unfinished Church still survived. To the right of the church is St. Peter's Rectory. (Courtesy St. George's Preparatory School.)

was diverted to rebuilding at the capital. Despite these difficulties, the new church was virtually completed by 1894 at a cost of £2,000. The roof was added in 1899 by private subscription.

Once Government House, now the Rectory, all that survives recognisable today from its glamorous past is the half octagonal bay, a not uncommon feature in late 18th century houses.

But attitudes were changing as demonstrated by the christening of the road which passes the church as Church Folly Road, and by popular consensus the congregation elected to renovate old St. Peter's, abandoning their new church on the verge of its completion. The western end of the church was badly damaged in the hurricane of 1926, and thereafter the walls and floor suffered from neglect, storms and erosion. The rest of the roof has since vanished and one side of the internal support pillars have toppled over. Today, the ruin is leased by the Bermuda National Trust, which is undertaking its stabilisation.

The buildings to the north served their intended purpose as the rectory for St. George's Parish. They are all that remain of the old Government House (see chapter 2) which occupied the hilltop before its front was demolished to lay the foundation of the Unfinished Church.

Besides being a notable monument to parish infighting, the Unfinished Church is the only rival in Bermuda to the Anglican Cathedral in Hamilton in the English 19th century Gothic revival style. Both are excellent examples and can give much larger versions in England a run for their architectural money. Faithfully adhering to an early Gothic form with plain lancet windows and arches, simple buttresses and low square tower, the church, once finished, might well have suited the town it would have dominated as well as the Cathedral that only now is ceasing to dominate Hamilton.

The Ebenezer Methodist Church, built in 1840, is a splendid example of late neo-classical design. It dominates the Duke of York Street ingress to St. George's. Visually, the façade is divided into three vertical sections, the central section having simple Doric pilasters surmounted by an entablature and above that a well-proportioned low pediment. A central door is flanked by arched fenestration extending uniformly for the full length of the building, which also continues the entablature and terminates with wider pilasters at the corners, each with raised definition.

Recent archaeological investigations conducted by the Bermuda National Trust have revealed part of the cellar and foundations of this earlier structure, completed in 1722.

Throughout the 19th century the Methodist Church was the greatest rival to St. Peter's in the contest for the souls of St. Georgians. The colony's introduction to Methodism came in the spring of 1748 when the famous evangelical preacher George Whitefield spent a few weeks in Bermuda to recover his health. Another 50 years were to pass before Irish missionary John Stephenson came to the colony with the express goal of converting the island's slaves and free blacks. The colony's leading politicians, all slaveowners, considered Stephenson's actions incendiary and gaoled him in St. George's for unlicensed preaching. They even went so far as to pass an act effectively prohibiting Methodism, an act which was disallowed by the Crown.

In 1808 Joshua Marsden arrived to continue Stephenson's work and the following year petitioned for a grant of land in Hamilton to erect a church. When Marsden departed in 1812, there were more than 80 Methodists in St. George's, led by the Higgs, Gibbons and Outerbridge families. By 1814 Reverend James Dunbar had erected a wooden chapel on the north side of Chapel Lane, but 15 years later this building was in ruinous condition. Its roof leaked so badly that services were impossible during rain. Clearly a new church was needed.

In March 1839, Reverend Theophilus Pugh and 15 trustees purchased a lot from Caroline Lewis which had originally been granted to Richard Somersall in 1761. The cornerstone for the **Ebenezer Methodist Church** was laid in June 1840 and the building was completed by New Year's Day, 1841, at a total cost of £1,000, £200 of which was given by the same House of Assembly that had once tried to outlaw Methodism.

Author William E. S. Zuill in *Bermuda Journey* states that the architect was a man named Dawson who had designed Napoleon's Tomb on St. Helena, but in this assertion he was apparently the victim of a joke. The late French emperor's grave on the island of his exile consisted of a small, simple slab with the words "Here Lies..." etched on it, and the tomb only housed his body until 1840, when it was returned to France for a grander burial. Historian Henry Wilkinson attributes the design to James Wright, a Royal Engineer then stationed at the St. George's garrison.

Authorship aside, the design of the 300-seat Methodist Church was brilliantly conceived. Its façade is dominated by long, narrow windows capped with fanlights, a feature common to Methodist chapels in Britain at the time. The south entrance was also capped with a fanlight. The front is decorated with dentil moulding, stout pilasters and a symmetrically placed capital. On the east side, there is a circular rose, or bull's eye, window above the door, while the original matching one on the west side has since been obscured by a stylistically harmonious porch added in 1962.

The ornamental wall in front, bordering Duke of York Street, was added in 1865. With the exception of the porch and a recent addition to the north side, the Ebenezer Church presents the same appearance as when it was completed in 1840. There is little doubt that the opening of this new, large Methodist church prompted the 1841 expansion of St. Peter's.

The large yard surrounding the church was used for various purposes. Soldiers from the garrison frequently

Even the Methodist Sunday School repeats with modest deference the classical splendours of its mother church, its central door and fanlight flanked by arched windows and pilasters supporting a plain pediment. The Methodist Church and its dependencies can claim to be the most architecturally coherent and splendid of any church environment in Bermuda.

In stark contrast to the nearby Unfinished Church, the Salvation Army Hall, built originally in 1879, but perhaps embellished in later years, seeks to infuse a Gothic treatment with a military sense. The result gives an effect of almost child-like fantasy and could almost have come straight out of Disney World. The Gothic details are picked out in white, as is the curiously elongated dentil decoration adding an incongruous note under the gable moulding. The stepped capping of the buttress setbacks lends a touch of Bermuda while the crenellations around the top of the tower remind us of the military overlay given to Christianity by the Salvation Army.

attended services and many of those who succumbed to yellow fever or other fatal ailments while stationed in Bermuda were buried in the graveyard before the practice was discontinued in 1854.

The Methodist Parsonage to the northeast of the church was erected in 1865 at a cost of £550. The most striking feature of this one storey U-shaped structure is the many top hung blinds. The flat roofed section to the north, flanked by parapets, was added to the original building at a later date.

The Methodist Sunday School (formerly the Ex-Home Sunday School) to the west, built around 1874, has survived virtually unaltered with its well proportioned gable roof structure whose front façade closely matches the style of the main church to the south.

On Sundays, the one room schoolhouse was used primarily for the religious education of the parish's black children. During the other six days each week, it was rented to the St. George's Grammar School and housed the school until 1912, when it moved to Park Villa.

St. Paul's Church, the Reformed Episcopal Church, built deliberately near the Unfinished Church, was completed in 1879 and named for a rival apostle. This build-ing, now the **Salvation Army Hall**, fronts on Governor's Alley and was erected on the site of the 18th century house of Reverend Andrew Auchinleck. His house was long gone by the time the "free" or Reformed Episcopal faction of the town congregation broke away in the early 1870s, led by William C.J. Hyland, former director of the parish Sunday school and founder of the YMCA. They hired a brilliant, charismatic preacher in Reverend R. Anthony Bilkey who drew crowds from Hamilton each Sunday.

The colonial government consistently denied Bilkey the right to perform marriages and the insulted preacher left Bermuda in 1880. Thus

"The Dedication of the YMCA" by Edward James, 1865. (Courtesy St. George's Historical Society Collection: Bermuda Archives, Hamilton, Bermuda.)

the newly finished St. Paul's Church was vacated almost immediately after it was consecrated. A less inspiring replacement for Bilkey was found, but the congregation dwindled and eventually rejoined St. Peter's, abandoning St. Paul's.

The church is rather typical of the period, an ornate single storey building with a high gable roof, whose eaves are graced with dentil mouldings. The arched windows are notable for the eyebrows above them. The tower appears to be a later addition, as is the wing to the east and the Sunday school to the west. The deserted building was rescued by the Salvation Army who still occupy it today.

The **YMCA Building** on the corner of Duke of Clarence Street and Duke of York Street is one of the easiest buildings to date. It has 1862 etched on the gable above its three fanlight windows. The edifice is a paragon of Victorian excess, by far the most elaborately decorated structure

in St. George's. Its corners are covered in quoins and the gable ends and cornices positively drip with dentil mouldings. Stocky architraves cap the side windows, while three symmetrical windows in front allow light into the large hall on the top floor. The arcaded porch is flanked by balustrade-capped walls.

At the beginning of the 18th century, the lot on which the YMCA now stands was the site of Miriam Briggs' house, but this building had vanished by 1812, when the governor granted an empty lot to Freemasons' Lodge 266 of St. George's to build a meeting hall. Work had still not commenced three years later when the lodge secured the use of the State House, so the lot remained vacant.

In September 1862 it was transferred to William C.J. Hyland, James A. Atwood and William Tudor Tucker, trustees for building a new hall for a branch of the Young Men's Christian Association. Hyland had just returned from New York City where he had come

to appreciate the benefits of the organisation. The building went up within a few months and nearly fills the original grant.

The YMCA sought to wean the town's youth and the garrison soldiers away from the many grog shops on Water Street by directing them towards more wholesome activities in its reading room and lecture hall. By the 1910s, however, the organisation had drifted a bit from its original purpose.

The late Frank Gurr recalled that although the lower floor still housed a Sunday school, a "gentleman's club" met upstairs. In 1935 the building was transferred to the parish church and became known as St. Peter's Hall. Twenty years later it was purchased by Frederick C. Outerbridge who merged it with his grocery store next door. At present, the lower floor is storage for Somers Market, while the upper floor has been converted into an apartment.

Somers Market next door is decorated similarly to the YMCA. The

The Good Templars' Hall admirably represents the plain, utiltarian style that the decline of St. George's in the high Victorian period produced, instead of any number of bad, but more expensive alternatives.

core of the building dates to 1825 or earlier, but the façade was altered to match the building next door, probably in 1875, when James A. Atwood briefly owned the store. Throughout the late 19th century, a verandah with cast iron balustrades graced the front of the store. The present market is actually a conglomeration of four buildings, composed of the YMCA, Frederick Outerbridge's old grocery store flush with Duke of York Street, the converted sail loft of Thomas Wright, which is the rear portion of the store, and a two storey store built about 1838 by Benjamin Higgs, the northernmost room. The front yard of the sail loft was enclosed in the 1950s, and the exterior walls of this enclosed yard were decorated with quoins to match those on the grocery store and YMCA

While the town's churches attracted citizens each Sunday, a number of fraternal organisations

and friendly societies vied to occupy their weekdays, providing a venue where merchants and workmen might gather informally. Freemasonry was the oldest and most elite social club in St. George's. Bermudians were first introduced to the Masonic order in 1744, when Governor Alured Popple was appointed Provincial Grand Master for the island. Popple died before he could establish a lodge, but his brother, William, succeeded him as both Governor and Grand Master.

For reasons unknown, this lodge became defunct some time in the 1780s. The earliest permanent lodges came with the British military in the 1790s, and some survive to the present.

The St. George's Lodge was founded by John Van Norden and members of the 47th Regiment who came to Bermuda from Halifax, Nova Scotia. To hedge their bets, they applied to both the English and Scottish

orders and received charters from both. Van Norden and his brothers retained the Scottish Registry for Lodge 266, since renumbered 200, dated August 7, 1797, while the Atlantic Phoenix Lodge 307, chartered by the Grand Registry of England, moved first to Flatts and later to Hamilton.

In 1812 the St. George's Lodge was granted land to build on the corner of Duke of York and Duke of Clarence Streets. Three years later, they still had not begun construction when the State House became vacant and Mayor Van Norden obtained it for his lodge. The YMCA was built on the lot.

During the 19th century, Freemasonry in St. George's proliferated, largely due to the strong British military presence. By 1900 there were seven lodges. These all shared the State House building and met on different nights, while Hannibal Lodge 224 met occasionally on Queen Street.

Membership in the town's various Masonic lodges was chiefly limited to British military officers and the town's leading gentlemen and merchants.

More modest St. George's citizens created their own clubs. Carpenters, masons (the stonelaying kind), storekeepers, painters and other craftsmen formed the backbone of The Order of Good Templars, a society based in Nova Scotia. By the mid 1870s there were no fewer than 23 chapters in Bermuda, four of which met in St. George's.

In 1874, 12 trustees of Eureka Lodge 20 purchased an old house and lot on Shinbone Alley for £90 to erect a lodge building. Within ten years, they had raised the **Good Templars' Hall** on the site. The lower floor contained four apartments, each with its own garden and outdoor privy, which were rented to help supplement the operating costs of the lodge. The large chamber upstairs was where the Templars met.

Membership in the Templars significantly overlapped with the Order of the Sons of Temperance, also of Nova Scotia, which shared the lodge building. One Temperance chapter had the fitting name, Anti-Bacchus Lodge. By 1915 the Order of the Good

Decorative Detail in St. George's

Decorative detail in Bermuda's 18th century architecture is rare, so rare that it is almost never introduced without a specific practical purpose. Eyebrows, now liberally splashed about on buildings in the mistaken belief that they will look Bermudian, were used to divert rainwater from flush window frames containing casement windows. As windows were recessed and sashes replaced casements, eyebrows disappeared. Simple architraves served a similar purpose.

The arrival of cement late in the 18th century allowed for the introduction of elements which were decorative rather than practical, but only the grandest houses used them at first. When Andrew Durnford was introducing his pilasters, belt course and plain eave moulding at Durnford in St. George's, Thomas Butterfield was introducing quoins as corner pilasters at Clermont in Paget. It is quite possible that his corner quoins were structural and believed to strengthen the building.

Quoins, dentil moulding and architraves over the windows were also common.

As the 19th century progressed, so did decorative treatments on buildings, most frequently cornice and gable mouldings, but as time went on dizzying treatments such as the YMCA and Salvation Army church appeared.

Fortunately, the 20th century vernacular revival put an end to these Victorian excesses. However, a failure to understand the nature and uses of butteries or the practical purpose of eyebrows or window architraves gave rise to the notion that these "decorative" elements were what 18th century Bermudian architecture was about. They have been used to excess and are now being combined with a Victorian revival to produce new excesses of pointless embellishment.

The affectionately regarded Longbird House was an example of a 20th century Bermudian house that had it all—quoins, keystones, elaborate architraves, fan lights, arches, everything except curved eyebrows. It has now been demolished.

The simplest but most common form of decoration included keystones, concrete sills, moulding at the corners and eaves, and belt or string courses.

Samaritans' Lodge, although of less sophisticated construction, has much of the dignity and good proportion of the original Town Hall. Its awkward site required a narrower building than might have been desired, but the dignified wide entrance with its elegant fanlight provides presence.

The Independent Order of Good Samaritans, Rechab Lodge 7, and its sister organisation, the Daughters of Samaria, Princess Louise Lodge 12, were founded in St. George's in 1876, chapters of a larger New York based society established in 1847. There were at least eight chapters active in Bermuda by 1878.

The St. George's branch met in the store to the south of Bridge House until 1900, when it purchased at auction a storehouse built by John Davenport about 1844. They named the building **Samaritans' Lodge** and renovated it in 1907 after they redeemed a mortgage and dismissed tenants who had been occupying the lower floor as a workshop. They added a fanlight and side lights around the front door, with the initials of their organisation above.

About 1915 the St. George's chapter of Good Samaritans quarrelled with the national branch in New York, who threatened to suspend their charter and withhold the password sent out each year. The outcome of this dispute is not clear, but the chapter had lapsed by 1970. The building is at present owned by the Bermuda National Trust and is rented to the Bermudian Heritage Association which is developing a museum to showcase the history of black friendly societies and lodges.

The Grand United Order of Odd Fellows was another active organisation which erected two lodges: one on Cut Road about 1851 and another more recently at the foot of Rose Hill which has since been converted to a cinema. Unlike the Samaritans, this organisation has survived into the 1990s, although the average age of its members is considerable.

Templars was defunct, and the upper floor became the Temperance Hall School. Later, the St. George's Colts cricket club and the Carnation Girls' Club met there.

In 1947, Victor Trott, the sole surviving trustee of the Good Templars, inherited the building and converted the upper floor into a carpenter's shop. It was recently renovated and is now private apartments.

The black community of St. George's emulated white social and charitable clubs in the decades after the abolition of slavery. The benevolent societies they created, linked to English and American friendly societies, provided a number of services which included relief for the poor, job training and extending small loans and insurance for funeral expenses. Like the Freemasons, these groups staged pageants in town to foster solidarity and community support.

Seal of the Rechab Lodge. (Among the Samaritans' Lodge papers. Courtesy of Ross Smith: Bermuda Archives, Hamilton, Bermuda.)

Clubs and social organisations play a much smaller role in communities today than they did a century ago. Cinemas, television and sports offer more accessible distractions. Government social services and Bermuda's prevailing prosperity have eliminated the charitable and aid-driven causes which brought the Samaritans, Templars and Odd Fellows together. St. George's churches, however, continue to shape the lives of those living in the parish, and thus are the enduring pillars of the community.

CHAPTER FOUR

On The Waterfront

Often sketched and photographed, this view of St. George's from the east is taken from Barrack Hill. Ordnance Island with its only surviving house is on the left, while Fort George still crowns its hill on the right.

St. George's has always been first and foremost a port. The site is ideal, with close proximity to a natural sheltered harbour and easy access to the sea. The inlet which once dominated the centre of the town enabled Bermuda's early settlers to moor their boats close to the State House and church.

By 1620 Governor Butler had built a storehouse on Ducking Stool Island to receive Company goods sent out in the magazine ships. In an era before reliable roads and with the virgin forest only partially cleared, boat traffic was the fastest and most convenient means of transport. Planters from the main island, who visited the capital regularly for civil, social or commercial reasons, came first to the town's waterfront.

The waterfront of the 17th century bore little resemblance to that of today. The original coastline lay just to the south of Water Street, so named because it once ran directly along the shore. Land grants from the early 18th century reveal that only 30 to 35 feet

of land separated the street from the harbour. Two natural coastal features, Stile Point and Powell's Point, today lie buried beneath Hunter's Wharf and the storehouse at 50 Water Street respectively. Much of the shoreline to the east and west of the town was inaccessible, shielded by extensive shoals which deterred waterborne traffic, and cliffs which made a landward approach difficult.

During the Somers Island Company period, the harbourfront changed little. All trade was conducted aboard the magazine ship from London or regulated by the government, so there was little private commerce and thus no need for individual storehouses and wharves.

When the Company was abolished in 1684, Bermudians could, for the first time, legally trade with other colonies without prohibitive regulations. They built dozens of swift and nimble sloops for commerce abroad and needed wharves and storehouses to support their fleet at home.

Between 1693 and 1721, the

Crown granted land on the south side of Water Street to merchants in need of wharves and storehouses. Indeed, the earliest properties granted were water lots for wharves. Many of the grantees were merchants who lived in the western parishes and needed facilities in St. George's.

For much of the 18th century all vessels were legally required to load and unload at the capital under the watchful eyes of the colony's customs officers. The early builders erected combination dwelling-warehouses, often living above their stored merchandise. Light draught vessels moored alongside the wharves which extended into the harbour, while larger ships moored in deeper water in the centre of St. George's Harbour and unloaded their cargoes into lighters which ferried the goods to shore.

Of the town's early storehouses, few survive. The front portion of **Block House** is now greatly changed. It was originally granted to the Reverend Andrew Auchinleck in 1731,

A close-up of the front of the Esten House on King's Square shows recent alterations to the verandah to permit commercial access to the upper, once residential, level. The original internal access survives.

although there had been a timber frame building on the site belonging to Mary Pearman.

On this lot, described as "voide ground neare unto the Town Dock", Auchinleck or his successors built a house, warehouse and wharf. This complex belonged to Nathaniel Butterfield in 1791, when it was used as the Customs House. In 1839 two of Butterfield's daughters exchanged with their sister and brother-in-law Catherine and Benjamin Tucker this building for Tankfield in Paget. Later owners included Henry E. Higgs and Nicholas C. McCallan. In the 1870s McCallan ran a bakery and grocery on the property.

In the early part of the 20th century, Block House became a showroom and base for the Bermuda Electric Light Company. The storehouse immediately to the east of Block House, also owned by BELCO, was granted to Paget merchant John Trimingham in 1713, and within 20 years he had built

a house and wharf on the lot. This property was inherited by Butterfield, his grandson, and joined with the Block House lot by 1791.

The **Esten House**, just north of The White Horse Tavern, with its fine verandah on the corner of King's Square and Water Street west, dates back to at least 1782, on the site of a structure erected in 1709 by John Dickinson. The property was one of six chosen by lot and given to merchants living on the main island in 1707. Two years later the parish vestry accused Dickinson of encroaching on the Town Bridge Wharf while erecting a building on the lot and ordered him to pull it down. The merchant appealed to Governor Bennett who overruled the vestry on the grounds that Dickinson's building did not prejudice access to the bridge.

The Esten family acquired the house from Dickinson's heirs, probably in the early 1740s. In 1782, John Esten received a grant to extend his wharf

further south into the harbour, which he accordingly did. In 1805 Esten's son sold the property to William Tucker who, the following year, built the attractive verandah which graces the eastern side of the house to give outside access to the upper floor. Tucker also extended his wharf another 12 feet further south.

The building was the ideal merchant's residence. It was centrally located for business right on King's Square. It had its own wharf with ample retail and storage space on the ground floor and living space above, with separate access via the verandah from which the family could look down upon the activities of the town.

During the War of 1812 William Tucker made a considerable fortune as Deputy Prize Agent for George Redmond Hulbert, secretary to Admiral Warren. Tucker handled more than 200 captured vessels and their cargoes worth in excess of £600,000, netting him at least £15,000 in commissions.

The Brick House on west Water Street as it was shown in a stylised sketch drawn c. 1731. (Bermuda National Trust Collection: Bermuda Archives, Hamilton, Bermuda.)

There is little doubt that his store-house and wharf were constantly crammed with French and American prize goods during the war years. Tucker built a grand house on Rose Hill and in 1818 sold the Esten House property to another up-and-coming merchant, John Davenport, who apparently lived there in the 1820s. Davenport had married into the Forbes family, prominent merchants originally from Scotland. Rose Hill was demolished in 1905 to build the St. George Hotel.

William E. S. Zuill's *Bermuda Journey* contains an entertaining oral history account of Davenport hoarding his gold and silver profits in arrowroot kegs kept in the cellar of his house. The treasure was said to have amounted to more than £75,000 by the time of Davenport's death in 1857. The only catch is that Esten House has no cellar. Later in the century, the Higinbothom brothers operated a drugstore known as The Medical Hall on the site.

In 1929 William Frith purchased the property and converted it into a bar and hotel, expanding the building to the south on land reclaimed by Esten and Tucker from the harbour. Frith's new White Horse Tavern opened its doors the following year and has been a St. George's landmark ever since. The restaurant and bar were extensively renovated in the mid 1960s and in 1980, when yet another extension into the harbour was made.

To the west of the Esten House and the White Horse Tavern is the site of the **Brick House Wharf**, which, in the 18th century, was the most substantial house and wharf complex in the town. Robert Dinwiddie purchased no fewer than six lots, now 34-40 Water Street, between 1725 and 1750 and combined them into one large property. In 1726 he built a great wharf extending 100 feet into the harbour, the largest built in the colony up to that period, complete with its own fishpond.

He lived in an elegant red brick house which could not fail to impress. It stood out sharply amidst the Bermuda stone houses and announced Dinwiddie's wealth, since all of the bricks had been imported from England or America at vast expense.

Dinwiddie left Bermuda in 1738 and eventually became Governor of Virginia from 1751 to 1758. His house and wharf were used as His Majesty's Customs House in the 1760s. During the following decade, Dr. Robert Forbes purchased the property and, after his death in 1785, his widow Mary and daughter lived there off and on. In 1790 Mary Forbes married William Grant, a schoolteacher, but was widowed again three years later. She operated her own shipping firm under the name of Mary Grant & Co. in the 1800s, stocking goods to the value of £3,500.

In 1848 the property was divided into smaller lots and sold. The Brick House was demolished in the 19th century and replaced by a monolithic four storey building that has also since been levelled.

The **Smith House** (now Taylors) on Water Street west is another rare survivor from the 18th century. John Hilton had already erected a storehouse and wharf on the lot when it was granted to him in 1697. The alley to

Lieutenant H. S. Clive's 1864 painting looks west from Ordnance Island. It shows the buildings on Hunter's Wharf with Durnford behind. Fort George is to the right of the flag. (Bermuda National Trust Collection: Bermuda Archives, Hamilton, Bermuda.)

the west of his store led to the Gaol Dock, down which many condemned prisoners walked to the boat that would take them to the gallows.

The house which stands today appears to be a replacement of Hilton's earlier structure. Its U-shape and hip roof suggest it was built about the middle of the 18th century by Samuel Smith, who owned the property in 1759. John and Catherine Smith were living in the house when they mortgaged the property to Edward Goodrich in 1786.

John Smith was a vendue master who made his living from his commission on the sale of the prize goods, marine salvage and cargoes of trade goods, which he auctioned to the public for other merchants. Goodrich apparently foreclosed on the property and sold it to merchant Isaac Cox, but the Smiths continued to live there. John died in 1816 in his eighties. Catherine was still living in the house in 1825 when it was sold at auction to John Barr for £750 by Isaac Cox's heirs.

Originally from Scotland, Barr was an active merchant in St. George's.

He married Edward Goodrich's daughter Frances and inherited many of his father-in-law's lucrative trade connections when Goodrich died in 1817. He added the long storehouse reaching to the wharf's edge on the east side of the lot.

After Barr's death in 1853 his widow and most of their children emigrated to England. His remaining son in Bermuda sold the property to Robert C. McCallan in 1875. McCallan did little to change the layout of the buildings but may have added the wooden verandahs at the ends of the southern wings.

By 1917 there was a small blacksmith's shop on the wharf, perhaps to cater to the many people who left their horses at the stables run by the Spurling family on the lot. Roy Taylor acquired the property from the McCallan family in 1960 and ran a clothing store. In 1970, he converted two of the original three doors opening onto Water Street into windows.

The basement may be the island's only remaining example of a salt cellar. Loose salt raked on the Turks

Islands may have been stored there until the autumn months when it would fetch high prices in Virginia and the Carolinas during the slaughtering season.

Between 1743 and 1751, St. George's expanded westward into an area known as Stile Hill. The name comes from the early 17th century stile erected where the road to the Ferry intersected with a livestock palisade. This palisade stretched all the way from St. George's Harbour to the North Shore. It was built by Governor Daniel Tucker in 1617 and was maintained by succeeding governors, but it is doubtful whether this ancient feature still stood by the 1740s.

Governor William Popple made three large grants in the area, although these did not contain the building clause found in earlier grants and, as a result, were slow to develop. The area that is now the site of Long House Wharf was granted to George Forbes, who perhaps erected a small wharf to support his shipping business. Stile Point, a natural rock outcrop extend-

The large, U-shaped Hunter Building is one of the most elegant of St. George's late 18th century houses with particularly beautiful original windows and fine quoined pilasters on the corners. Discordant though it undoubtedly is, the long verandah, built in the 1920s of reinforced concrete, derives its elegant proportions from the house it obscures. There is no better example of such a verandah in Bermuda.

buying the property from Atwood's estate, Shedden borrowed heavily in 1816 to build an extensive new wharf by enclosing the entire Stile Point within sea walls and building into the harbour to the south.

By the early 1820s, the house and wharf were worth £4,800, perhaps the most valuable non-military piece of real estate in St. George's. Unfortunately for Shedden he over-extended himself financially and in 1826 the property was seized by the Provost Marshal and given to the Hon. Tudor Hinson and Dr. Joseph Hutchison, to whom Shedden owed £3,000.

In the 1830s the wharf was used by Hinson's son-in-law, Dr. Joseph S. Hunter, who purchased it outright in 1842 and for whom the houses and wharf are named. Throughout the mid 19th century, Hunter's Wharf and the residence and storehouse nearby bustled with shipping activity.

L ong House, which today faces a Shell Oil service station, and its wharf to the southeast, were built by John Paynter, a merchant from Bailey's Bay. He took a lot worth £100 in 1788 and by 1794 had erected a house and wharf worth £700. Paynter's building retained the same approach as the residence over storehouse buildings of the early 18th century, but was executed on a much larger scale.

ing into the harbour, was given to London merchant John Piggott, who apparently failed to develop the grant. A 300-foot stretch of land between the harbour and the Ferry Road (today's Wellington Street), to the west of the Forbes and Piggott grants, was awarded to another London merchant, William Selby, who likewise failed to improve his property.

Of the three grants, the one at Stile Point was the first to be built upon. Captain Anthony Atwood acquired the lot and erected a house and wharf worth £1,300 which he rented in part to the firm of Place and Paynter in 1781.

Now known as the **Hunter Building** (or sometimes the Meyer Building), it is a large two storey U-shaped building with four large chim-

neys flanking the front ends and wings. Aside from the concrete verandah added in the 1920s, the present building looks much the same as when the Atwood family lived there in the 1780s.

Captain Atwood was an extremely active merchant and ship captain who traded extensively throughout the West Indies and the newly-formed United States. He died in 1801 and was survived by a wife and two daughters. After Atwood's widow died in 1810 the property was sold to Archibald Shedden.

Shedden was the son of Robert Shedden and Agatha Goodrich, loyalists who were driven from Portsmouth, Virginia, during the American Revolution. Archibald came to Bermuda in 1803 to work as a clerk in his uncle Edward's firm, Goodrich & Co. After

The small commercial building or workshop behind the Hunter Building was probably built on the site of an earlier detached kitchen. The base of the chimney appears to be from the 18th century, but the upper part is a clumsy addition. Just below the wall plate there is a series of blocked embrasures, perhaps to carry large beams to support machinery.

Long House is a now-unique example of a double house, the other having been the Mussons' now-destroyed Frascati in Flatts. Arched alleys lead through the building to the yard behind, which was quarried out of the hillside to provide stone for its construction. The upper floor has narrower walls than the lower, the Flemish gable is supported by an elegant, narrow chimney. By St. George's standards the gates are very plain.

Long House is an enormous structure, nearly 100 feet long, with a small west wing on the northern end of the house. The top floor was devoted to living space, reached by side stairs on the west side. Rows of wide, arched double doors open into the extensive cellars on the ground floor, where a variety of goods brought from across the seas or awaiting export were housed. The building is flanked at each end with enormous chimneys which support decorative Flemish gables, while a third, internal, chimney can be found at the end of the northern wing.

After John Paynter's death in 1800, the house was divided into northern and southern halves and given to John and James Musson. In 1819 the Musson brothers extended their wharf another 55 feet into the harbour. Until 1895 the two halves of the house were owned separately and each side had its own privy, garden and walled backyard.

The large lot granted to William Selby west of Hunter's Wharf was sub-divided between Joseph Gwynn, William Outerbridge and George Ball by the 1780s. Gwynn, a silversmith, built a workshop and modest gable roofed house. The other lots were consolidated, first by merchant James McDowall and then, in 1791, by Captain Andrew Durnford of the Royal Engineers.

Durnford, a veteran of the American Revolution, briefly visited Bermuda in 1783 and prepared a report pointing out to his superiors the colony's strategic military position. Five years later he was dispatched with Governor Henry Hamilton to put the island in a fit state of defence and to explore the potential for a major Royal Navy dockyard. Between 1789 and 1795 the captain built or rebuilt four forts with the help of military and slave labour.

From 1789 until 1791, Durnford lived in Stewart Hall with his mistress Elizabeth Lucas, with whom he had six children. In 1791 he purchased land on Stile Hill and set to work the following year building a grand house of his own design now known as **Durnford**. Durnford's parish assessments suggest that it took two years to complete the house. His assessment leaped from £750 in 1792 to £1,490 in 1794 and climbed further to £3,565 the following year.

With its perfectly symmetrical layout, the massive square two storey structure was a model of Georgian design. If original, the house has the oldest documented use of keystones over the windows. Its roof, with rafter feet protruding through the eave moulding (an architectural trait mostly confined to St. George's), is a 19th century re-

A very deep chimney terminates the wing forming an L behind the north end of Long House. There is no matching wing at the far end.

Durnford, built in 1793-5, was popularly known as the Fifth Fort, as its builder was believed to have skimmed from the four fortifications he was employed to build in order to create this massive, ponderous house for himself. Its austerity relieved only by plain mouldings, keystones over the windows and a version of welcoming arms steps that would have been better copied from any number of 18th century examples nearby, the house also earns its nickname visually.

placement of the original. Two large internal chimneys project through the hip roof capping this grand mansion.

The verandah on the south side of Durnford is a recent addition, revealed by the architraves that once shielded the windows from rain. Below the cliff to the south, Andrew Durnford built a wharf, storehouse, fishpond and bathing house.

Many of the Captain's contemporaries were more than a little suspicious about the source of the building materials used in the house and wharf, since Durnford was in charge of rebuilding the island's forts. The stone in the walls of Durnford, far thicker than any other private residence, was probably intended for public use, so it is not surprising that Durnford's enemies referred to this house as the colony's "Fifth Fort".

In October 1797 Andrew Durnford became the first Mayor of the newly incorporated Town of St. George. He died shortly before his term expired and left two wills. In the first he left his house and land in England to his wife Jemima and two sons, while in the second he gave his new house and land in Bermuda to his "good friend" Elizabeth Lucas and their four surviving children.

Lucas, who took the surname Durnford after Andrew's death, tried repeatedly to rent or sell the huge house with little success. After her children had come of age, in 1814 Elizabeth Lucas Durnford purchased a small lot to the east of the house and built a cottage where she lived. Three of the children moved to the United States while the fourth, merchant James A. Durnford, mortgaged his share and eventually lost it through foreclosure. In 1844 and 1845 merchant John Davenport, the alleged hoarder of gold who owned the Esten House, bought each child's share and reunited the property after 30 years.

After Davenport's death his daughter Jane and son-in-law William L. Penno inherited the house and wharf. In 1859 Penno, then Deputy Military Storekeeper for the British garrison, constructed the large wharf that bears his name over Durnford's earlier effort and the following year built a long two storey warehouse to better facilitate his duties. This building, dated 1860 above its main door, still stands today on Penno's Wharf.

After the American Revolution, British trade in general and Bermudian trade in particular became far more volatile. Trade with the new United States was problematic and subject to high duties and tight regu-

Privately built in 1860, Deputy Military Storekeeper William Penno's wharf shortly afterwards cashed in on the furious burst of commercial activity associated with running the blockade of the Southern States in the Civil War. It is appropriately large and utilitarian, but has now been "beautified" with the inappropriate addition of planters, palms, and heavy "Victorian" electric lights. Under the rafter feet is an example of the characteristic St. George's square moulding.

A detail from Thomas Driver's 1833 painting shows the eastern end of Water Street before the Davenport Warehouses were built. The cattle stalls on the wharf can be seen clearly, as can the Samaritans' Cottages. (Courtesy Fay and Geoffey Elliott Collection: Bermuda Archives, Hamilton, Bermuda.)

lations, but new markets were opening up elsewhere. Sailing vessels grew in size with correspondingly deeper draughts, and the town's early 18th century wharves became inadequate.

Between 1800 and 1820 many Bermudian merchants shifted their base of operations to the new deep water port of Hamilton, leaving mostly newcomers from England, Ireland and the West Indies to revitalise the old port. These 19th century merchants petitioned for and received grants to extend the old water lots a considerable distance further into the harbour, changing the face of the town's waterfront.

Many of the old houses and stores along Water Street continued in use, but new warehouses were built on the reclaimed land. These long, narrow buildings accommodated bulky goods like cotton bales, lumber, masts and cordage. The new storehouses were often two storey buildings, where the lower floor was used for storage while the upper floor, fronting on Water Street, housed a retail or wholesale shop. Notably absent were living spaces integrated within these new facilities. Business practices changed in the latter half of the 18th

This c. 1820 commercial building, the Upper Davenport Warehouse, is one of the finest of its kind. As Ocean Sails, it is still in commercial use. It has both pilasters and architraves over the windows, rare additions to such buildings which were more often left without decoration.

century, shifting from family operations to partnerships between unrelated merchants. The separation of home and workplace, which was occurring throughout Britain and America at this time, led to the construction of storehouses solely for business purposes. The merchants who owned them lived elsewhere in St. George's or Bermuda.

The **Upper Davenport Warehouse**, which today houses Ocean Sails on East Water Street, offers an excellent example of the larger storehouses built in the early 19th century.

The building occupies the entirety of the original grant to Margery Potter, so that its southern wall is roughly in line with the original 17th century coastline. Another 140 or so feet of wharf was added to the south, first by Thomas Handy in 1725 and later by John Davenport about 1820. The present building was erected between 1833 and 1842 on the site of an earlier wooden shed.

The upper floor is level with Water Street and probably housed a retail store. The lower floor, accessible from the wharf side, received goods landed from ships moored alongside. In the 1870s, Tom Pitt operated a ships' chandlery business out of this building and during the 1920s, the period of Prohibition in the United States, owner Frederick C. Outerbridge stockpiled liquor in the warehouse. It was destined for the holds of "rum runners" and, ultimately, American speakeasies.

Another building, the **Lower Davenport Warehouse** just to the south, was constructed over Thomas Handy's 1725 wharf by John Davenport about 1835, replacing a previous wooden structure. The lower floor originally contained cattle stalls for

One of a long series of 19th century buildings on the harbour side of west Water Street, the Perry Building shares the alterations made to suit the requirements of developing commerce. The arched "alley" serving the dock has survived where many others have not. The flush window frames upstairs are protected from water by small architraves and the side hung blinds are held back with the old style S catches.

livestock imported from America while the upper storey housed goods. A long series of arches once allowed light and air into the cattle stalls, but these have since been walled up. In 1854 the Corporation of St. George's regulated against polluting the harbour and closed all the slaughterhouses along the waterfront.

The building is in poor condition today but is well worth a visit. Its old strap-hinged double doors evoke an age when the town's waterfront bustled with activity and cattle milled on the quayside.

The **Perry Building** on Higgs' Wharf on west Water Street (now occupied by the Bermuda Railway Company) is another mid 19th century wharf complex, but executed on a more modest scale than Davenport's facility at the east end of town. In 1697, Samuel Stone owned the lot and built a storehouse there. A few decades later, it was acquired by William Riddell of Heron Bay, Southampton, one of the most prominent and successful merchants of the 1750s and 1760s. The Riddell family sold it to John Paynter in 1791, who passed it to John James Tucker.

Between 1818 and 1821 Tucker

extended the property from its original coastline 47 feet south of Water Street and added 129 more feet in two successive wharf building episodes until it jutted well into the harbour. The wharf face of today sits on a line of shoals that had earlier barred easy access to the town's west wharves and is still that built by Tucker more than 170 years ago.

Few of the warehouses thrown up to accommodate the increase in business supplying the British military have survived in anything approximating their original form. Nor indeed has this one, the Lower Davenport Warehouse, off the east end of Water Street, but this western side is little changed beyond the arch infills. It is one of the most important such survivors.

Tucker was a successful wharf builder but an indifferent merchant. After renting and mortgaging his water lot a number of times, he finally sold it to Robert Higgs in 1836. About 1841 Higgs erected the building which now stands, using the old style, with living space above and stores below. A public path once ran to the water's edge on the west side of the lot, but between 1854 and 1876 Higgs built a gate and a room above the alley to regulate access to the goods he had on the wharf. Higgs died in 1862 at the age of 85, just as blockade running out of Bermuda was beginning during the American Civil War.

Higgs' son Joseph moved to Nebraska in the United States and sold the house and wharf to Albert Inglis in 1877 for £1,000. Inglis was a typical merchant of the late 19th century, whose wide ranging stock-in-trade included West Indian produce, postage stamps, fresh meat, general groceries and wholesale provisions. He was famous for his aerated water which he provided to military messes and taverns in the town, and for importing ice from Nova Scotia.

In the early 20th century, Inglis operated the St. George's Ice Com-

As eccentric a house as any in Bermuda, to determine a possible layout for Glen Duror from the outside stretches the imagination to its limit. Its characteristically plain early 19th century features are relieved by an interesting pedimented entrance. The house has two half hexagonal wings projecting towards the west at an open angle and must have been built by a man of more determination than natural architectural ability.

pany, which manufactured ice artificially in a shop located on the wharf.

While merchants in town were extending their wharves deeper into the harbour and building new storehouses, others were developing new waterfront property to the west of Stile Hill.

In 1793 the same act that incorporated the Town of Hamilton included a provision to execute the Glebe Act of 1791. This act subdivided the 50 acres set aside for the use of the town's minister in the early 17th century, and auctioned the lots off to merchants interested in building new wharves and storehouses. The buyers were compelled to pay an annual quitrent of seven percent of the purchase price to the rector of St. George's and to build walls on the boundaries of their property within two years. On June 29, eleven water lots and three large land lots were auctioned for a total of £1,326, with one water lot reserved for the use of the rector. The

act made no provision for inflation in the quitrents paid to the rector, so that by the time the practice was abolished in 1941 the rents, some as low as £1.7.10, had become a pittance.

There were some serious obstacles to developing the Glebe water lots and a decade passed before the first substantial house and wharf were erected. Many of the lots were very small, in some cases only 20 to 30 feet deep between the road to the Ferry (Wellington Street) and the water's edge. A line of shoals about 100 feet offshore was a further hindrance preventing deep draught vessels from reaching any wharf which might be erected. The grants for the Glebe lots extended all the way to this line of shoals, and eventually most owners solved the problem by building the southern face of their wharves on top of the reef and filling in the gap with ballast stones, trash, quarry off-cuts and other debris.

Glen Duror (now Old Glenduror), built by John Stewart on

Glebe lots 1 and 2, was the first large house to be erected. The double lot was originally acquired by Royal Navy officer Thomas Hurd who sold it to the Hon. Samuel Trott. Stewart, a member of council and the colony's Collector of Customs, purchased the lot in 1805 and built a house worth £500 within two years.

Glen Duror is an odd shape because it does not conform to the perpendicular angles common to the Georgian style. Its long, rectangular eastern portion is typical enough, but two wings project at 45 degrees from the northwest and southwest corners, all capped with a hip roof. It has a single internal chimney and pilasters on the corners.

From about 1820 to 1835, Stewart's son Duncan and his wife brought up their family in this house. Duncan Stewart moved to Ardsheal, Paget, in 1835 to be closer to the seat of government. He later became the colony's Attorney General from 1855 until his death in 1861. Stewart's sons,

Glen Duror

ST. GEORGE'S
Bermuda

On the Water. . . . . . With Private Beach

A White Bermuda Limestone House
200 Years Old

with 3 acres of Garden and shady lawn sloping
to Private Beach with deep-water Dock
for Boating—and Diving.

Congenial crowd.   Never more than 8 people.
Meals that everybody talks about
Vegetables fresh from the Garden.

Fishing Parties, Carriage Trips, Riding, Horses,
Picnics, Arranged for at Moderate Rates

An Ideal place for people who want to avoid
the Tourist Atmosphere "of the usual hotel."

Rates: Five Dollars Per Day

Drop in for Tea! . . . Stay for the Season!

An optimistic advertisement for Glen Duror in 1930. Taken from <u>Bushell's Handbook</u>.

all of whom were barristers at Lincoln's Inn in London, sold the property to John R. Duerden in 1884. In the 1910s the house was the headquarters of the St. George's Yacht Club, and in the 1930s, Hattie Clinton ran a guest house there. Clinton, whose father ran the Globe Hotel, offered a private dock, swimming beach and three acres of gardens, all for only $5 a day.

During World War II the property was owned by Frederick C. Outerbridge who leased it to the US Government. Glen Duror was turned into an officers' club and the US Army Corps of Engineers built a huge canteen for enlisted men to the southwest, which has since been converted into a residence. The Outerbridge family still owns the property and in recent years converted the carriage house to the north of Glen Duror, dating to at least 1876, into an apartment.

To the east of Glen Duror lies an empty wharf which is now part of the house grounds. This property, auc-

tioned as Glebe lot 3 to John MacLachlan, was later purchased by John Esten, who erected a wooden house.

In the 1820s naval contractor Andrew Belcher owned several houses, wooden sheds and a wharf. The property has been known as Belcher's Wharf ever since. Belcher himself lived in Halifax, but his slave, William Archer, lived in the house and supervised his master's business until he was freed in 1829. Archer later purchased the Mitchell House, now the St. George's Historical Society Museum, and Foster House. Belcher's extensive commercial complex had vanished by the 1870s, perhaps the victim of a hurricane, but the remains of his wharf still resist the elements and can be seen by boaters from the harbour.

Clifton Vale, set against Wellington Street, was the next Glebe lot to be developed. Lot 4 was purchased by Samuel Adams, but neither he nor subsequent owner John Grove Palmer improved the lot. By 1800 Richard Fisher had bought the property. Fisher, a merchant based in Antigua, relocated to Bermuda in 1807 to join his brother John who had sold his wharf complex on Water Street to the Commissariat Department.

Richard Fisher built Clifton Vale about 1812 to serve both his family and commercial needs. Beneath the genteel interior of the upper floor is a building designed for work. The one storey house seen from the road sits on top of a vast storage area carved out of the bedrock. Its 18-foot ceilings and wide doors were designed to accommodate hundreds of tons of goods. The long, narrow middle room housed the longboats which Fisher used to ferry goods to and from ships anchored in the harbour. The line of shoals to the south prevented vessels from docking alongside Fisher's wharf until the wharf itself was extended out to the reef later in the 19th century. The boats were hauled into the basement and made fast to a bollard which still can be seen in the room.

The hip roof of the house is unusually wide and is supported by massive beams. Internal evidence suggests that in earlier times there were

Clifton Vale is an 1812 waterfront residence west of the town built over a substantial commercial basement fronting on a yard and dock. The high verandah, now partially glassed in, requires an unusual length of steps and the present owner created the double flight of curved steps as a satisfactory solution to the problem.

trap doors between the floors, and a crane installed in the rafters to haul goods into the attic for storage. The material of the roof itself is unusual. Instead of using Bermuda stone, the builder layered wide planks, up to 28 inches wide, sheets of zinc and then shingles which were tarred and caulked, so that from the outside the roof presents a smooth surface.

Richard Fisher died in 1813 and his widow married Reverend Alexander Nichol. The house passed to Fisher's children who lived there well into the 1890s. John Trott Fisher followed in his father's footsteps and became a successful merchant, Member of Parliament, and St. George's Magistrate for more than 25 years.

The Fisher family undoubtedly used their commercial connections with the British military to obtain the Dockyard-style cast iron pillars which support the verandah at the rear of the house and the Yorkshire flagstones found elsewhere on the grounds.

In 1897 Robert C. McCallan purchased the property and combined it with his other holdings to the east. After McCallan died in 1905, his son Robert acquired the house and operated a ships' chandlery out of the cellars. Robert's son Ralph inherited the property in 1955 and after his death his heirs sold it in 1974 to Launcelot Outerbridge. The present owner, Dr. William Outerbridge, purchased it from Launcelot's widow in 1987. Clifton Vale's fanlight door, lattice porch and front external chimneys present a typical domestic appearance on the street side which is not seen when the house is viewed from the harbour side, across the wide expanse of wharf.

By the middle of the 19th century Bermuda's trade was flagging. Shipbuilding dropped sharply in the 1820s and, facing competition from the enormous schooners, brigantines and steam powered vessels built in Britain and the United States, Bermu-da's merchant fleet declined further. The colony's trade shifted from carrying the goods of other nations to exporting locally grown produce and importing goods for the consumption of the British military. In 1861, however, the slow decline in commercial fortunes abruptly stopped and for a three-year period the port of St. George's became busier than it had ever been. The United States was at war with itself.

At the outbreak of the American Civil War, the southern states lacked factories, industry, arms, gunpowder, lead, machinery—in short, most things necessary to wage a successful war. They did produce cotton in great abundance, upon which the British textile industry depended. The inevitable exchange of British war materiel for southern cotton was hampered, however, by the northern navy's blockade of southern ports. The lure of profits, and support for the southern cause, led British merchants to outfit

The entrance front of Clifton Vale demonstrates the graceful proportions and symmetrical elegance that the building's living quarters presented to the street. The roof is of a particularly solid West Indian design and construction, apparently preferred by its Antiguan builder.

a fleet of blockade runners. These were specially designed fast steamers which ran through northern blockading warships in the dead of night to Wilmington, North Carolina and other southern ports.

St. George's, with its convenient access to open ocean, became the second largest transhipment base for these blockade runners, after Nassau in the Bahamas. Large ships from Britain unloaded their huge cargoes of arms, ammunition, cannon, gunpowder, lead and other tools of war into the town's warehouses, where they were stored until loaded aboard the fast steamers.

British speculators and Confederate purchasing agents rented every available wharf and storehouse, often at exorbitant rates. Hunter's Wharf and Penno's Wharf were stacked high with bales of cotton from the South. Long House and William Penno's new warehouse were packed to near-bursting.

The stealthy, speedy blockade runners loaded and unloaded alongside these wharves, while others of deeper draughts were prepared for their voyages by fleets of lighters and small sloops. Coal, especially non-smoking anthracite from Wales, was in

great demand, and thousands of tons of it were imported for the blockade runners. Coal sheds were built to the west of Hunter's Wharf, a cluster of shed roofed buildings which housed coal bunkers, workshops and stables. The warehouses on Todd's Wharf (now the site of St. George's largest car park) and Davenport's Wharf off Water Street received copious amounts of liquor, which was sold to thirsty blockade running sailors with more money than sense. Hundreds of barrels of gunpowder and saltpetre, enough to level the town, were stored at a safe distance at Tucker's Town and on Smith's Island. For a few short years, every storehouse was filled to capacity and every wharf was crammed with goods.

This remarkable boom came at a price. St. George's was overcrowded, polluted and downright dangerous with all the cash-rich but rowdy sailors in town between runs. In July 1863 a dockworkers' strike on the part of the predominately black workforce culminated in two cases of arson and an assassination attempt on Magistrate William Tudor Tucker, who moved to Nebraska soon afterwards.

The following summer a deadly yellow fever epidemic swept the town

after the disease was introduced from the Bahamas by a blockade runner.

In January 1865, Wilmington, North Carolina, was captured and the fleet of blockade runners vanished almost as quickly as they had appeared and with them the merchants and sailors who had brought prosperity. As a

The latticed entrance porch at Clifton Vale shows a distinctively military provenance, as do the double doors and fanlight.

Clifton Vale, McCallan's Warehouse and Edgewater stand together on the harbourfront just west of the town, where they were able to combine an advantageous commercial situation with suburban living. The dock in front of Edgewater is modern, the lawn behind it marking the location of the original little bay.

legacy they left dissolute paupers, unpaid bills and warehouses of unsold and unsaleable goods. There was not much of a market for uniforms, cannon and rifles after the war was over.

E dgewater and **McCallan's Warehouse** (now Godet & Young's Warehouse) on Wellington Street are visible testimonies to the success of the McCallan family during the American Civil War.

Claude T. McCallan moved to St. George's from Bailey's Bay in the 1820s. He bought a house on Duke of York Street and another on Queen Street, but was unable to purchase a wharf or water lot in town. Instead, in 1841 he paid £150 for an unimproved Glebe lot, sold by the Seon family to whom it had been granted in 1793. In 1848, he acquired another to the east for £25.

By 1851 he had constructed a wharf worth £500 extending to the line of shoals offshore. Rather than invest in a warehouse, the canny merchant employed the innovative and cheap solution of buying dismasted hulks salvaged from the reefs and using them as floating storehouses.

During the American Civil War

The street front of Edgewater has had its severity reduced by the addition of a small cantilevered shelter constructed over the fanlight of the front door and by planters.

he built the two storey hip roofed warehouse which has survived virtually unaltered. Despite the utilitarian purpose of construction, McCallan added a decorative fanlight over the front door, corner pilasters and a wooden addition to the back which overlooks the harbour. This shed roofed extension was probably added during the war to capitalise on the enormous sums the blockade runners paid for storage; it was certainly standing in 1876.

At the peak of this excitement, McCallan died in December 1863. His shipping business was assumed by his son, Robert C. McCallan, and business

A detail from an 1874 painting by Edward James shows Edgewater and McCallan's Wharf (now the Godet & Young warehouse). (Bermuda National Trust Collection: Bermuda Archives, Hamilton, Bermuda.)

associate George Wainwright. In 1866, Robert inherited the two Glebe lots and wharf, along with the considerable profits of shipping during the Civil War years. Using some of this fortune,

A painting by Edward James c. 1874 commemorates the repair and relaunching of the Norwegian ship Gramma (or Grenmar) at the St. George's Marine Slip Company. (Courtesy Bermuda Historical Society Collection: Bermuda Archives, Hamilton, Bermuda.)

Robert built **Edgewater** on the unimproved eastern Glebe lot in 1867 and lived there with his wife Mary, George Wainwright's only daughter.

The street side of Edgewater has fanlights above its front door and windows, similar to its westerly neighbours. There are also fanlights over the upstairs and downstairs southern doors. An interesting feature of this two storey hip roofed residence is the hexagonal kitchen chimney projecting from a recent western addition to the original house.

Edgewater has to be viewed from the harbour side to appreciate its original close proximity to the water. Only a score of feet separated the rear wooden verandah from the first sea-wall. McCallan built a breakwater over the line of shoals by 1876 to protect his house from the full force of waves during stormy weather, but this was washed away during a hurricane in 1899. One wonders whether

Edgewater would have survived the hurricane if the breakwater had never been built.

Although the backyard has since been extended, the Edgewater property is the only Glebe lot that was not built out to the line of shoals mentioned in the original 1793 grant and is thus unique among the ten original grants. The house remained in the McCallan family virtually undisturbed until 1980. It is now owned by David L. White.

After the excitement of the Civil War faded, shipping continued on a much smaller scale in St. George's. John S. Darrell used Hunter's Wharf as his base, and converted the upstairs living quarters into offices, while William E. Meyer occupied Musson's Wharf.

Vegetables, onions, arrowroot and Easter lilies grown on St. David's Island were common exports, bound for America's sprawling coastal urban

centres. The town's merchants also sold coal to passing steamers, many of which were too large to enter St. George's Harbour and had to anchor in nearby Murray's Anchorage or Five Fathom Hole.

One of the lessons learned from the American Civil War was that, other than the Royal Naval Dockyard at Ireland Island, there were no facilities for ship repair. To remedy this, a group of St. George's merchants formed the St. George's Marine Slip Company and built an extensive complex on the Secretary's Land near Mullet Bay, which is still in operation today. The *Gramma* (or *Grenmar*) was repaired and re-launched there in 1876, and is commemorated in a painting by artist Edward James.

William Eugen Meyer emerged as the most prominent St. George's merchant of the late 19th century. Originally from the city of Danzig, Germany (modern Gdansk, Poland), on

The west façade of The Palms with its sweep of neo-Palladian arches, classical pilasters and grand balustraded entrance steps was added in 1904. The pairs of two-over-two plate glass windows look perfectly at home.

the Baltic, William E. Meyer ran away to sea at the age of 16. At the age of 18 he went to Rhode Island with the specific purpose of fighting against slavery in the American Civil War. He joined the Rhode Island Cavalry and fought for the North for three years. After the decisive Battle of Gettysburg, Meyer was captured and spent the last six months of the war in the notorious Confederate prisons at Castle Pemberton and Danville.

After the war he studied engineering and navigation and in 1872 was part of the team which built the Brooklyn Bridge. The following year he married into one of New York's most prominent families when he wed Mary Anna Stonebanks.

Chance brought Meyer to Bermuda. His ship was dismasted during a storm in 1874 and while awaiting repairs he was offered a job by mer-

An oval pediment supported by decorative corbels reflects the arched window panes at the north end of The Palms.

chant William C.J. Hyland. Meyer flourished and in 1881 he purchased at auction from the heirs of Charles A. Hayward a small house built about 1845 by John Murray on a waterfront lot to the east of town.

Meyer built a grand Victorian residence which blended continental European, nautical and Bermudian elements to create a unique house which he named **Gluckauf**. A most striking feature is the tower and widow's walk projecting from the hip roof, affording Meyer a fine view of the harbour and of the wharf and warehouses he erected below the cliff to the south of his house and the motley collection of hulks he acquired and moored nearby.

One of Meyer's business pursuits was buying ships wrecked or damaged on Bermuda's reefs and stripping them for salvageable parts. A skylight in the house reputedly came from an old tugboat stripped by Meyer. Several of these hulks are still visible today.

In 1903 Captain Meyer gave Gluckauf to his son William Eugen Jr. on the occasion of his marriage to Alice McCallan and moved across Cut Road to Caledonia Park. William renamed the house **The Palms**, by which name it is known today. He added the front porch, with its gingerbread skirting and balustrades, and an ornate arcaded addition to the south.

The younger Meyer was no less interesting than his father. He was at various times a Freemason, Italian Consul (although he spoke no Italian), acting American Consul, Mayor of St. George's, partner in the firm Darrell and Meyer, and, with Sir Stanley Spurling, God father of the St. George's Historical Society.

He collected old cannon from 17th and 18th century shipwrecks which he mounted on the high parapet wall he built between The Palms and the workshops and wharf below. During World War II he was forced to dismount the old guns, lest an enemy confuse the house with a fort and shell it.

William's wife, Alice, purchased **Eastcliffe**, next door, in 1919 and the couple built a tennis court between the two houses. Senator Noela Hay-

This view demonstrates the sophistication of the details of The Palms. Finely moulded cornices reflect the style of the double octagonal chimneys, while the chimneys relating to the service areas are more simply treated. The main roof is smooth and, from the ground, hidden behind the parapet roofs. The skylight was salvaged by the builder from a derelict tug to light his study.

cock, the present owner, is the great granddaughter of the extraordinary seafarer from Danzig who made The Palms so distinctive.

In the 20th century the growing size of merchant ships prompted the House of Assembly to widen and deepen the approach to St. George's Harbour. Rather than work on the original long and winding channel between Paget and Governor's Islands, a new cut was made between the southeastern tip of St. George's Island and Higgs Island, christened the New Town Cut. Between 1911 and 1917, the channel was widened to 250 feet and deepened to allow passenger ships into the harbour. In 1935, New Town Cut was further deepened to 27 feet, and in recent years a training wall has been added to improve the channel.

St. George's still depends upon its waterfront for its livelihood, but the huge vessels moored at Penno's Wharf and Ordnance Island today discharge American visitors rather than cargoes.

Designed and built in 1995 by the Ministry of Works and Engineering, this passenger terminal on Ordnance Island is the first modern building in St. George's that fits into the 19th century tradition appropriate to its site. Its size requires the flanking wings, which in the 19th century would have produced a second storey. On the dock a lower profile was called for and the pleasing result has won awards and prizes for its appropriateness to both its location and to traditional St. George's architecture.

The steady trade of the 18th century and the frantic rush of the American Civil War era have long since passed into the pages of history.

The new **Customs Hall** or **Cruise Ship Terminal** on Ordnance Island built in 1995 respects the proportions and architectural style of the 19th century and almost atones for the destruction of the fine early 19th century house previously on the site. It is inevitably dwarfed by the massive ocean liners. One wonders what Bridger Goodrich, John Davenport or Captain Eugen Meyer would have made of the cruise ships of today.

CHAPTER FIVE

St. George's Early Vernacular Houses

A fine double chimney at Skerrett's Cottage has bake oven flues piercing the assembled lean-to outbuildings. This part of the house has a Flemish gable in contrast to the predominance of hips.

Although the Town of St. George was founded in 1612, none of its earliest buildings survive. Indeed, very few standing today date even to the last decade of the 17th century.

The houses built during the Somers Island Company period (1615-84) were mostly timber frame structures, with wooden posts set in holes cut into the bedrock or set upon cedar sills resting on the ground. Over time, even durable Bermuda cedar timbers succumbed to rot and vermin. Given the abundance of trees, settlers simply replaced their timber frame houses with new ones for much of the 17th century. Stone was rarely used as a building material. In 1688 only 29 of the colony's 579 houses were made of stone. The rest were timber frame buildings topped with thatch or shingle roofs.

All this changed in the 1680s when Bermudians turned to trade and shipbuilding after the dissolution of the Somers Island Company. The island's cedar was a superlative shipbuilding material and was highly valued and conserved. As older timber frame houses fell to rot or hurricanes, they were replaced with stone ones, often exact copies of their predecessors.

The accelerated pace of building in stone in St. George's occurred for two reasons. In 1702, in order to curtail the danger of fire, the government passed an ordinance which required all buildings in town to be built of stone within four years and the land

Skerrett's Cottage is an early 18th century house abutting the road, with its garden characteristically shielded from the road by high walls. The upper windows are appropriate to the period, while those at street level are modern and metal which are unsatisfactory in St. George's restorations.

Seen across its banana patch, hidden from the street by a high wall, Stockdale's typical cruciform construction and fenestration suggest an early 18th century date. The crispness and symmetry of the Flemish gable, however, suggest recent additions or repairs, perhaps following hurricane damage to which gables unsupported by chimneys are prone. The idiosyncratic extension of the wing on the right is easily visible.

grants in town made by the Crown required that the recipient "erect, build, sett up and compleatly finish a sufficient stone house or building", usually within 18 months of the grant.

This chapter reviews the oldest houses in the town. Many were built to secure the free land given by Benjamin Bennett and other governors to promote the growth the town. Some predate the grants and a few contain elements of timber framing within their walls. With the exception of the Globe Hotel, which was built by an English governor and reflects urban taste, all the earliest St. George's houses are vernacular buildings, designed to suit the needs of their builders with little regard for symmetry or exterior decoration, aside from the occasional Flemish gable. Although these houses were organic in nature, with rooms added to meet needs, a few common floor plans emerge. The two room "hall-and-parlour" is most common, with a large hall next to a smaller parlour which doubled as a bedroom, built in either one or two storey versions. Sometimes

a kitchen wing was added to make a T-shaped house, but more often a detached kitchen was built nearby, both to keep the house from getting too hot when cooking and to minimise fire hazards. A cruciform plan arose when a porch chamber was added to the front of a T-shaped house. In all of these buildings, the original roofs were gable ended, often with steep pitches, and were usually supported by robust chimneys on the ends. The rooms were invariably narrow and the windows usually high under the roof rafters and with top hung blinds. Of course, there are exceptions to these rules, but these features are good indicators that one is looking at an early 18th century building.

Stockdale and Skerrett's Cottage on Printer's Alley are two typical early 18th century residences. They were originally laid out on a cruciform plan, with porch, hall, parlour and rear kitchen or bedroom, but have been added to over the years. **Skerrett's Cottage** is the older of the

Stockdale's unusual entrance porch, a 19th century replacement for whatever served the house previously, is a defining eccentricity, added to the side of the south gable to take advantage of available space and still serve the configuration of the house.

two. It was standing in 1706 as the home of James Wright and was probably built in the 1690s. Wright died in 1708 and left it to his son Benjamin, to whom it was formally granted in 1713.

The Old Rectory presents several problems in dating. The chimney to chimney length of the front is clearly very early indeed. The chimney to the right is set away from the roof, suggesting that the original house may have had a thatched or shingled roof which needed to be protected from the heat. The windows are set close under the wall plate. The asymmetrical porch room with its Flemish gable seems to have had the extension to the left added.

The property was inherited by William and Eleanor Higgs, who by the 1780s had built a larger house to the east. The house is now a ruin. Skerrett's Cottage stayed in the Higgs family until the 1930s, when it passed first to the Clifford family and then to the Ming family. The house takes its name from English school teacher John W. Skerrett who, according to local tradition, taught school in the cellar at the turn of the 20th century. Although a room added to the northeast spoils the original cruciform layout, the house has several interesting early architectural features. The Flemish gable on the west end and the large external chimney to the north are typical.

Stockdale was built shortly after 1706, for in that year Joseph Wright was given a grant next to his father's house on the condition that he build a stone house within 18 months. Wright's house mirrored his father's in its cruciform layout and in its employment of a Flemish gable. The younger Wright's house differed in that it had

two external chimneys attached to the hall-and-parlour, rather than the single chimney on the northern chamber found at Skerrett's Cottage.

The house is named for Joseph Stockdale, a London printer who brought the first press to Bermuda in 1783 and published the colony's first newspaper, the *Bermuda Gazette*, the following year. Stockdale leased the house in 1801 from John Briggs for 1,000 years for £180 and a rent of one peppercorn a year. After Stockdale died in 1803, his three daughters, Frances, Priscilla and Sarah, carried on the printing business, probably in the cellar of the house.

In 1816 this sibling syndicate was dissolved after Sarah Stockdale married professional printer Charles Rollin Beach and moved the press to Hamilton. With the Beaches gone to the new capital, Frances and her husband John Bryan Tucker moved into Stockdale. In 1848, their heirs sold the house to John McKean, Royal Engineers Foreman of the Works, for £160. McKean, in turn, sold it to George

Wainwright in 1865, who bequeathed it to his daughter Mary McCallan two years later.

The simple wooden porch which gives access to the upper floor was probably built by the Stockdales to separate the printing work and commercial transactions in the cellar from the domestic family space above. After passing through a number of hands in the 20th century, the house was acquired by current owners Lt. Col. and Mrs. Gavin Shorto in 1969.

Built in or before 1699, the **Old Rectory** is one of the oldest houses in St. George's. The lot was granted to Captain George Dew in 1700 in consideration for the great cost he had laid out in buying the house already there, which consisted of only a hall-and-parlour and, perhaps, the entry porch which graces the front of the building today.

The odd taper of the chimneys flanking the eastern gable end of the house suggests that the original roof was thatch or shingle which had to be

This view of the roofs and chimneys of the Old Rectory clearly shows the extension of the kitchen wing and subsequent wing added to the west. The slightly different chimney on the right may have been added when that end of the house was lengthened to provide closets. There is an extra ring of moulding below the top.

kept away from excessive heat. Dew's lot was large, 140 feet square, bounded by roads on every side. At the time, a now-vanished street separated the house from the Whitehall lot to the east. Broad Alley to the south once bisected the Whitehall lot on its way to Duke of Clarence Street.

George Dew was a ship's captain with a chequered past. He first came to Bermuda in 1691 to obtain a letter of marque and a ship from the colony's Governor, Isaac Richier. Enroute to Africa, Dew's vessel was dismasted and he returned home empty handed. His consort, the *Amity,* under the command of Thomas Tew, turned pirate, and took several rich prizes in the Indian Ocean before founding a short lived, radical democratic settlement called Libertaria on the coast of Madagascar.

Dew next turned to the slave trade but had no more success than in his privateering venture. While sailing from Barbados to Africa as captain of the brigantine *Marigold,* he was struck by a storm and his crew muti-

nied, forcing him to sail to Bermuda. Dew promptly retired from maritime pursuits and made his home in St. George's. He entered politics as an assemblyman, married the daughter of merchant John Welch, and had three children before he died in 1702. In his will he left the house to his widow Ann and then to his children.

Records do not reveal ownership of the house after Ann's death. In 1763 it was owned by mariner Richard Somersall. In May of that year, Somersall gave it to his daughter Ann and son-in-law, the Reverend Alexander Richardson, rector of St. George's parish church, "for the better maintenance and preferment" of the couple. Ann died four years later but Richardson continued to live there with his second wife Mary until his own death in 1805. The house was never owned by the parish and never officially a rectory, but Reverend Richardson's occupancy of the house led to the name which has remained with the house for nearly two centuries.

The rear wing of the Old Rectory has been extended beyond the chimney, perhaps in two stages, which would account for the discrepancy in roof pitch. The very steep roof pitch, suggesting thatch, and the matching chimney mouldings of the two chimneys visible in this picture suggest that the house was always T-shaped.

The Broad Alley Cottages are difficult to date. The one on the right seems to be from the 18th century, the one on the left from the 19th. The connecting wall and yard gates have the clean finish of the 19th century but the rough and ready yard wall visible on the right clearly goes with the 18th century.

Richardson bequeathed the house to the Esten family and it became the home of Martha Dickinson (née Esten) after her husband James died in 1807. She carried out a major refurbishment and lived in the house until the 1850s, when she left Bermuda to join her only surviving daughter in Guernsey. She died there in 1857 and the property was sold to Dr. Frederick A.S. Hunter. The doctor, as it turned out, bought the house mainly for its large lot. He lived in the much larger Poinciana House to the northwest which was surrounded by rather small grounds, so he annexed most of the western portion of the Old Rectory property to Poinciana House. When his heirs sold the house to Robert H. James in 1903, much of Dew's original grant did not accompany it. James also owned neighbouring Whitehall, and he transferred a small portion of the Whitehall lot to the eastern side of the Old Rectory.

James' heirs sold the ancient house to the Bermuda Historical Monuments Trust in 1950, who undertook a much needed renovation. It is now in the hands of that group's successor, the Bermuda National Trust. Its small size and Jacobean style offer a sharp contrast to Whitehall next door.

To the south of the Old Rectory is a pair of small but well preserved houses, the **Broad Alley Cottages**. They were built on a lot occupied by John Norman in 1700 and one of them may be the house in which he lived. His daughter Susannah was formally granted the property in 1713 after her father died. Neighbouring grants make it clear that he was raising potatoes and corn in the fields surrounding his house.

Little is known about the property for the next century. Dr. Joseph Hutchison acquired the lot and "houses near the church" in the 1780s

or 1790s, and the cottages were, perhaps, the homes of some of Hutchison's slaves. In 1854 both cottages appear on a map much as they are today. The gable ended, single room northern cottage is exactly the same shape as it was in 1854, while the southern cottage has acquired a small northern extension. In 1863 the cottages were joined to William Hayward Fox's property to the west, which thereafter encompassed the entire block. In the 20th century the properties were once again divided by one of Fox's heirs. Today they serve as poignant reminders of how St. George's more humble citizens lived. For every Whitehall, there were, perhaps, five Broad Alley Cottages, many of which have not survived.

The **Pearson House** at the foot of Duke of Cumberland Street or Old Maids Lane, is another rare survivor from the late 17th century. A house

A construction sequence for the Pearson House is not easy to discern without access to its interior and possibly to its roof. Entirely built in the 18th century style, the two gables suggest an earlier construction than the hipped wing. All the windows are close below the wall plate. There is a residential floor above a quite substantial storage level. As is so frequently the case, there is absolutely no decorative element.

tury. A house and garden had already been built by 1704 when it was the home of mariner Francis Harris, who was a freeholder in 1696. In form, the house is typical of the period. The L-shaped original core has small rooms and a gable roof with a massive chimney on the west side and cellars below. Although not original, the hip roof addition to the south is quite old, probably added in the mid to late 18th century. The room added to the northeast corner of the house dates perhaps to the early 19th century, while the chimney attached to it, capped with dual clay pipes, is even more recent.

Francis Harris died in the early 1720s and was succeeded by his sons Francis and Moses, who were also mariners. The brothers died in quick succession in 1742 and 1746. Probate inventories of the house taken after each death reveal little. Francis' three slaves made up £60 of his £66 probate, while Moses' worldly goods were

worth only £19. Moses Harris Jr., yet another mariner, inherited the house and lived there with his wife and five children until his death in 1782.

By 1800 William Gibbons had acquired the property from Harris' heirs. Originally from Hamilton, Gibbons and at least two of his sons were merchants in St. George's. He was also a very active Methodist, one of the 15 trustees who supervised the purchase of the lot and construction of the Ebenezer Methodist Church. He must have found it convenient to have the church next door, at the end of his own private path. Gibbons' heirs sold it to Anna Maria Outerbridge in 1903, who passed it on six years later to engineer James R. Pearson.

The construction of the **Globe Hotel** has already been discussed in chapter 2. Using public funds, labour and material, Governor Samuel Day built the house in 1700 and then kept

it for himself when he was ousted from office. In 1714 it was granted to Day's brother Thomas, a merchant from Bristol, England. He evidently sold it to a Tucker in the 1720s or 1730s. Although he left much to be desired as a governor, Samuel Day as architect produced a finely proportioned residence which contrasted sharply with traditional Bermudian building methods.

Its large gable roof spans two rooms, an ambitious feat made possible by an elaborate internal system of braces. Day's house is also the earliest firmly documented structure to have Flemish gables. The four chimneys buttressing the north and south sides anticipated the symmetry so prevalent in Georgian architecture, but the internal layout of the house remained irregular.

Although the two storey porch facing east may look original, a probate inventory of Day's goods reveals that

The Globe Hotel, built in 1700 by Governor Day for his own use, is one of only three buildings on the island built in this style. Both the others, Verdmont and Bridge House (now Somerset Rectory), have been substantially altered. The four chimneys give strength to the very wide Flemish gables and help support the roof, the span of which is very much wider than came to be used when stone construction superseded wooden buildings in the island. The building probably had casement windows which were replaced later in the 18th century with the existing windows. The small, east entrance wing containing a staircase is a 19th century addition. The house is notable for its complete absence of decoration, despite its imposing size and intended use as Government House. (1898 Business Directory, Bermuda Archives, Hamilton, Bermuda.)

it is a later addition. An external staircase attached to the northwest corner of the building which survived up to the 1940s provided access to the upper floor. In the late 18th century, this was the home of Captain Henry Tucker.

In 1800 his house and garden were worth £600 and home to 11

A detail from a stylised sketch c. 1731 shows the Globe Hotel building with its paired chimneys on the left. (Bermuda National Trust Collection: Bermuda Archives, Hamilton, Bermuda.)

slaves besides Tucker's considerable family. In his 1801 will, he gave the house to his wife Aletta and his three sons.

An archaeological excavation sponsored by the Bermuda National Trust and Bermuda Maritime Museum uncovered a rich array of artifacts, including musket balls, gun parts and a collection of fine ceramics, as well as a five-foot deep quarry, perhaps dating to the 1760s, and dug for stone to repair the house or build the porch tower.

In the 19th century the house passed through a succession of Tucker heirs, but after 1860 none of them appear to have lived there.

During the American Civil War, Confederate shipping agent Major Norman Walker used the upper floor as the office from which he coordinated the flow of desperately needed guns, am-

The Globe Hotel today.

munition, uniforms and other war matériel through the Union blockade.

In 1867 the house was rented to Ralph Foster, the first of many proprietors of the Globe Hotel. Foster died the following year at the relatively young age of 33 but his widow continued to run the hotel and bar with billiard room for another 14 years.

In 1884, the Globe Hotel was remodelled by A.J. Richardson, who in-

Seven Gables actually has seven gables and is one of St. George's most picturesque 17th century houses. The original half timbered walls were changed to stone before 1702. There is a storage basement too low to have been of much commercial use. Where the flush window frames are not protected by the overhanging eaves, there are architraves. The owner has recently undertaken a careful and sympathetic restoration.

stalled an elevator, long since removed. Proprietorship had passed to George Clinton by 1892, and he added a horse and livery service by erecting a wooden stable and coach house in the yard to the west.

Samuel Crofts Rankin purchased the Globe Hotel from the Tucker family in 1899 and soon afterwards the operation went to one of his grandsons.

The Bermuda Historical Monuments Trust bought the house from Rankin's estate in 1951. Six years later, the Confederate Museum was opened to highlight Bermuda's role in the American Civil War, featuring the reconstructed office of Major Walker. In 1995 a major restoration of the building was carried out and a new museum created. It is now the Bermuda National Trust Museum, featuring "Rogues and Runners", a new exhibit on Bermuda in the 1860s.

S even Gables, opposite the Police Station, traces its history back to the 1650s when a timber framed house occupied by Hannah and Christopher Ming stood on the site. In 1662 the widowed Hannah married tailor Alexander Smith, who moved into the house. Daniel Tucker had acquired the property by 1702 when it was granted to him with a building already standing. He had evidently rebuilt the earlier building in stone on the same foundations, for timbers in the cellar bear the mortises where vertical wooden joists once slotted into place. Although Seven Gables appears to be a cruciform house, architectural evidence suggests that the original core was a rectangular hall-and-parlour house, possibly with a wing to the north. The southern room was added in the early 19th century. The massive chimney attached to the west side was originally outside, and only later when closets were added in the late 18th century, was it brought inside the house.

Daniel Tucker was a very active St. Georgian. As a surveyor, he was responsible for laying out most of the early house grants. He ran at least two shops, one near the Town Dock just south of Bridge House and one immediately to the east of Seven Gables on the lot presently occupied by Gosling Brothers liquor store. He was also a lieutenant in the militia and active in local politics.

After Daniel Tucker's death in 1730, Seven Gables was inherited first by his son Henry and later by his granddaughter Margaret Trott. In the 1790s it was home to Ordnance Storekeeper Simon Fraser while he was building Ordnance Island. In the 1830s and 1840s, William and Elizabeth Outerbridge lived there and were probably responsible for adding the southern wing. The small entry porch to the east and a matching room to the north were added between 1854 and 1876.

Seven Gables' three chimneys are modest compared with the array found on other St. George's houses, but nevertheless graceful in design.

Somerled is a typical chimney to chimney gabled house with its downstairs commercial or storage level now converted to an apartment. The rather grand steps leading to the entrance take an unusual turn and the newel posts have a lozenge decoration which suggests a much later date. The roof ventilators are of a style borrowed from the British military and are frequently found in St. George's.

In the first decades of the 20th century, Seven Gables was owned by E.A. McCallan, author of *Life on Old St. David's*. The present owner Nea Stack is a direct descendant. A careful restoration was launched in 1995.

S omerled is one of the "grant houses" dating back to the beginning of the 18th century. Joiner Stephen Wright was given the land in 1702 and erected Somerled within 18 months to keep the lot. The house stayed in the Wright family for four generations before Esther Wright married Henry Roberts in 1823. Roberts added to the north and west side of the house in 1825, reflected in the building's assessment increasing from £100 to £300 that year. He died in 1828 and Esther lived another 38 years, dying in 1866 at the age of 80.

The house was inherited by Esther's daughter Susan, the widow of Claude T. McCallan. She died in 1870 and left it to her son Samuel Crofts McCallan, who passed it on to his son Ernest A. McCallan.

McCallan gave the house to his sister Essie, who passed it to her daughter Nea Smith in 1950. The property was inherited by her cousin Dianne Mary Green after Nea Smith died in 1992. Thus, Somerled has the rare distinction of never having been sold since it was built. The old home has been passed down with little modification through the same family for 11 generations.

Seen from Duke of York Street, the much photographed Samaritans' Cottages are more easily recognisable as two separate dwellings. Chimney details vary and the one in the centre has been heightened to clear the higher roof of its neighbour. The wall is high to shield the two yards from the dust, noise and animals of the main road.

Like all the early St. George's houses, it has a gable roof. Two large chimneys buttress the ends of the house to add structural support. The side staircase leading to the upper floor is original, but the attractive lattice porch attached to the entrance to the lower floor is a more recent addition.

A small detached outbuilding against the northern wall of the property dates to the early 19th century and may have housed Henry Roberts' four slaves. Somerled is an excellent example of the hall-and-parlour floor plan of the early 18th century.

Samaritans' Cottages date back at least to 1704. The eastern cottage was standing when the lot was granted to carpenter William Pearman in that year and may be the building he purchased from John Briggs in 1676. It is a hall-and-parlour house with a porch projecting to the south. The western house, built by Pearman's daughter Martha and son-in-law Thomas Handy in 1719, is hall-and-parlour style running north and south, much

like Pearman's but without a porch chamber.

The land for the Handy house was originally granted to the widow Margery Potter, one of the last women accused of witchcraft in Bermuda. She was presented for trial in July 1693, charged with using diabolical means to make John Middleton sick. A trial in December returned a verdict of *Ignoramus*, meaning there was not enough evidence to convict her. Potter gave the land to her daughter, widow Honora Harding, who gave part of it to her niece Martha Handy.

The eastern cottage was occupied by Alexander White, a tailor, from the late 1750s until his death in 1786. The cottages were then acquired by Benjamin Fox, but were sold upon his death to John Trott in 1806. Trott passed them to John Davenport by 1820, who merged them with his other properties next door and across the street.

In 1900 the eastern cottage was sold, along with the storehouse to the west, to the Independent Order of Good Samaritans', from which its mod-

ern name, Samaritans' Cottages, is derived. It is a Bermuda National Trust property rented on a long term lease. These two houses are excellent examples of the architecture prevalent when St. George's was rebuilt in stone, and have survived with very little external modification.

Samaritans' Cottages (seen from Water Street) are two small early 18th century cottages now combined into one house. The windows directly under the wall plates, gables and chimneys are characteristic of the period. The garden wall on this side of the house is low by the standards of the town and the absence of gate posts is very unusual.

The west end of the Taylor House is a late 18th or early 19th century addition of charming simplicity but quite out of keeping with the long low one storey cottage to the east, with its liberal array of low chimneys, of which the west end is a mere appendage.

Clifford Rowe purchased it in 1977. Rowe launched a much needed restoration which took five years to complete.

Reeve Court, an imposing three storey structure beside the State House, was for centuries the tallest building in the town. It was erected about 1705 by the Reverend Dr. Thomas Holland, minister of the parish church. The lot was granted in 1706 in recognition of the minister's expense in putting up a substantial house. By October 1706 Holland and his wife Elizabeth had sold their house for £110 to Samuel Smith and moved to Hampton, Virginia.

Smith, a considerable landowner in Smith's Parish, obtained a grant for the detached kitchen lying on the Bridge House side of Pound Alley and the present front yard and side garden to the east. In 1729 Smith willed the property to his only surviving son Seth, a merchant in Guadeloupe, and died three years later. Seth then died and left his real estate to his four children, Seth, Thomas, William and Elizabeth, after his wife's death. By 1760 Dr. Richard Tucker had acquired the house, perhaps through his wife Mary. Tucker was assessed 10 shillings for his property in that year, indicating a substantial house.

In 1770 the Tucker family moved to St. Eustatius and lived there until Richard's death in 1782. During this

Set alongside Queen Street to the south of Stewart Hall, **Taylor House** is one of the most photographed houses in St. George's and has been a favourite subject of artists for more than a century. The exact date of the building's construction is elusive, but it was certainly standing when the property was granted to pilot Edward Colson in 1712. The grant to Seven Gables to the south mentions a garden belonging to Colson on the southern part of the lot in 1702, which suggests a house was close by. The early core of Taylor House is an L-shaped structure with a massive external chimney on the southern end, one storey over a cellar, all capped by a gable roof. As with the Old Rectory, timber frame partitions survive inside,

although in this building they remain buried beneath layers of plaster. From its granting until 1864, Taylor House was home to five generations of Colsons. In the 1770s the house was briefly the home of William and Sarah Sears, when John Colson leased it to his daughter and son-in-law, but it reverted to his son Stephen after John Colson's death. Higher parish assessments suggest that by 1800 Stephen had added the cluster of rooms and chimneys to the west side of the old house, along with the two storey portion at the extreme western end.

The house was apparently leased during the mid 19th century after the Colson family line died out. The Roberts family acquired the property in the 1890s and held it until

The north side of the Taylor House shows its comparatively humble status with low eaves and the simplest of fenestration. The number of chimneys suggests a commercial use.

Reeve Court suggests an early 18th century construction date, with its gable and windows set close under the eaves. Lower windows have been aggrandised, probably when the rear wing was added. The roof over the porch seems to be a later addition and is similar to, but larger than, the one at Tucker House. Like its neighbour Buckingham, it has two residential floors above a storage or commercial use basement. The garden is surrounded by a standard pillar and railing wall and serves to screen the yards and outbuildings from people and animals in the neighbouring alleys.

property was inherited by Richard's son William Tucker, whose wife, Hester Louisa Tucker, was the "Nea" celebrated by Irish poet Thomas Moore. William, a merchant, had been extraordinarily successful during the War of 1812 and built a fine house on Rose Hill. But the premature death of his wife in December 1817, cast a considerable pall over his life. He died in 1867 after serving the town for many years as a JP and magistrate.

Reeve Court then passed to his son Territt Fraser Tucker, who lived there with his wife Sophia. In his 1873 will, Territt gave lifetime occupancy of the house to his wife, and then bequeathed it jointly to his children. After Sophia died in 1889, Reeve Court was apparently occupied by Catherine, the youngest daughter, who married Frederick Basham the following year. The Bashams bought out the shares of Catherine's brothers and sisters for £487.10.0.

After changing hands a number of times this century, the building was purchased by the Bermuda National Trust in 1987.

The three storey core is apparently that built by Holland in 1706, and additions to the north and northwest were put on in the late 18th or early 19th century. The roof is unusual in that it has one gable end and one hip end centred on a large old internal chimney, perhaps indicating a partial earlier conversion from a gabled to hip roof style, or a small western addition

The back of Reeve Court demonstrates the way the building was enlarged over time. The two wings on the left seem to have been added sequentially with the one to the left containing the staircase, perhaps suggesting seniority. The wing on the right, with its lower pitched roof, altered floor levels and more refined window muntins, clearly was the last addition and serves to complicate the floor plan considerably.

sojourn, Tucker's daughter Elizabeth was courted by English merchant Thomas Reeve. When Admiral Rodney sacked St. Eustatius in 1781, Reeve lost nearly £400 in goods. Later that year, Reeve came to Bermuda and married Elizabeth in St. George's. The newlyweds moved to St. Croix, where Reeve started a shipping business after his widowed mother-in-law, Mary Tucker, returned to Bermuda in 1782. Five years later, Richard Tucker's estate was assessed at £600 for the house, and Mary's assessment reveals that, besides furniture and goods amounting to more than £900, she owned another house worth £325 elsewhere in town.

About 1800 the Reeves returned to Bermuda. Thomas Reeve died on July 30, 1805. Elizabeth, on the other hand, died in 1844 at the age of 87. By 1822 Mary Tucker had died and the

Detail of Reeve Court from a 1731 stylised sketch. (Bermuda National Trust Collection: Bermuda Archives, Hamilton, Bermuda.)

The chimney to chimney gable ends of Stewart Hall and the placement of the windows close under the eaves suggest an early 18th century date, but the symmetrical arrangement of windows and door and the stone window sills give the house a later Georgian appearance. The doorway and stoop have avoided the later addition of any form of porch. The roof on the far side extends to the end of the chimney to create a closet.

The baffling collection of chimneys on the west wing of Stewart Hall, a double one at the gable end of the kitchen and two flanking oven chimneys, suggests that there may have been a commercial bakery there at one time. The chimney at the extreme right of the picture is the north chimney of the main house.

Mitchell married Sarah, the widow of Daniel Johnson, through whom he acquired a wharf and lot to the east of Block House. In the 1720s Mitchell was an active architect. He supervised the construction of the new Government House and built the Mitchell House, now the St. George's Historical Society Museum, for his nephew William. By the time he died in 1731, Walter Mitchell owned several ships and possessed furnishings, trade goods and gold worth more than £4,100, making him one of the richest men in Bermuda. Sarah Mitchell followed him to the grave two years later, and Stewart Hall was bequeathed to her daughter Martha, the wife of Alexander Herron. The Herrons spent the 1730s living in the house before they moved to the colony of Georgia, where Alexander became Lieutenant Governor. In 1751 they sold the property to George Tucker, the Colonial Secretary.

George Tucker was a model citizen. He had inherited the posts of Colonial Secretary and Provost Marshal from his father, who had served in those offices in the 1720s. He was a member of the Governor's Council under both Governors Popple. His house was a crowded one, since he had a wife, five children and 11 slaves.

The detached two storey cottage to the north of the main house that encompassed the original gable end.

Stewart Hall on Queen Street was already built when the land on which it stood was granted to Walter Mitchell in 1707. An active militia commander and officer in HM Independent Company, Mitchell was a third generation descendant of a family which migrated to Bermuda on the *Plough* in 1612 and eventually settled in Southampton Parish. The house he built was one of the grandest of its day, a large two storey hall-and-parlour house set right against the street, with two massive flanking chimneys and a steeply pitched gable roof. An even larger chimney was built on the end of the kitchen wing to the rear of the house and, over the centuries, no fewer than seven chimneys have been added to this building.

Even the northern one storey extension at Stewart Hall has its own chimney. This may have been built to accommodate a silversmith's workshop c. 1820. There are seven chimneys in all, two of them double.

The last addition to Fanny Fox's Cottage is a narrow wing with a Flemish gable, probably in imitation of the other lengthened section, or perhaps accomplished simultaneously. The chimney is less graceful than the others and suggests an early 19th century date. The stone gutter running around it is a good example, now not often surviving.

was probably home to some of Tucker's slaves, whose duties undoubtedly included looking after the small herd of livestock which Tucker kept in the yard. An archaeological excavation in 1991 uncovered a watering trough for these cattle, over a mid 17th century grave dug long before Stewart Hall was built.

A probate inventory made after George Tucker died in 1766 reveals the wealth and refinement of the Secretary's home. He had created a "cross chamber" on the ground floor by dividing the larger hall with a partition, reflecting the Georgian predilection for symmetry and its emphasis on creating private spaces by increasing the number of doorways in a house. Tucker had a writing closet off the hall where he attended to his official duties. Silver plate, Chinese porcelain, English salt-glazed stoneware and lead crystal graced the Tuckers' dining room and exhibited their wealth and status to all visitors.

George Tucker's widow Mary lived in Stewart Hall until her death in 1787. The house was then rented to Andrew Durnford for six years while he was improving the colony's fortifications and building Durnford. The house was purchased at auction in 1795 by Hannah Stockton, who was the late George Tucker's niece. She died two years later and the house went to her two young children.

The direct impact of the arrival of the British military in the 1790s can be seen in the fate of Stockton's children. Her son John became a purser in the Royal Navy and her daughter Sarah married Lieutenant James Robinson of the Royal Fusiliers.

The Robinsons lived in Stewart Hall until 1819, when they departed for England and sold the house to silversmith John Trott Cox. He was responsible for the one storey addition to the north, which housed his workshop and retail store.

Barrister Duncan Stewart purchased the property in 1849 and, although he never lived in the house himself, the name Stewart Hall commemorates his ownership.

In the early 20th century, it was owned by the Higinbothom and Clifford families before the Bermuda

The original chimney to chimney gable of Fanny Fox's Cottage, built c. 1707, is easy to discern here. The windows are close below the wall plate and the building is notable for its simplicity. The Flemish gable visible at the far end is the result of an 18th century lengthening of the original cottage. The door stoop and low garden wall are probably later additions too.

Historical Monuments Trust purchased it in 1949. Until recently it housed the St. George's branch library. One of the largest of St. George's early 18th century houses, this important property is now owned by the Bermuda National Trust.

Fanny Fox's Cottage is nes tled in the northern end of town, fronting on Old Wells Lane (now the top of Duke of Clarence Street). The lot was originally granted to Edward Jones, the colony's Provost Marshal, in 1700. Jones was later dismissed from his post by Governor Benjamin Bennett for gross negligence. As keeper of the gaol, he allowed prisoners to come and go at will and operated a dry goods shop out of the front cell. Jones sued Bennett and the Gov-

ernor countersued, and it was 30 years before the case was resolved, by which time both men had returned to England. Given his difficulties, Jones had not had time to build on his lot before 1706 when he sold it to mariner James Burchall. It was Burchall who erected the core of the house that now stands: a two room gable roof structure facing the road, flanked by external chimneys.

After Burchall's death in 1738, ownership of the property is unclear. Burchall or his successor enclosed the northern chimney to create a small room, the exterior of which is decorated with a fine example of Flemish gables. The eastern wing of the house was also added around the middle of the 18th century, perhaps to accommodate a larger family.

Roof Pitch in St. George's

Early Bermuda stone roofs were almost always pitched extremely steeply. One possible reason for this is that their precursors, thatched roofs, must be sharply pitched to throw off rainwater, and builders were either used to doing it that way, or were slating an existing roof frame with stone instead of thatch. Another reason is that Bermudians must have learned early that the lateral thrust of their very heavy roofs increased as the pitch decreased. If the pitch was too shallow, the thrust would soon push out the walls and, in extreme cases, collapse the entire building.

As the 18th century progressed, however, cedar became so prized for shipbuilding that people were unwilling to waste long straight lengths of cedar on something with as little commercial return as their own roof. The result was that rafters were shortened as far as they safely could be, and collar ties were reduced by raising them as far up the rafters as the builder dared. The result was a reduction in both pitch and strength. Buttresses were often necessary to shore up spreading walls.

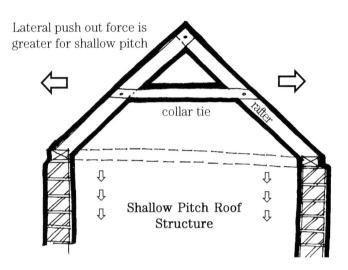

Lateral push out force is greater for shallow pitch

collar tie

rafter

Shallow Pitch Roof Structure

The introduction of unlapped smooth stone roofs at the end of the 18th century or early in the 19th may have been an attempt, made possible by the introduction of cement, to reduce the weight of stone on deliberately weakened wooden frames. Pitch was even further reduced at that time.

Experience and science have shown that the aerodynamics of low pitched roofs in hurricane winds create a lift over the lee side of the roof which can literally lift the roof off the walls. Being much more prone to storm damage, low pitched roofs remained the exception.

There is another theory to suggest why roof pitches got shallower fairly soon after stone roofs came into general use. Masons quickly discovered that they could use their new non-porous roofs to collect rainwater by channelling it into their tanks via stone gutters, and that flatter pitches harvested more water because in a downpour the gutters would not be overwhelmed. Hip roofs, when introduced in the mid 18th century, offered a flatter and greater area to collect water in a storm, while presenting glancing surfaces to winds from any direction. So a combination of shallow pitch and a hip roof made for the most efficient collection of water.

Whatever the reasons, the angle of a roof is a useful dating tool for estimating the age of a building.

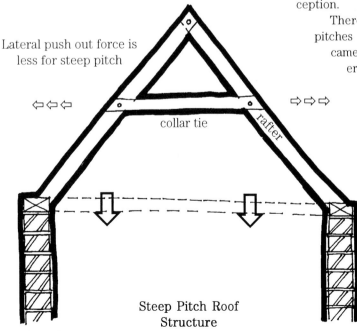

Lateral push out force is less for steep pitch

collar tie

rafter

Steep Pitch Roof Structure

The south wing of Bridge House has a massive chimney and a southeast wing which appears to be a later addition. The verandah is from the 19th or even 20th century. The remaining chimneys belong to dependency structures, the nearest of which was an early separate kitchen later converted to a stable for the neighbouring Reeve Court.

In 1802 the property was in the hands of Henry Adams, who died six years later and left it to his wife Sophia. She died in 1810, bequeathing it to her husband's nephew, Benjamin Fox, when he reached the age of 21.

In 1816 Fox married Frances Zuill, the Fanny Fox for whom the house is named. There is a legend that the marriage lasted only one night but, whether she remained married to Benjamin or not, she lived in his house while he was away at sea. Benjamin drowned in Kingston, Jamaica in 1834. The following year, Fanny gave the house to her brother, William E. Zuill of Orange Grove, Smith's Parish.

Fanny apparently lived in the cottage in St. George's until she was quite old, when she moved to Orange Grove. She died there in 1881 at the age of 85. The cottage was sold by the Zuill family after William's death in 1872. It is presently owned by the Bermuda National Trust.

Bridge House is one of the oldest and best documented locations in St. George's. The original building was a timber framed two storey house erected by planter and shoemaker Roger Bailey, whose father, John Bailey of Devonshire, arrived in Bermuda before 1623. The exact date of the construction of this precursor to Bridge House is unknown, but it certainly predates Norwood's 1662-63 survey. Roger left the house and "garden plott lying before it" to his wife Mary, in 1686. She died just three years later and after her seafaring son Moses died in 1694, her other son Aaron inherited the house. In 1702 the newly married Aaron and Miriam Bailey sold the house to John and Jane Follett, newcomers from Barbados, for the substantial sum of £110.

A sketch of the Bailey house accompanying this deed gives us a rare glimpse of Bermuda's 17th century timber frame architecture. The two storey gable house had an entry porch with a chamber above, wide casement windows on the ground floor with smaller ones above tucked close under the eaves, a large chimney attached to the north wall and another one, probably at the end of a room extending to the east. The building was apparently L-shaped, with a steeply pitched roof. A decorative finial graced the peak of the southern gable.

Bridge House was named for the bridge believed to have existed nearby. It may merely be a corruption of Bridger's House, after its most famous owner, Bridger Goodrich. Not quite a cruciform house, it has, nevertheless, many characteristics of one and dates from that period. Here the high double chimney and upper windows directly set under the eaves lend credence to the notion.

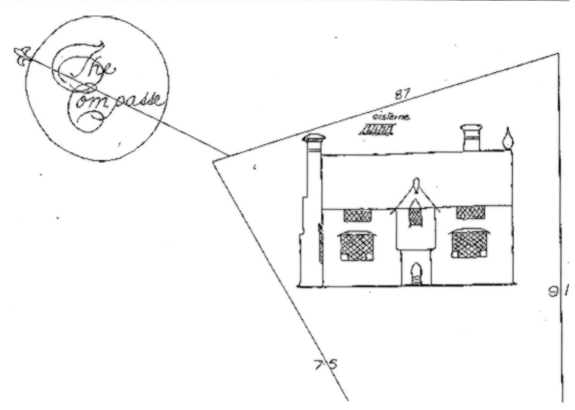

A 1702 drawing of a wooden Bridge House seems to be evidence that stone houses followed the plans of their predecessors. The sketch is traced from the deeds of Bridge House. (Bermuda National Trust Papers.)

The Folletts had a turbulent past. John was an English merchant and ship captain who traded with the West Indies. In 1685 he rose with the Duke of Monmouth against James II and was deported to Barbados after the rebellion failed. His earlier commercial connections quickly reestablished him in the West Indies and by 1698 he owned three houses in Bridgetown and a number of trading vessels. In that year, he married Jane Massey, née Thorowgood, who had already been widowed twice. In 1702, they migrated to Bermuda.

After they purchased the house from Bailey, Governor Benjamin Bennett formally granted the land to them. It is clear that they contemplated a major renovation of the building, for the grant noted "the great costs, charges and sums . . . laid out and expended and which will be laid out and expended in the rebuilding and refitting" of the house. But the Folletts never lived to complete the job. John died in 1704 and Jane died a year later. In her will, Jane directed that "my house in the town of St. George's be without delay well and sufficiently repaired, built, fitted and

completely finished in workmanlike manner in windows, doors", and then rented out with the proceeds going to an orphan boy named Thomas Newtham.

The Folletts were good friends of their neighbours at Reeve Court, Thomas and Elizabeth Holland. According to Jane Follett's will, Elizabeth Holland became overseer of the rebuilt Bridge House. As it turned out, however, the Hollands did not stay in Bermuda long enough to witness the rebuilding.

The refitting of the house was completed by 1708 and, following the precedent set by Governor Day, the builders made use of stone originally quarried at public expense to build a gunpowder magazine. In all likelihood, the stone house which stands today was built on the foundation of the earlier Bailey house, perhaps incorporating the same cellar. The present building bears a striking similarity to the sketch of the earlier house, with two differences. A chimney was added to the southern gable end and a larger porch and stair tower replaced the more modest one on the timber frame structure.

By 1709 the new house was the residence of Governor Benjamin Bennett, who had moved from a build-

A view over a dependency to the southeast wing of Bridge House shows that the window has a small protective architrave. The top hung blind is of the old style, with broad slats comfortably spaced to admit air while excluding sunlight or moderate rain. The window frame itself is set flush with the unplastered masonry, both usually signs of considerable age, but not necessarily so in the case of unimportant dependencies such as this one.

A detail from Thomas Driver's 1824 painting from near Government House shows Banana Manor on the extreme left. The Mitchell House, Davis Cottage and the now ruined Longford House align Duke of Kent Street. Whitehall without its verandah or parapet additions looms behind Longford, and Durnford can be seen to the right of the church spire. (Courtesy Fay and Geoffrey Elliott Collection: Bermuda Archives, Hamilton, Bermuda.)

ing next door to the north. A walled garden or courtyard separated the house from King's Square and a detached kitchen to the rear that belonged to the Reeve Court lot was rented for the Governor's use. The house was the site of many council meetings and informal courts.

Bennett continued to live in Bridge House after he was replaced as Governor, perhaps until his death in 1736. By 1742 the orphan Newtham had apparently died and the house was sold by Jane Follett's heirs. In that year, merchant John Esten was living in the house, but it probably belonged to Robert Dinwiddie.

The Glasgow born Dinwiddie had served as Receiver General, Collector and councillor in Bermuda between 1721 and 1738, but when he was appointed Surveyor General of Customs for all of Britain's southern and West Indian colonies his new office required him to leave Bermuda.

In 1748 Esten's heirs apparently exchanged Bridge House for the Brick House Wharf with Robert Dinwiddie, then resident in Williamsburg, Virginia. Dinwiddie never returned to Bermuda.

He served as Governor of Virginia from 1751 until 1758 and then retired to England.

John Esten Jr. was a prominent merchant in St. George's and lived in Bridge House until 1782, when he sold it to Bridger Goodrich, a Virginia loyalist who had made a fortune as a privateer captain from prizes taken from the American rebels. Goodrich, a young man of 25 at the time, had escaped from gaol in Baltimore where he had been imprisoned as a traitor. He reached Bermuda and outfitted a fleet of privateers which wrought vengeance on American shipping. He married Elizabeth Tucker, a member of the pro-American Tucker family and a cousin of Virginia patriot St. George Tucker. His fortune in prize money allowed him to pay £1,000 in cash for Bridge House.

In 1787 Goodrich transferred ownership to his brother, Edward, but continued to live there. This was probably a legal sleight of hand to protect the property in case he was sued or went bankrupt.

When war with France broke out in 1793, Bridger Goodrich once again assembled a fleet of privateers and had great success capturing American vessels in the West Indies. His personal assets rose from £5,410 to £18,775, and his company assets rose from £500 to £6,300 by 1795. When the British Admiralty reversed itself two years later, declaring that US vessels were not liable to capture, Goodrich was faced with having to compensate American shipowners £100,000. He died suddenly in June 1795 at the age of 38, probably from the stress of impending financial disaster. Bridge House was in his brother's name, along with most of his other Bermudian assets, so his creditors got little. He was buried in St. Peter's Church, where a white marble memorial was placed in his honour.

Soon after his death, Goodrich's widow Elizabeth, departed for England with her children, never to return to Bermuda. Elizabeth advertised the house for rent in the *Bermuda Gazette* and sold the household furniture, which included a silver mounted harpsichord, a sideboard with pedestals and vases, carpets, a very fine library, mirrors, and a genteel assortment of

Gateposts in St. George's

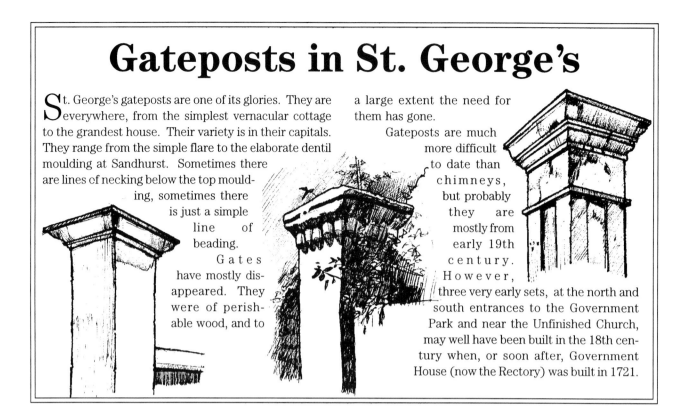

St. George's gateposts are one of its glories. They are everywhere, from the simplest vernacular cottage to the grandest house. Their variety is in their capitals. They range from the simple flare to the elaborate dentil moulding at Sandhurst. Sometimes there are lines of necking below the top moulding, sometimes there is just a simple line of beading. Gates have mostly disappeared. They were of perishable wood, and to a large extent the need for them has gone.

Gateposts are much more difficult to date than chimneys, but probably they are mostly from early 19th century. However, three very early sets, at the north and south entrances to the Government Park and near the Unfinished Church, may well have been built in the 18th century when, or soon after, Government House (now the Rectory) was built in 1721.

china, glass and queensware, clearly the trappings of one of St. George's finest residences.

Edward Goodrich lived in the house until his death in 1817. In his will, Edward Goodrich gave his wife life tenancy in Bridge House, but when his accounts were settled she found that his estate was insolvent. Their son John slowly sold off his late father's properties to keep creditors at bay. Bridge House was one of the last to go, sold at auction in 1821. A sketch by Thomas Driver in 1824 shows Bridge House much as it looks today, with a wooden verandah on the front of the porch.

The house was purchased by silversmith George Samuel Rankin for £1,800 and remained in the Rankin family for more than a century. The property by then consisted of the entire block, except a coach house or stable in the southeastern corner which belonged to Reeve Court. This was the same building or a replacement of the earlier kitchen that Governor Bennett had rented in the 1710s. It was added to the Bridge House property in 1887.

Most or all of the outbuildings standing today were built by the mid 19th century and included a detached

kitchen to the east of the house and a multi-unit privy to the northeast. One of these buildings, perhaps the store to the south, was Rankin's silversmith shop, where he worked and displayed items for sale. When George Samuel Rankin died in 1876 at the age of 82, he gave his unmarried daughter Henrietta life tenure in Bridge House before it passed to his many heirs.

Henrietta took full advantage of her father's bequest by living to be 98 years old. She died in 1921 and while various Rankin heirs decided what to do with the house, it was rented by Frank Gurr and his wife. Three years later Gurr purchased the house. During Gurr's tenure, the house acquired the name Bridge House, perhaps christened by Gurr himself after some preliminary research into the history of the building.

Roadwork on Duke of York Street to the north of the house revealed what he took to be the footing of a bridge, which he conjectured must have crossed a stream which flowed down to the harbour past the front of his house. Recent research places the bridge on the other side of King's Square, near the intersection with Water Street west, and argues against the presence of a stream, since the

"pond" in Somers Garden was dug by Daniel Tucker in 1617.

The Gurrs lived in Bridge House until 1968, when the house was sold to Hereward Watlington. Watlington undertook a major renovation of the building and altered its internal layout by removing a staircase and sealing up several doors and passages. In 1971 he sold the building to the Bermuda National Trust.

In 1993 the Trust's Archaeological Research Committee dug a number of test excavations to help date the various buildings on the site, and the following year the Trust completed another major renovation.

On the west side of Duke of Kent Street, a sprawling ruin of a house is slowly being reclaimed by a lush growth of vegetation. The history of this ruin, called **Longford House** by some, has long remained a mystery. Clearly this large two storey residence was an important landmark. In the early 1700s the lot was a garden for widow Ann Levinz's house built to the west. In 1709 the land was granted to Dr. Roger Thomas who built a house by 1713. Thomas gave the house to his wife Sarah and son William before he died in 1715. Sarah died three years

at least 1717, for Davis retained the lot.

The oldest part of the house lies to the south. Its western end is slanted, reflecting the triangular shape of the original lot and is buttressed by a large internal chimney. Its entrance on the east end is reached via a set of side stairs fronting on Duke of Kent Street.

Jehoadan Davis remarried in the 1730s to merchant William Martindale, and the couple had two children before Martindale died in 1757. Their son, also William, moved to Barbados and after Jehoadan's death it is unclear who occupied the house. By 1797, however, it was the property of Ann Gwynn, who wed an American mariner, Benjamin Pindar.

The Pindars tried repeatedly to sell the house but could find no buyers, surprising for a residence that boasted six rooms and a closet, with a storeroom and floored kitchen in the cellar below, a walled garden and a good well.

The size of the house offered in the *Bermuda Gazette* strongly suggests that the two storey gable roofed addition to the northeast of the original house had been added by this period. The house was worth £450.

In November 1828, the body of Benjamin Pindar was found floating at Blue Hole. He was returning from at-

The awkwardness of the addition of a two and a half storey apparently early 19th century commercial building to the early 18th century Davis Cottage has been ameliorated by a particularly graceful extension of the original steps.

later and Walter Mitchell was appointed guardian of the young William. Mitchell, a hugely successful merchant, taught the boy well, for in 1737 William Thomas moved to Barbados to set himself up as a trader.

By the 1760s the house had been purchased by another successful merchant, William Foot. He was the son of a poor lieutenant who had been stationed in Bermuda as part of HM Independent Company. Foot amassed a considerable fortune before his death in 1807, and also served as an assemblyman. He bequeathed his property to his daughter Jehoadan Lagourgue, the widow of French merchant Denis Victor Lagourgue. The Lagourgues had been living in Santo Domingo during the bloody slave rebellion of 1793 and had only narrowly escaped with their lives. The widow Lagourgue lived out her final days in her late father's house on Duke of Kent Street while her four children scattered.

After her death in 1835, the house was sold to another prominent merchant, John Davenport, and became the home of his son Robert. The

Davenports later sold it to Samuel Crofts Rankin, who placed it in trust after his death in 1904. By the time it was finally auctioned in 1951, Longford House was described as a "building in ruins, no value". The cause of the house's demise was not stated, but more than likely it was the terrible hurricane which struck Bermuda in October 1926.

The house has a deep cellar and three chimneys and the ruin remains, despite the neglect of more than 50 years. The remains of the house's detached kitchen stand to the west, and on the south are traces of the alley which once ran from Church Lane to Blockade Alley.

Davis Cottage to the south of Longford House is its close contemporary. In 1713 widow Jehoadan Davis was granted an odd shaped triangular lot on the condition that she build upon it within four years. The following year she was also granted a garden lot across the street, in the northwest corner of the Governor's Garden. The gable roofed core of the present day house thus dates to

Top hung blinds provide contrasting angles to the severity of the plain porch roof at Hillside. Older blinds have wider slats set to allow the breeze to come through while keeping out both rain and sun, an early form of air conditioning. Today blinds are made with narrower slats and are primarily used to protect glass from flying debris in hurricanes.

Hillside is a long, asymmetrical early 18th century house with a large double chimney and windows set close below the wall plate. Its porch has been created by adding a roof, here on simple wooden posts, at the top of the steps leading up to the living floor (hidden by the hedge). The further gable has Flemish decoration. The commercial level of the house has undergone recent alterations to create apartments.

tending court at Hamilton when two of his friends reported seeing him fatigued, pausing often on his way home. An inquest ruled the death accidental, speculating that perhaps he had

An excellent example of a stone gutter skirting an intervening chimney at Hillside to take advantage of every possible inch of roof water catchment. The height of this chimney suggests that it was an oven chimney, rather than one for a full fireplace.

stumbled and fallen into the sea. The widowed Ann occupied the house until her death in 1850, whereupon the property was purchased by Charles Pickthorne, an officer originally from Devonport, England, who was attached to the convict establishment in St. George's. The Pickthorne family occupied this house for more than half a century. Charles and his wife Betsey died in 1876 and 1871 respectively. The last of their four daughters died in 1908. The property was sold to Richard Higinbothom and has not been substantially changed since the early 19th century. A rustic detached shed to the south of the house, probably built by Higinbothom, was once a cobbler's shop.

Hillside, overlooking Shinbone Alley, was built by mariner Phineas Wright between 1714 and 1717. He died as the house neared completion and the lot was inherited by his sister Lydia, who successfully petitioned Governor John Pitt for the garden in front of the house. Lydia never married and lived in the house

until her death in 1747.

She left the property to her great niece Mary Adams, who moved into the house with her parents, William and Elizabeth. Mary was probably the "Miss Adams, daughter of the pilot" listed in the assessment records. She died in 1770, and the house passed to her father. In his 1783 will, he left the house to his other children.

In the 19th century, ownership passed to the Roberts family. In 1866 widow Esther Roberts gave the house equally to her two daughters Elizabeth Outerbridge and the widowed Susan McCallan. Outerbridge promptly bought out her sister's share, but the house returned to the McCallan family upon Elizabeth's death when she bequeathed it to her nephew Samuel. In 1895 the property passed to Ernest A. McCallan who owned Seven Gables. In 1979, McCallan's son sold the house to Steven Masters, who undertook a renovation of the property. Hillside is a good example of an early grant house, with a Flemish gable, massive old chimneys, and windows set high under the eaves. The side

The Southern façade of Ming House is extremely simple, thus making it difficult to date. During the late 19th century its front garden was removed to facilitate the widening of Duke of York Street.

In 1713 Captain Robert Burton obtained the grant for a lot to the south of the State House on the condition that he build on it within three years. He already owned a tall house in the northern part of town, which he had inherited from his father. He began to erect a house but his health failed. In May 1715 he wrote his will, directing that in the event of his death his wife was to completely "finish, glaze and make fit for habitation the house which I have begun to build on my lott neare the Sessions House". He died less than a year later and it is evident that his widow carried out his instructions, for the grant did not revert to the Crown.

Thus, the building known as the **Casino** on Water Street dates to 1716. Burton's widow Esther married Thomas Smith, who was living in this house and owned the wharf across the street when he died in 1742. In 1764 the aged Esther Smith gave the house, kitchen and lot to her granddaughter Esther, wife of George Ball. The widow Smith died a year later. Esther and George lived in the house and had at least one son, Alexander Forbes Ball. In 1768 they apparently mortgaged the property to George Forbes for £140, for, in

stairs in front and an eastward wing on the southern end of the house seem to have been added between 1867 and 1876, when William and Elizabeth Outerbridge lived there.

The **Ming House,** near the steps to St. Peter's Church, dates to about 1715, when Caleb Wright sold a portion of his larger lot to his daughter Rhoda for a pittance. Rhoda married John Colson and the couple built the present house. Most of the building's interesting architectural features are in the rear and include a Flemish gable and two chimneys on its north side.

In 1765 the house was sold to the recently widowed Sarah Ming. She passed the house to her son Joseph, who wed Jane Hayward in 1779. Joseph died in 1799, but his widow lived in the house until 1844, when she died at the age of 91. Joseph and Jane's son, David Glegg Ming, became a reputable silversmith and operated a shop on the premises. After his marriage to

Susannah Wright in 1810, the couple moved into the Ming House and had two children, Joseph and Mary. David died prematurely in 1819 and his seven year old son died four years later of tetanus after stepping on a rusty nail.

Mary Ming inherited the house and after her marriage to Anthony B. Hayward in 1834, the property passed into the Hayward family. It was the birthplace of St. George's Mayor, Joseph Ming Hayward, and was later occupied by Lillian H. Hayward, founder of the St. George's Historical Society, until her marriage to Reverend Arthur C. Tucker.

In the 18th century there was a front garden with a red brick path, but this disappeared during the following century when Duke of York Street was widened. The front façade has not changed substantially since the early 19th century. Its windows are set high under the eaves of the roof and the ground floor doors and windows retain the same configuration as shown in John S. Humphrey's 1923 book.

Just behind the State House on Water Street stands Casino, another prominent example of an early 18th century building surviving relatively unscathed. Standing on a hillside, it has the usual residence over commercial level with a gate protecting a substantial flight of entrance steps. The porch protecting the front door is a later addition.

The large chimney on the western gable of the Casino is typical of its period, but much of the stone guttering has been replaced with more modern down-pipes.

1781, Forbes' heirs sued the Balls in chancery court for the money. Neither George nor Esther left a will when they died in 1792 and 1796 respectively, and Alexander inherited the house.

Alexander Forbes Ball was one of the founding members of the Masonic Lodge in St. George's. He married Mary Augusta Hinson, a widow, in May 1800 in St. Anne's Church, Southampton, and they had one son, Joseph, the following February. Mary Augusta died in 1807 and Alexander Ball never remarried. The year that they married, his house had been worth £325 and he had furniture and merchandise worth another £1,000. His fortunes steadily declined until by 1813 his total worth was only £582. In 1821 he was forced to mortgage his house to John Barr for £400 and three years later advertised it in the *Bermuda Gazette*, hoping that its "five rooms upstairs with closets, excellent kitchen, large cellar, tank and outhouses" and the fact that it was enclosed with a substantial wall might

attract a buyer. It did. Joseph Gwynn, merchant and keeper of the clock in the parish church, purchased the house in March 1824. He would enjoy it for little more than a year before his own rash actions drove him forever from the house.

Gwynn's son, Joseph Jr., was involved in a scuffle late in 1825, for which he was sentenced to a short gaol term by St. George's magistrate, Dr. Joseph Hunter. The father became enraged and set off for Hunter's residence on the night of December 6, armed with a pistol and dirk. Word travels quickly in a small town and Hunter was warned before Gwynn arrived, so he pretended to be out. The frustrated Gwynn set off for home in an angry mood. Just as he turned up Princess Street to go home, he saw his neighbour Henry Folger, whom he mistook for Hunter. Gwynn drew his pistol and fired it at point blank range, wounding Folger, whom he left to die in the street.

The murder caused a sensation, since it was the first killing of a Ber-

mudian in 20 years. Gwynn, along with his two sons, Joseph Jr. and Benjamin, was arrested and tried in May 1826. The court room in Hamilton was packed and when the jury returned a guilty verdict against the elder Gwynn, he protested his innocence, claiming he never meant to kill either Hunter or Folger. The sons were acquitted for want of sufficient evidence.

The Governor pronounced a death sentence upon Gwynn which was to be carried out on the site of the murder. A scaffold was erected near the corner of Duke of York Street and Princess Street and at 11:25 in the morning, the *Bermuda Gazette* reported that Gwynn "with calmness and resignation . . . was launched into eternity". After hanging for half an hour, the body was cut down.

Richard Cotter, a Royal Navy purser who claimed to be an eyewitness to the execution, adds a detail notably absent from the *Bermuda Gazette* account. Cotter related that the hangman was a mulatto man hired by the Provost Marshal for $100, who accompanied Gwynn from the gaol dressed as a woman and would only perform the execution after removing his gloves and mask.

As a felon, Gwynn's property was forfeited to the Crown. The colony's Provost Marshal auctioned it in June 1826, and it was purchased by William Tucker, the owner of Rose Hill, Reeve Court, the White Horse Tavern (in the days when it was Esten House) and several other properties. In 1849 he sold it to James Mitchell, a grocer, who moved his family into the house. In 1861, Mitchell's wife Eliza died, leaving him to raise six children with only the help of his sister-in-law, who was living with the family. By 1882 James Mitchell had died and two of his daughters had moved to New York City.

Over the next four years Thomas W. Foster tracked down and purchased all of the individual shares in the house from Mitchell's heirs, for a total of £530. Foster kept the property until 1920, when it was sold to Reginald H. Higinbothom. Higinbothom added the three storey northern wing to the old house, replacing a smaller extension which had been

The fine 1731 Mitchell House stands over a storage basement and has one of the best sets of welcoming arms steps to be found. The benches can still be seen at either side of the door at the top of the steps. Two handsome chimneys punctuate the length of the house which is externally symmetrical and has a formal Georgian dignity despite its severe simplicity.

built before 1854, as part of the hotel and tavern that he ran. The property acquired the name Casino about this time, perhaps because Higinbothom encouraged gambling in his establishment. After passing through a number of hands, the property was purchased by the Bermuda Historical Monuments Trust in 1966. Since 1980, it has been leased for 999 years by the Bermuda National Trust to the Jehovah's Witnesses as the Kingdom Hall, a place of worship.

The original southern portion of the building, built, according to Burton's will about 1716, is typical of an 18th century merchant's house, with living quarters above and storage space in the high ceilinged cellars below. The house was conveniently located near the wharves. The asymmetry of the windows predates the arrival of Georgian architecture. The west gable is buttressed by a massive old chimney, while the eastern side, perhaps a one room addition to an older core, is decorated with a finely executed Flemish gable. Casino's side

steps are typical for the town, although the porch roof may be a later addition. The building bears a striking resemblance to Tucker House and gives a good idea of what that building could have looked like as built by Thomas Smith about 1753, before President Henry Tucker made additions to the structure.

The northeast corner of the Governor's Garden was one of the last lots granted in town. In 1726 the land was given to mariner Joseph West. By the time West died in 1736, he had built a "new mansion house", which he gave to his wife. This building has survived with little alteration and is now known as **Chandler's Cottage**. The roof of today has replaced an earlier one, but the massive chimney against the eastern end of the house clearly dates to the 18th century. After West's widow died, ownership becomes unclear, but in 1796 James and Eleanor Service moved into the L-shaped building. The newly married couple ran a tavern out of their

home, dividing their time between tending bar and raising three children. Later, during the American Civil War, the cottage was the home of Joseph Johnson, a merchant from Liverpool and one of the principal blockade running agents in Bermuda. At the end of the war, Johnson fled the colony and the house and all its furnishings were auctioned to pay his debts.

Along the western edge of the lot was a stable used by Banana Manor resident Joseph Martin in his horse livery business in the 1890s. From the late 1960s until 1992, the southern wing of Chandler's Cottage adjoining Shinbone Alley was in a ruinous condition, but has since been restored by the current owner, Thomas Wadson. The Flemish gable on the southern end dates to this restoration.

The Mitchell House, which houses the St. George's Historical Society Museum, was erected about 1731 by Major Walter Mitchell for his American brother's son, William Mitchell. Walter had apparently ac-

A splendid array of roofs and 18th century chimneys at the Mitchell House: the very wide chimney on the right clearly serves the kitchen while the central one seems to have been heightened to clear smoke over the higher roof of the outbuilding on the left.

quired the lot and an older house through his wife Sarah Briggs, who inherited it from Charity Briggs Hilton, to whom the lot was originally granted in 1712.

A 1994 archaeological excavation revealed a post hole carved into the bedrock in the old kitchen, which supported the timber frame walls of Hilton's house or predecessor.

William Mitchell moved into the new stone house with his bride of four months, Mary Tucker of Southampton. Walter Mitchell died the following year, confirming his gift of the house and including a storehouse on Water Street east, part-shares in several sloops and £300—a nice gift with which to start married life.

William Mitchell was a successful merchant and militia officer. He traded frequently with his father John, who was based in Philadelphia, and went to sea himself on a number of occasions. He was an officer in HM

Independent Company and Captain of Paget Fort in the 1730s.

Mitchell was granted a garden lot across Duke of Kent Street in 1734 and added a chimney to the southern end of his hall in 1740. When he died in 1749, his incomplete will left all his property to his wife Mary. She lived another 23 years in the house and was frequently visited by her Tucker relatives. She carried on her husband's shipping business, specialising in articles such as fabrics, needles, tea and gloves. In 1772 her niece Effie and her family moved into the house after Effie's husband, Captain Thomas Smith, lost a court case and with it Tucker House.

The following year, Mary Mitchell willed her house to Effie's single daughter Marianne Smith. She also directed that her executors were to fashion her coffin from the wood of a large cedar tree growing in the front yard. An inventory of the house made

in 1774 reveals the house much as it stands today, with a hall, hall chamber, passage, kitchen and "Mrs. Mitchell's bedchamber". After the widow's death, Smith's inheritance was unsuccessfully challenged by the illegitimate daughter of William Mitchell, who alleged that Mitchell's will was defective.

Marianne Smith retained the house until 1820. She never married but some evidence suggests she may have had an affair with Collector John Stewart which produced two children. To support herself, she taught "reading, writing and needlepoint" at her house for £3 a year tuition and rented the cellars to the Commissary of Provisions Department of the British garrison.

In 1820 Marianne Smith sold a small lot in the northwest corner of her property, upon which was erected the short-lived Independent Chapel of St. George's. Later the same year, she

The south wing of the Mitchell House shows the storage basement very clearly. The problem of how to paint a Bermuda chimney is clearly seen in the unsatisfactory compromise which changes colour half way up the lateral stepping.

gave the property to her niece Elizabeth, who married Major Edward Moore, then commander of the colony's gunboats. The Moores were posted abroad and did not live in the house.

In 1842 it was sold to William and Isabella Archer, former slaves, who were proprietors of The Gun Tavern. William Archer's fate is chronicled in chapter 6 (see Foster House.) After Isabella's death in the late 1860s, the house escheated to the Crown and was regranted to Jonathan J. Trott, a

farmer from Tucker's Town, who sold it to Alfred Burch within a year. Burch and his successor, Thomas Ward Kelly, operated a hotel and tavern there called City Hall and added the cottage to the west of the main house. From 1900 to 1914, the house, renamed the Commercial Hotel, was run by George and Annie Wailes.

George C. Wailes originally came to Bermuda in 1883 as a private in the 84th York and Lancaster Regiment. Within five years, he had purchased his discharge and was a warden in the

military prison. In the 1890s he became a victualler and, with his wife, opened a tavern elsewhere in town. In 1914 Wailes gave the property to his son George Jr., who promptly mortgaged it to Claude McCallan, who foreclosed upon it six years later.

When the property came up for auction, a group of historically minded St. Georgians, led by Lillian Hayward, rallied to save the house. They formed the St. George's Historical Society, which purchased the building and converted it into a museum and library. This new group saved the old building, then on the verge of ruin. The Society launched a three year restoration of the house and has recently completed another.

The building, with its jumbled roofs and sprawling layout, offers a fine example of a well preserved 18th century house with early 19th century additions. Furnished with period pieces, it gives visitors to St. George's the rare opportunity to examine both the interior and exterior of an old town dwelling.

In the original building, there was a wall separating the large hall at the top of the front welcoming arms stairs from the bedroom to the right. The wall was removed in 1956. It is thought that the old kitchen, with its wide hearth and brick bake oven, was once detached, and was joined by a covered passage some time in the early 19th century. The well in the front garden was there in the 1820s, and was probably the town well of the 17th and 18th centuries.

St. George's is blessed with many early buildings that offer insights into the first sustained forays into building with stone as well as the timber frame architecture that came before. These ancient survivors readily stand out among their more elaborately decorated or larger Georgian and 19th century neighbours.

Had Bermuda's capital not moved to Hamilton in 1815, there would probably be far fewer examples of early 18th century houses, for undoubtedly they would have been replaced by taller and more sophisticated modern buildings.

The loss sustained by St. Georgians of the 1810s is our gain today.

CHAPTER SIX

Georgian Style St. George's Residences

Whitehall, the town's grandest and probably largest house, was built in 1815 by Mayor John Van Norden. The main house is rather severe, classic in style, and heavily parapeted to hide its roof. This splendid Edwardian verandah is a later addition. The house is in sad disrepair and has been divided into small apartments.

The Bermudian vernacular architecture of chapter 5 was a home-grown style which evolved out of an older timber frame tradition brought from England by the first settlers and modified by local builders during more than a century of isolation. The Renaissance, or Georgian style, on the other hand, was an import, introduced to Bermuda by British government officials and foreign merchants, and by Bermudian seafarers and traders who had seen houses built in this new style in foreign ports and then duplicated them at home. The Renaissance mode of building was adopted throughout Great Britain in the late 17th and early 18th centuries and spread to the American colonies where it became known as Georgian, named after the four Hanoverian Georges who reigned from 1714-1830.

The Georgian style, emphasising order, was a fundamental break with

the past and reflected in a physical form the Enlightenment in thought. While political philosophers were articulating new, ordered and contractual ways of governing and scientists were ordering the natural world by fashioning the Great Chain of Life, architects ordered the space of everyday life. They stressed symmetry within and without. The house floor plan was divided into a greater number of separate rooms proportional in size to the building as a whole, usually with balanced chimneys, while the exterior presented a deliberate and uniform appearance. The entrance shifted to the exact centre of the house and opened onto a central passage which controlled access to more private interior rooms. The placement of windows was balanced around the entry, and decorative elements, seldom present in the earlier vernacular style were introduced. Cornices adorned the eaves, keystones the windows,

quoins the corners and pediments the entries of the new Georgian houses.

Beside these ornate mid and late 18th century houses, the simple, earlier vernacular ones paled in comparison, and a few were "Georgianised" by cutting new and more regularly placed windows through the old walls. The ideal of the Georgian builder was to mirror perfectly the two halves of the house, in both façade and layout.

The Georgian style itself evolved in the late 18th century into the Regency style in Great Britain and Federal style in the United States. Since a systematic architectural assessment of Bermuda's houses remains to be done, the subtle nuances of this change in Bermuda have not been explored.

This chapter examines the Georgian buildings of St. George's, starting in the 1740s with the house built by Scotsman George Forbes and concluding with the construction of

The roofs of Banana Manor demonstrate the series of mainly 18th century additions to the c. 1740 house in the background. The extensive sweep of smooth roofs in the foreground cover the later 19th century stables and outbuildings at the back of the house. They are connected to the main house, despite the fact that the drive passes between them.

Whitehall in 1815, a structure that epitomises the Georgian style in its form, layout and appearance.

Banana Manor on Blockade Alley just north of Shinbone Alley, was built by Dr. George Forbes on land formerly owned by one of his professional predecessors, surgeon George Ramsey. The lot was granted by the Crown to Susannah Tucker, whose father, Daniel Tucker, had surveyed the land in question. Susannah married Dr. Ramsey a few months later so the grant amounted to a free dowry, compliments of His Majesty the King. The Ramseys apparently moved elsewhere and the lot was obtained by Forbes around 1741.

George Forbes was an immigrant to Bermuda. Born in Strathdon Parish, Aberdeenshire, Scotland, in 1710, he learned "phisick and surgery" at the University of Aberdeen and graduated in 1734. Late in that year he came to Bermuda, where he promptly fell in love with Mary Jones, the daughter of prominent merchant, councillor and militia general, Francis Jones. Forbes' letters of recommenda-

tion from the Duchess of Gordon and his kinsmen Lord Forbes, Sir Arthur Forbes and Sir Duncan Forbes, were impeccable, and the couple were married in 1737. Their first child Francis was born at Brackish Pond in Devonshire in 1740, but succeeding children were born in St. George's.

The house that Forbes built was originally T-shaped, with a single wing extending to the north from the centre of the main building. Each end terminated in a large internal chimney, but only the eastern one has survived. The house offers the first example of the Georgian style in St. George's, with a central passage leading from the front door to hall, parlour and bedroom. Doubtless Forbes was exposed to the style in Edinburgh and London before he emigrated, so it is not surprising that he duplicated it in his own home. The front windows are extremely tall, suggesting perhaps that there may have been French doors opening onto a long, now-vanished verandah. Later, as the Forbes family grew, northern wings were added to the east and west ends of the house,

Under Banana Manor is storage space, reached through this arch. The house, built on a low, damp site, is raised over a basement.

creating a structure with an E-shaped floor plan. In 1768 Forbes purchased the land behind his house from neighbour and business partner John Slater.

George Forbes had a true 18th century intellect. As a physician he pioneered smallpox inoculation in the colony. He was the personal doctor of Governor William Popple and sent two of his sons to medical school in Edinburgh. A successful merchant, he used personal connections in Britain to good end, sent two other sons to the West Indies as factors and built a wharf near Stile Point (see chapter 4). As an amateur scientist, Forbes regularly subscribed to the *Philosophick Transactions* and exchanged specimens with John Fothergill and others in London. He was an avid gardener and attempted to raise everything from China tea plants to Portuguese cork trees in the upper and lower gardens surrounding his house. Forbes also had a long and distinguished career in public service; he was a councillor and vestryman from 1752 until his death, Justice of the Peace in 1763, and, briefly, Chief Justice in 1749 and President of the Council.

In George Forbes' 1774 will, he gave his wife Mary the use of all his property for her life and then directed that his estate be evenly divided among their six children. Sons William and Thomas were merchants in St. Kitt's and Charleston, South Carolina, in 1774 and died before their mother. Francis and Robert were doctors, both of whom lived in St. George's. James failed as a merchant in Georgetown and Charleston, South Carolina, and returned home to Bermuda. He evidently suffered from mental illness, for his sister, Ann, was appointed his guardian.

Ann herself had considerable experience with the insane. Her husband John Hinson went mad after a bad business deal in 1774 and had to be confined when he "began to rave". After Dr. Forbes' death, occupation of Banana Manor fell to Ann Hinson. Francis and James lived on Paget Island, their mother Mary Forbes lived in the Forbes' house and farm on Smith's Island and Robert lived in the Brick House Mansion (see chapter 4) on Water Street until his death in 1785.

After Ann Hinson died in 1817, the house became the residence of her son, Francis Forbes Hinson, who in turn, left it to his wife and children when he died in Nassau, Bahamas, in 1832. Tragically, his 15-year-old son, George, and several other Bermudian boys were washed overboard from the brig *Recruit* while returning home from college in Windsor, Nova Scotia, a few months later. Hinson's widow,

Sarah, died in 1840 and within a year, his daughter Mary Lough bought out her sister Lucy's share in the inheritance. Mary was the widow of Reverend John Lough, the Oxford educated rector of St. Peter's Church who quarrelled frequently with his vestry. He died during one such fight in January 1839.

During the American Civil War, the Widow Lough rented Banana Manor to Confederate shipping agent Major Norman Walker. His wife Georgiana ran the blockade in March 1863 to join him in Bermuda and set up house in the "cottage", as she called it. George Forbes' garden was still flourishing, for Mrs. Walker found her new home "embowered with trees & flowers which bloom throughout the year. We can count a dozen different kinds of fruits."

In June Mrs. Walker gave birth to a son in the house, whom she named Randolph St. George Walker. But her joy was diminished by the worsening condition of her daughter, "Little Georgie", who had chronic eye troubles and had to be confined to a dark room in the back of the house most of the day.

The house played host to a variety of Confederate dignitaries passing through Bermuda, but never more so than at Christmas 1863, when the Walkers gave a party attended by more than 100 Southerners. "The Confederate Flag," Walker wrote, "gaily decorated my little cottage. We had Confederate songs, dancing and games. . . We parted almost at 'rosy dawn' & all declared that they had been happier than they believed they could be out of Dixie."

The following month, the house was transformed into "a fairy scene" when Walker held an amateur dramatics night for the children of garrison officers, attended by the 39th Regiment Band. The Walkers stayed until yellow fever drove them, and the blockade runners, from Bermuda in the summer of 1864.

In the 1870s Banana Manor went quickly downhill, its Enlightenment garden and southern hospitality forgotten. Thomas W. Foster owned the house for six years before selling it to Daniel Lane, a livery stable keeper who originally came from Ireland. Lane

built a large complex of stable buildings behind the house and set up a number of watering troughs in the front yard. He competed with the Spurling family for the business of the increasing number of visitors to St. George's after The Causeway was completed.

Lane himself lived in Devonshire, far from the stink of horse manure, and the house was presumably rented. The liveryman died in 1886, and seven years later his widow sold the property to Ole Edward Jensen, a grocer and "xylographer", one who carves wooden blocks for printing. In 1900 Jensen sold the property to another stable keeper, Joseph Martin, who expanded operations by purchasing Chandler's Cottage across the street and building more stables on that property. In 1933 the property was acquired by yet another liveryman, James Robinson, who sold it four years later to Frederick C. Outerbridge, the owner of nearby Greig Hall and Somers Market.

Outerbridge converted the old stables into cold storage, combining those near Banana Manor with others belonging to Greig Hall to the north. He used this extensive new storage complex to stockpile food during World War II and supplied the troop ships and convoys bound for Europe. Outerbridge channelled his wealth into real estate and at one time owned perhaps a tenth of the buildings in the Town of St. George.

Since 1994 Banana Manor has been restored to some of its former glory. The banana grove in front has been trimmed back to reveal George Forbes' house and lower garden once again. The old pillared gate on the west side of the house reminds us that once this alley, The Governor's Walk, extended from the gate of Governor's Garden to the front of Government House on the site of the Unfinished Church. The northern part of the path was enclosed in 1940 and became part of the front lawn of Greig Hall.

Banana Manor in the town was complemented by a summer home on Smith's Island built about 1770 by Dr. George Forbes. As a physician, Forbes was mindful of the diseases which spread quickly in towns,

The Forbes House on Smith's Island reaches beyond its grasp architecturally. The central placement of the steps emphasises the asymmetrical pilasters, windows and entrance door. It was built in the 1770s as a summer home and farm.

so he probably built **Forbes House** for his family as a refuge from epidemics. The house was more typically Georgian than his older residence in town. The large L-shaped building has an asymmetrical northern façade bolstered by decorative buttresses. A chimney dominates the end of the kitchen wing to the south. A cluster of outbuildings appears on early 19th century maps of the island, most of which have since vanished. After his death in 1778, his widow Mary lived at the farm for another two decades. Her son, Dr. Francis Forbes, joined her there in 1787. Francis eventually acquired the whole of Smith's Island and left the house to his son Francis after he died in 1815.

Francis Forbes Jr. was destined for bigger and better things than a country home on Smith's Island. A gifted lawyer, he became Attorney General of Bermuda in 1810. He left for Newfoundland in 1818 to take up

the post of Chief Justice of that colony and later occupied the same position in New South Wales, Australia. He was knighted in 1837. Soon after he left for Nova Scotia, he sold the house and middle section of Smith's Island to Thaddeus A. Outerbridge.

In 1882 Claude William McCallan moved there from St. George's and launched an experimental farm on Smith's Island while renovating and expanding the old house. McCallan grew mostly onions on the western half of Smith's Island, while Robert James grew Easter lilies on the eastern half.

After passing through a number of hands, the Forbes House and two adjoining lots were purchased by Eric and Rita Rothwell. Rita Rothwell is the daughter of Frederick Robertson of Robertson's Drug Store. The house is now in need of substantial repair, but retains a long tradition of rural grandeur.

Buckingham visually dominates the view of the State House from King's Square, preempting the ancient building with its size. When the land on which Buckingham stands was

The wings of the Forbes House are relieved with shallow bays. This may have served to increase interior space somewhat but the single windows added no light.

Extreme simplicity is the keynote of the c. 1750 Buckingham. Despite the windows being set well below the wall plate and a definite formal Georgian symmetry, they are set in flush wooden frames characteristic of an earlier era, clearly demonstrating the difficulty of dating Bermudian houses from architectural details. The plain architrave over the front door served to keep rainwater away from the door. The windows are protected by the top hung blinds, suggesting their introduction by mid century. The unusual flight of steps to the front door was required by the proximity of the alley below and the need for the usual storage basement.

widow died a year later, leaving the property to their sons. Samuel III apparently died or sold his share to brother Thomas by 1803. In that year, Thomas, a huckster by profession, was in sole possession of the house when he mortgaged it to neighbours William and Henry Todd for £64. Three years later, Mills was sued by several parties for business debts amounting to more than £315 and the house was seized and auctioned.

The winning bid of £415 was placed by Miss Martha Wright. She married Joseph Hayward in 1810 but when she died just five years later, Buckingham went to her mother, the widow Sarah Wright. Sarah rented the property, and it was occupied by another widow, Anna McDonald, when Wright made her will in January 1823. She directed that the property continue to be rented by her executors, with the proceeds going to support her sister Jane Ming and her nephew, seven-year-old Joseph Glegg Ming, until he died or reached the age of 21, when the house was to be sold. Sarah Wright died a few weeks later and the young Joseph Ming likewise perished in November of the same year (see Ming House, chapter 5). For a decade, Buckingham was occupied by one of Wright's executors, Anthony Atwood Jr., but in 1833 the house was sold at public auction to William Hayward Fox for £600.

Fox, a newly married 25-year-old when he purchased the house, was a victualler by trade and operated a dry goods store out of the basement of Buckingham. The Fox family lived there until 1864, when William bought a house worth £1,000 near St. Peter's Church. The timing of the move coincided with the addition of a kitchen wing to the north side of Buckingham, reflected in a £140 increase in the building's assessment. By the time he died in 1867, William Fox had acquired a number of houses and a waterfront property. He gave life tenure of all his real estate to his wife Susan, who died in 1891, and then ownership passed to his four children.

His two sons, William Davenport Fox and Joseph Fox, followed in their father's footsteps and operated dry goods and grocery stores in the town. In 1879 William bought the two quar-

granted to Thomas Brooke, Collector of Customs, in 1703, the site was vacant. This seems odd, given its proximity to the State House. It had probably once been part of the enclosed yard surrounding that building in the early 17th century. Brooke was not required by the terms of his grant to build a stone house, so he did not do so. He already possessed a fine house with an extensive library near today's Somers Market, a house which has long since vanished. Brooke died about 1727 and his widow married Jonathan Burchall. In 1745 she sold the property to Samuel Mills for £5, a sum that strongly suggests there was no building on the lot.

Mills probably built Buckingham soon after he acquired the property and certainly before 1768. In that year he made his will leaving his dwelling house to his wife for her life and then to his son Samuel, on the condition that he paid each of his sisters £5. They could live in the house until he paid. Samuel Jr. and his wife Sarah, were modest residents in St. George's. Samuel, a mariner, was away at sea for long stretches, leaving Sarah to look after their two sons, Samuel and Thomas Burt Mills. The house was assessed at an average of £150, considerably less than its grander neighbours Bridge House (£950) and Reeve Court (£600). Samuel died in 1795 and his

The elegant Tucker House, built c. 1752, is a classic example of a residence over commercial basement. The large double chimney serves fireplaces on both floors and the small windows flanking the chimney provide light and air to the small closets, while the larger windows serve the two principal rooms. The verandah roof over the entrance is probably a 19th century addition. The lower walls are of heavier stone than the upper, creating the slight setback.

flush against the front of the building perhaps now buried under the considerable amount of fill composing the front lawn of today.

Tucker House, on west Water Street, is a Bermuda National Trust museum, furnished with pieces from the late 18th century which give visitors a sense of what it would have been like to visit the well-to-do home of President Henry Tucker, a prominent politician of the period.

The house lot, along with a water lot across the street, was granted to Sarah Tucker in 1699, and again in 1713 because she failed to build upon it within three years of the first grant. Sarah Tucker outlived two husbands, mariner Nicholas Hinson and silversmith Daniel Hubbard, and gave the property to her two daughters, Jane and Rebecca, both of whom had also been widowed by 1749. In 1752 they sold the unimproved northern lot to merchant and mariner Thomas Smith, while Jane continued to live in an earlier, now demolished house to the south, built on the water lot. Smith built Tucker House much as it stands today.

In layout, it is like Casino (see chapter 5) in that it has living space for the family above and cellars below for storing the merchandise which

ter shares in the property owned by his sister. He had presumably obtained the other quarter from his brother, and so became the sole owner of Buckingham. William became the US Vice Commercial Agent in 1890, an important post, since much of Bermuda's produce went to that country. He was a member of the parish vestry and Masonic Lodge 200, and died in 1907.

Two Flemish gables at the back of Tucker House seem more elaborate than their nearly invisible location justifies. Until the northern neighbours were built in the American Civil War boom, however, they had been readily visible from Duke of York Street.

In 1901 William D. Fox belatedly settled his father's estate, ten years after his mother had died. At the time, the upper floors of Buckingham were used as a boarding house operated by Thomas Spicer. The building was purchased for £300 by Samuel Crofts Rankin, who had grown up in nearby Bridge House, and continued to be leased to tenants by him and his heirs until 1951. After Rankin acquired the property, the building was christened Buckingham. Perhaps it complemented Windsor, another house owned by Rankin at Turkey Hill.

The Bermuda Historical Monuments Trust purchased the building to preserve the architectural integrity of the neighbourhood surrounding the State House. This rather plain Georgian structure remains essentially as it was built by Samuel Mills about 1750. The present entrance steps to the first floor were added after 1876, replacing an earlier staircase built

The Tucker House steps rise to an asymmetrical landing to leave room for a basement door. The asymmetry allowed for a bench for visitors to sit on at the top of the steps. The archway has a simple eyebrow to deflect rain from the door serving the basement storage area.

The Barber's Alley entrance to the service buildings of Tucker House is an excellent example of how St. George's looked in the late 18th century. Water Street at the bottom of the Alley then fronted the harbour. The Alley has recently been repaved in a particularly satisfying treatment.

agent in London in 1782, Colonel Henry secured for his son the lucrative posts of Secretary and Provost Marshal, which came with an annual salary of £800. Tucker used some of this money to expand his house to accommodate his growing family. He built a long addition to the north on the western side of the house, only half of which survives today, as well as several detached outbuildings. He also remodelled the hall and dining room to accommodate the genteel entertainments which he was required to give, according to his new station in government. In the 1790s and early 1800s, Tucker was President of the Council and served as Acting Governor on no fewer than four occasions. By 1807, however, all of his children were grown and had left home, and his wife, in poor health, wanted to return to England.

The Tuckers made preparations to depart Bermuda by selling their household furniture and offering to lease their house, but before they left Henry died suddenly of influenza in February 1808. The following year, Frances Tucker sold the property for £3,000 by instalments to John Till, a former East India Company purser and now agent for Gosling & Co. of London.

When that firm went bankrupt in 1811, Till could not pay the mortgage on the house and Frances Tucker foreclosed. She offered the lot and its many buildings for sale and found a buyer in Liverpool merchant James Richardson, whose brother George lived in the house from 1813 until 1825. Richardson extended the wharf another 40 feet into the harbour in 1815 to better accommodate his merchant fleet when his ships called at Bermuda.

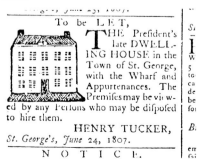

An advertisement to rent the Tucker House in 1807 when President Henry Tucker prepared to go to England.

Smith carried in his sloops. The Flemish gable end of the northern extension may have been inspired by decorated houses in Curaçao, St. Eustatius, St. Maartens and other Dutch colonies visited by Smith while in pursuit of markets for his cargoes.

In 1760 Thomas Smith acquired the water lot from Rebecca Outerbridge, Sarah's daughter, and built a wharf, storehouse and fishpond to further support his shipping business. In 1771 disaster struck in the form of an adverse decision in a lawsuit, and Smith was forced to sell his house and move in with his wife's aunt, Mary Mitchell, who lived in the Mitchell House. The Honourable Thomas Smith, owner of Verdmont in Smith's Parish, another Bermuda National Trust museum, in Smith's Parish, purchased the house and owned

it for three years before he sold it to Henry Tucker in 1775.

Henry Tucker was the son of Colonel Henry Tucker of The Grove in Southampton, the ancestral Tucker seat at the Overplus laid out by Governor Daniel Tucker in 1618. His father sent him to St. George's in the late 1760s to act as his commercial agent in the capital. There, he successfully courted Frances Bruere, the Governor's daughter, and married her in 1770. Later that same year, Tucker was appointed Colonial Treasurer by his new father-in-law and was appointed to council in 1771. When Henry and Frances "went housekeeping" in 1775, they already had a sizeable family which would eventually grow to include 11 sons and one daughter.

While serving as the colony's

Steps in St. George's

Everywhere in Bermuda one finds an abundance of the traditional "welcoming arms" steps, and there are many of this type in St. George's. They are flared, rising fairly steeply from the ground to an upper storey. Those of the Mitchell House, which houses the St. George's Historical Society, are an excellent example and they probably date from the building of the house about 1731. At the top they have space for the benches which were placed there for callers to sit and wait before being admitted to the house.

However, St. George's has unique examples of two far less common types of steps. The first is probably the earliest version of the welcoming arms, before the wide flung arms started to be built. The sides of the steps are not flared but parallel. The Carter House steps (see photo in chapter 9) and the much shorter ones at the Old Rectory are typical. Both these buildings are known to be very old.

Welcoming arms steps, whether parallel or flared, project a considerable distance from the house and were often impracticable for structures built flush against the town's narrow streets. So St. Georgian's modified their staircases to run along their houses to the street level. These are known as side (or lateral) staircases. Two typical examples are attached to the Tucker House and Casino, but there are many other examples in the town. Dual approach sidestairs were also once common, but have now disappeared. A documented example is the building which stood on the western side of King's Square just north of Water Street.

In 1825 Benjamin Dickinson Harvey bought the property for £1,110. Harvey lived in Hamilton Parish, but some of his 11 sons and daughters lived in Tucker House. Harvey was a ship owner and lawyer noted as a champion of American causes in Bermudian courts in the 1780s and 1790s, for which he was branded by one critic "a most determined democrat". He had been an assemblyman for nearly 40 years when he died suddenly in 1833. His daughter Althea, and perhaps other children, continued to live in the house after his death.

In 1860 the property was briefly transferred to William T. and Richard T. Tucker, who sold the house back to Althea but retained the water lot and land to the north of the house fronting on Duke of York Street.

Althea Harvey died unmarried in 1876, and the house was sold to Irishman Robert Boggs, keeper of HM new prison built at the foot of Rose Hill. Buildings to the north and south of Tucker House obscured the once unobstructed view of the north side of the house. In 1939 the Bermuda Historical Monuments Trust purchased the house from Boggs' heirs, the first on a long list of important historic properties in St. George's acquired by the group.

Tradition has it that during the American Civil War, Joseph Rainey, a free black man from South Carolina, rented the detached kitchen to the northeast of the main house and operated a barber shop while his wife made dresses. The couple returned to the US in 1866 after thanking their many St. George's customers for their support. In 1870, Rainey became the first black man elected to the US House of Representatives, a post he kept until 1879.

In 1953, the Bermuda Historical Monuments Trust opened the President Henry Tucker House Museum, filled with original 18th century furnishings, paintings and pieces owned by the Tucker family which had been generously given by one of the family's descendants from Baltimore. From the walls of Tucker House, President Henry's parents, brothers and sisters look down upon visitors.

Archaeological excavations carried out between 1988 and 1990 shed light on the diet, trade, wealth and taste of the Smith and Tucker families, and many of the recovered artifacts are on display in the cellar area.

The complex of buildings surrounding **California House** at the foot of Barrack Hill dates to the 1760s. In 1761 Richard Wright Jr. obtained ungranted land at the east end of town. He had erected a house by the time he died in 1770. Wright's two storey house and detached kitchen went to his grandson, Jacob Johnson Wright. Jacob's wife Sarah ran the household while he, a ship's captain, was at sea for much of the year. In 1808 Jacob died while in Grenada and Sarah inherited the house. She continued to live there until 1820, when she moved and sold the house to James Barclay. Before she did so, she freed her slave Kate and Kate's two children and gave her "a certain room or building . . . at the East End of town on rising ground above my now mansion house at the foot of Barrack Hill". This cottage was later incorporated into or replaced by the house set into the cliff to the east which hovers over California House today. Sarah Wright required the children to care for their mother Kate in her old age as a condition of their inheriting the cottage.

James and Honora Barclay owned the house for ten years. For part of the time it was rented to Mary Catterall, a free black woman who may have operated a tavern on the premises (see The Redan Hotel in this chapter).

James Barclay died in 1831 and his widow sold California House to James A. Bell for £500. In 1848 the Bell family sold the property, advertised as

The St. George's Hotel in 1890. It clearly shows the quoins and chimneys of the original Stiles House. St. Peter's Church and the old single storey Sunday school are seen on the left. (Plimpton Album: Bermuda Archives Collection, Hamilton, Bermuda.)

"first rate for carrying on retail, grocery and dry goods" establishments, to William Hayward. A map made in 1876 shows that the small cottage in front of the main house was used by the police, perhaps as a lock-up for the often drunk soldiers who frequented the bars on Shinbone Alley.

Two years later the McCallan family purchased California House. They held onto the property until 1923, when it was acquired by the Outerbridge family.

The California House property offers a good example of a late 18th century domestic complex. The upper floor of the main house was used for sleeping and entertaining, while the lower floor provided storage and work space. Food was prepared in the detached kitchen in the yard and shuttled into the main house through the lower floor and an internal staircase. Elsewhere in the yard are a privy and buttery.

By the middle of the 18th century the Town of St. George was in decline, largely as a result of the island's merchants shifting their commercial operations to storehouses near their homes "up the country". By 1764 things had reached such a low ebb that the vestry was willing to sacrifice a portion of King's Square, prime real estate in the very centre of town, in the hope of luring country merchants

back to revitalise the port. They approached Edward Stiles of Southampton, the richest merchant in Bermuda, and offered him the land on the condition that he build a substantial two storey stone house, at least 56 feet long and 20 feet high. Stiles accepted, and within a year had completed **Stiles House**, which is now the Bank of Butterfield. He donated a further

The prominent Stiles House dominated King's Square when it was built in 1766, but had fallen on hard times as a hotel in the 19th century and became structurally unsound. Faithfully restored by the Bank of Butterfield, it has resumed its local pre-eminence.

£30 towards building a market house elsewhere on the Square, but the money was diverted to repairing the parish church. Much to the dismay of St. Georgians, Stiles moved to Philadelphia a few years later and the house became the residence of his brother Copeland.

During the American Revolution, this building was a mess house used by British troops garrisoned on

the island. In 1791 Copeland Stiles went bankrupt and his creditors seized his furniture and auctioned it on King's Square. Captain Thomas Hurd of the Royal Navy lived in the house while he surveyed the island's reefs and channels in the 1790s. About 1812 the property passed from Edward Stiles to his son-in-law, Scottish merchant John Millar. Millar rented the building to Walter Stennett, who opened The George, a hotel, tavern and coffee house.

Stennett and his brother had originally come to Bermuda at the start of the War of 1812 and unsuccessfully set themselves up as portrait painters. Walter Stennett's hotel flourished un-

A detail from Thomas Driver's 1823 painting of King's Square shows the Stiles House before a verandah had been added. (Courtesy Fay and Geoffrey Elliott Collection: Bermuda Archives, Hamilton, Bermuda.)

The steep roofs of the Judkin House, hidden between Duke of York and Water Streets, suggest a cruciform plan and its gables also suggest an 18th century date. So surrounded by other buildings has this house become that it is very difficult to assess it visually, but there is no reference to this building before 1764.

til a prize ship he had purchased to supply the hotel with fresh food was captured by the French, and thereafter Stennett plunged into debt, for which he was put in prison. There, the failed hotelier convinced the gaoler and a fellow prisoner to run off and the three were last seen in an open boat heading for America.

In 1819 John Millar died and his son James inherited and mortgaged the property to a Stiles cousin to pay his father's debts. Seven years later he was forced to sell the property at auction to avoid foreclosure. A sketch by Thomas Driver made in 1823 shows this grand Georgian edifice with four large flanking chimneys and a wide hip roof.

James Musson purchased the building and lived in the house. He built a number of storehouses in the rear for his shipping business. About 1851 the Stiles House once again became an inn, the St. George's Hotel. A long wooden verandah was added to the front of the building about the time the hotel opened.

In the 1870s it was known as Kennelly's Hotel, and in the 1930s it was renamed the Somers Inn Hotel. The Bank of N. T. Butterfield opened its first St. George's branch on the lower floor in 1940. Fourteen years

later the bank purchased the building outright. A renovation in the 1960s removed the 19th century wooden verandah and returned the building to its original appearance. Inside, however, the old hotel floor plan survives with room numbers attached to the doors.

Behind the 20th century façade of the two storey shop front at 20 York Street lies a large three storey house built by Stephen Judkin in 1765. The lots upon which this building was erected were granted to George Tucker and Robert Burton in 1713. The northern Tucker lot served as a garden for Seven Gables in the late 17th century, while the southern Burton lot was the site of an earlier house. Judkin acquired both properties by 1764 and owned the entire block. Between 1764 and 1765 his parish assessment increased from 16 shillings to £1.10.0, reflecting the construction of **Judkin House**.

The house originally faced west, and consisted of a long, main section running north and south, with three one room extensions to the east, all covered by gable roofs. At one time a room projected west from the main house toward Barber's Alley, perhaps an entry porch, but it was removed in

the late 19th century. The long low shed to the east of the house also may have been built by Judkin.

Stephen Judkin, a sailmaker by trade, served as a juror, constable and assemblyman for the parish. A year after his death in 1794, Judkin's heirs

The unusual matched triple gables on the Judkin House suggest that the central one, original to the 18th century building, was embellished to match the early 19th century style of its neighbours. The chimney also suggests that later period, with its abrupt angles and graceless shoulders.

sold the house to Samuel Adams for £680. Adams lived there with his wife and seven slaves until he died in 1824. In his will, he gave life tenure to his widow Eleanor and daughter Mary Mills Sears, before ownership passed to his three Sears grandsons.

In 1828 the Sears brothers sold the house to Daniel Seon for £800 but retained the northwest corner of the

Lyncliffe dates from the end of the 18th century but with a replacement roof. The widely spaced fenestration with flush window frames seem to be original; the door, however, now has no steps and cannot be used. Once the front door of the house, it was reached by a narrow pathway. The house is now reached by an equally long narrow alley from Old Maids Lane on the other side of the house.

lot upon which a building had been erected, perhaps for the use of their mother. This is now York House, occupied by the H. A. & E. Smith's store. In 1838 they sold this house on the corner to their brother-in-law William E. Zuill, for £250. Merchant Daniel Seon owned Judkin House for seven years before he sold it to shipwright Claude Thompson McCallan for £500.

During McCallan's tenure, the house had an open porch on the west side of the house. He built a smooth stone wall dividing his property from Zuill's house to the west, and a long, single storey storehouse fronting on Duke of York Street to the south. McCallan was probably responsible for the two storey hip roofed northern addition fronting on Duke of York Street which housed a retail shop.

After Claude T. McCallan's death, the house went to his son Claude Wright McCallan. His heirs sold it to Frederick C. Outerbridge in 1929, who kept the southern storehouse and

sold the house to photographer William S. Cooper. A decade later Cooper sold the house to Somerset merchant William Perinchief, who moved his family from Sandys Parish to St. George's. The building is at present divided into apartments, owned by the late William Perinchief's daughter, Miss Lois Perinchief.

Brown House on Old Maids Lane is named for Esther Louise Brown, who owned and lived in the house in the 1930s, but it could just as easily have honoured Roger Browne, who dwelled in a timber frame house on the lot in the late 17th century. The land was granted to his unmarried granddaughter Mary in 1717. Some time in the 1770s, the Campbell family acquired the property. The house which stands today was probably erected by Samuel Campbell, who in 1783 left it to his wife Jane. The passage, hall, chamber, and cellars were split between Jane's children,

Samuel and Mary Ann, after her death. In 1820 the house was bequeathed to Samuel's daughter Jane, the wife of Andrew Cochrane Hayward. The Haywards sold it in 1844 to Nathaniel Roberts, making it the third house in the block owned by a Roberts.

About this time, an addition was made on the eastern side to the original rectangular core, turning it into an L-shaped building. The addition replaced an earlier detached kitchen, and the builders incorporated the old chimney into the newer structure, which can be seen on the exterior of the east wall. A small buttery, an architectural feature rare in St. George's, lies to the east of the addition.

Tucked between Tower House, Brown House and Somerled, **Lyncliffe** makes the most of its narrow lot, which measured just 25 feet by 70 feet when Josiah Basden purchased the land in 1794. The following year he erected the house

Part of a complex of buildings to the north of the State House, this building on Duke of York Street, once the Redan Hotel, is a plain late 18th century structure of fine proportions, commercial at street level, residential above. The unfortunate concrete verandah masks the graceful proportions of the building.

which stands today and gave it to his brother, Samuel.

A shipwright by trade, Samuel Basden died in 1828 and left the house to his four daughters. In 1844, Mary Murray, the only one of the four who married, sold her share to her single siblings. Of the remaining three, Margaret Basden lived into the early 20th century. Perhaps the Basden sisters were the old maids who inspired Old Maids Lane, the alternative and more frequently used name for Duke of Cumberland Street. The building has several features typical of the late 18th century: a hip roof, symmetrical placement of windows, architraves over the ground floor windows and top hung blinds.

The massive exterior chimney on the north side of the house is common to buildings of the period. The traces of mortar around the middle of the east side suggest that an entry porch may have been attached to this side when the front of the house faced east, and hark back to an earlier style of building.

The **Redan Hotel**, more commonly known today as Clyde's Cafe, was built on land granted to John Harlow in 1729 which had been in his family's possession at least four decades earlier. His father, also John, was a ship's captain in the 1680s and 1690s. He died in 1698, leaving his widow Rachel to raise their four children in their home abutting the State House. The cottage called Rendell House which fronts on Princess Street is probably this earlier house.

The exact date of the construction of the Redan Hotel is unknown, as are its owners after John Harlow, but it was certainly standing with much in its present appearance by 1815, when the lot and building were granted to Mrs. Sarah Crawford Magdalene Bazalgette, the wife of a captain in the 99th Regiment and the daughter of then Mayor John Van Norden (see Whitehall).

The grant stated that the building was formerly the home of Captain John Lewis of the 47th Regiment, stationed in Bermuda from 1783 until

1802. He had died intestate and without heirs, and thus his property had reverted to the Crown. This was probably the same John Lewis who died in 1809 and left a widow and three children, two of whom were dead by 1815. The third, Samuel, refused to administer his father's will. Assuming these two Lewises are the same man, the Redan was probably built about 1783, when Lewis' parish assessment jumped from £800 to £1,200. In 1786 he owned real estate worth £626 and by 1790 it had jumped again to £788. Regardless, Sarah Bazalgette claimed the property in 1815.

Two years later her father John Van Norden advertised the property for sale in the *Bermuda Gazette* as "a building 58 feet long, on the south side of Duke of Kent Street [modern Duke of York Street] with an upper floor divided into one spacious room and three of lesser dimensions". Underneath was an extensive cellar, well adapted for a grocery store and nearby were two rooms with cellars below, one of which had a fireplace and

The west wing of the L-shaped the Redan Hotel building, until recently Clyde's Cafe, maintains the graceful proportions of the Duke of York Street front. Further up the hill is the Flemish gable ended Rendell House which has been much restored, but perhaps dates from the early 18th century. The steps leading to the residential level are typical of the town.

Stephen Egan, an immigrant from Ireland who catered mainly to the needs of the garrison. Egan rented the building to various tenants over the next two decades.

In 1833 a free black woman named Mary Catterall leased the building. The fact that she had obtained a tavern licence from the Corporation of St. George's marks the first documented use of the Redan as a public house and restaurant, doubtless patronised by the British soldiers from Barrack Hill.

In 1848 the building was the home of Captain G.W. MacQuarie of the 42nd Highland Regiment, who paid £38 a year in rent to Egan. Nearby Rendell House was the garrison's billiard room. In 1849 Stephen Egan sold the property to John Edwards, Assistant Storekeeper to the Commissariat Department, who continued the tradition begun by Mary Catterall; he operated the Redan Hotel and Tavern, named for a fortification element, a two sided salient, well known to the Royal Engineers and soldiers who frequented the establishment. By 1876 Edwards had added a long wooden verandah to the front of the building which provided a commanding view up and down Duke of York Street.

Late in the 19th century, the Redan was purchased by Thomas Ward Kelly, who also bought neighbouring Foster House. Kelly died in 1895, possessed of no fewer than nine houses in St. George's. Redan House, as it was then called, was auctioned in 1901 to John Kendrick, son-in-law of postman Andrew Greig of Hillcrest. Kendrick transferred the building to his sister Fannie in 1907 who, by 1911, had moved to Oregon and sold it to widow Elizabeth Rankin.

Under Rankin's tenure, the building once again opened its doors as a restaurant. In 1947 she sold the eatery to chef Clyde Basden, who renamed it Clyde's Cafe. In 1990 this landmark closed its doors, breaking the building's 150 year chain of use as an inn, tavern, hotel and restaurant.

Except for a few sheds added by Elizabeth Rankin, the Georgian main building is much as John Van Norden described it in 1817. The 19th century wooden verandah added by Edwards

was "well calculated for a cook room". Elsewhere on the property were two excellent cisterns. The cook room was almost certainly Rendell House, which was on the same lot granted to Bazalgette.

Four years would pass before Van Norden sold it to Alexander Holmes, a printer who had arrived in Bermuda in January 1819. Holmes printed, among other things, a weekly newspaper *The Bermudian - A Com-* *mercial, Political and Literary Journal*, in the building, a competitor of the *Bermuda Gazette* based in Hamilton. Holmes published and edited *The Bermudian* until 1823, when he halted production. By 1831 Holmes had moved to Jamaica where he was publishing the *Cornwall Chronicle* and offered his property in St. George's for sale to his former rival, the *Bermuda Gazette*, in March. He found a buyer two years later in merchant

house and lot to William and Isabella Archer.

William Archer was born a mulatto slave in Dominica. In the 1820s he worked as a cooper and overseer for Halifax merchant Andrew Belcher and lived in the storehouse adjoining Belcher's Wharf on Glebe Lot 3 (see chapter 4). While still a slave, Archer married Isabella Budd, a "free woman of colour", on Christmas Eve 1826. William was emancipated by Belcher in 1830 and the following year he purchased the Foster House lot for £400, which he and his wife apparently had been renting since their marriage.

Like their neighbour Mary Catterall, the Archers were licensed to run a tavern and in the 1830s the pair of Duke of York Street bars were favourites of soldiers, sailors and St. Georgians. By 1842 the Archers had acquired enough money to purchase both the Mitchell House (see chapter 5) for £300 and another store. In 1845 their real estate, furniture and stock-in-trade exceeded £1,330, a figure which established the Archers among the most successful members of the black community in St. George's.

But success had its price for William Archer. In May 1848, he was admitted as one of the first patients to Bermuda's new Lunatic Asylum in Devonshire, because he suffered from

A difficult to find view of the Foster House, over the roofscape of the buildings between it and the State House, shows a small two storey 19th century tower rising above the generally single storey height of the older buildings.

was replaced with a concrete one in the early 20th century. The western half of Rendell House to the south has attractive Flemish gables and a side staircase. These early features suggest that it probably dates back to the John Harlow grant in 1729. The eastern half is more recent, added some time after 1876.

Foster House, to the east of the Redan, was built on land granted in 1713 to Florentius Richardson, a sailor who left no will and about whom little is known. The main core of the building, perpendicular to One Gun Alley, is a gable roofed house flanked by two massive chimneys and decorated with Flemish ga-

bles. It was built between 1770 and 1780, probably by Benjamin Richard Wright. His grandfather, mariner Richard Wright, bequeathed a lot near the "Government House" to him in 1770, but by the time Richard's widow Rachel made her will in 1780, a house had been erected. She confirmed that the property was to go to Benjamin and his siblings.

By 1800 the Wrights had sold the house and surrounding garden to mariner Anthony Atwood Sr. He mortgaged the property in 1824 to Hezekiah Frith who, after making a fortune as a privateer, had plenty of money to lend. Atwood, an old and respectable inhabitant of St. George's, died a year later. In 1831 his children sold the

Rendell House is part of a complex of buildings dating from early in the 18th century to the 1920s just to the north of the State House, this section defies dating, but may be 18th century with much later changes of fenestration. It has a typical St. George's Flemish gable.

The long 20th century stone verandah at Hillcrest gets its elegance of proportion from the late Georgian house it now hides. Similar to the Hunter Building, this verandah is more severe.

"mania" brought about by "intemperance" and from chronic delusions. After five years of unsuccessful treatment, Archer's sudden death in January 1853 was as remarkable as his life. Before doctors had a chance to perform an autopsy, Archer's friends broke into the asylum and stole the body in the middle of the night. By 1871, Isabella Archer and William's sisters in Bermuda had all died, so the property reverted to the Crown. Their daughter Nancy, living in Basseterre, Guadeloupe, petitioned for and was granted the property which she sold the following year to Thomas Ward Kelly for £325. Kelly presumably leased the building to the operators of a tavern who called it The Gun.

Grocer Thomas William Foster purchased the property in 1901 from Kelly's estate for £175 at public auction. Although he also owned Casino to the south, the fact that this building came to be known as Foster House suggests that this is where he and his family lived. He died in 1927 and the property passed briefly through a number of hands before it was acquired by Clyde Basden in 1944 and joined with Clyde's Cafe next door. The

1854 Darrell map of St. George's reveals that, with the exception of a small addition to the southwest corner built between 1854 and 1876, the building had a footprint identical to its present layout. The stone porch and projecting stairs are 20th century additions which obscure the original Georgian façade.

The fine house known as Hillcrest was built on two early land grants. On the northern half stood the 17th century home of widow Alice Finney. To the south Daniel Jones erected a stone residence soon after it was granted in 1699. After Finney's daughter married Jones, the two properties were joined to form one of the largest lots in the town. Ownership remains unclear after the Jones family died out in the 1750s, but a house was standing on the lot when Mary Leacraft and Richard Minors sold the property to Richard Prudden in 1789. The deed to a neighbouring property reveals that Prudden was living there three years earlier as a tenant.

Originally from Southampton, Prudden was a highly successful merchant who channelled his profits into

purchasing many of the lots surrounding Hillcrest. The symmetrical layout of this U-shaped building suggests that it was probably built shortly before Prudden acquired the house, although the quoins on the front of the house and the triple keystones over the windows, decorative elements dating to the late 1790s, raise the possibility that the merchant levelled an earlier structure and built afresh about 1800.

After his death in 1814, his extensive landholdings were willed mostly to his two granddaughters,

The U-shaped roof and chimneys at Hillcrest are the main indication of the gracious c. 1780 house beneath. The crisp detailing on the chimneys places them in the 19th century and the chimney pots betray the influence of the British military presence which is so common in little details all through the town.

The Old Armoury at the west end of Water Street has much of the impressive late Georgian effect so brilliantly achieved at Clermont in Paget. An incongruous balcony with attendant door spoils the regularity of the fenestration, and the street level windows have been altered to commercial store windows. But none of this can detract from the basic good proportions and elegance of the building.

Ruth and Eliza. Hillcrest went to Eliza, who married William Higinbothom, a merchant from Baltimore, Maryland, and the first Commercial Agent for the United States. Their daughter Elizabeth married William Tudor Tucker in 1832, and Tucker assumed the post of Commercial Agent after his father-in-law died later that year. Thus, in the 1840s and 1850s, Hillcrest functioned as a place where Americans abroad could turn for aid.

Following an assassination attempt during the dockworkers' strike in 1863, William Tudor Tucker emigrated to Nebraska and the house was rented. In 1873 the Higinbothom heirs sold Hillcrest to Warwick merchant Samuel Chapman, who continued to let it to tenants. In 1900 it was purchased by Scotsman Andrew Greig, whose wife Anna was William Tudor Tucker's daughter. Greig had come to Bermuda during the height of the American Civil War when he courted and wed Anna Tucker, but the couple departed when trade collapsed follow-

ing the fall of the Confederacy. The Greigs returned in 1879, when Andrew took a less glamourous but more secure position as postal clerk.

The Clifford family purchased the property in 1912 and sold it to John Wright in 1916. He replaced the house's original wooden verandah in 1920 with the present concrete one. The current owner, Ellen Trew Robinson, converted Hillcrest into a guest house in 1961. Today, Hillcrest offers visitors the rare opportunity to stay in an 18th century home in the heart of Bermuda's oldest settlement.

The commanding three storey building at the foot of Blacksmith's Hill known as **The Old Armoury** was built between 1794 and 1796 by shipwright Adam Brown. The land had been granted to Lieutenant John Foot in 1751, but neither he nor his son William had improved the lot when it was sold to Brown in 1794. The 60-foot long mansion took at least three years to build, as reflected in

Brown's parish assessments. These went from £655 in 1794 to £885 the following year, increasing to £1,355 in 1796. The building was sufficiently completed in September 1796 for John DuMont to open a dancing school in "Mr. Brown's Long Room", presumably on the top floor. The hip roof building has two internal chimneys, one at each end, although the one on the west end is set on a flat platform and may be a later replacement. Brown decorated this large structure with ornamental quoins on the corners (but on the front only) and triple keystones over the symmetrically placed windows. When assessed in 1800, the building was worth £1,600, making it one of the most valuable residences in St. George's.

Adam Brown's activities and properties were not confined to the Town. He owned a shipyard near Secretary's Point to the west, as well as land in St. David's. The fact that Brown was regularly licensed to retail rum strongly suggests that he was running a tavern on one of the floors of his house. He gave the western portion of his lot to his brother Samuel, who erected a blacksmith's shop on the corner where Water Street and Duke of York Street join, and thus Samuel Brown was the blacksmith for whom Blacksmith's Hill was named.

When Brown made his will in 1828, he gave his two sons lifetime use of The Armoury, and the use of part of Armoury Cottage to the north to his

The Armoury Cottage dates from the turn of the 18th and 19th centuries. The four symmetrically balanced windows are more than would have been included at an earlier date. Two have now unfortunately been replaced with a shop window. They have triple keystone ornamentation.

The charming Harbour View of the early 19th century is in considerable disrepair. This does not detract from its simple elegance of proportion, enhanced by the corner quoins and austere inset chimney. Unfortunately all the blinds and most windows will have to be replaced rather than restored.

Water from the street regularly flowed into the buried rooms when it rained. Its owner at the time, Reverend Richard Tucker, complained to the St. George's Improvement Committee responsible for the roadwork that this was "anything but an improvement".

Harbour View on Aunt Peggy's Lane was built between 1801 and 1808 by Samuel Adams Higgs on land given to him by his aunt Mary Minors. Construction probably commenced soon after his marriage to Elizabeth Rankin in 1804. Higgs' original two storey house was rectangular, running parallel with Aunt Peggy's Lane, with an internal chimney on the southern end breaking the lines of his hip roof. On the two corners of the house facing the road, Higgs applied decorative quoins and added keystones over the windows. It was a respectable home for a merchant with a family of five, a modest size house with simple decorations in the Georgian style worth £500 in the 1820s. It was also home to Higgs' seven slaves, who lived under the same roof. Higgs died in 1830 while visiting the United States.

His widow Elizabeth lived in Harbour View until her death, adding the garden lot to the north in 1838, purchased from the estate of Richard Prudden. In 1870 blacksmith Samuel Rankin Higgs purchased the property from his siblings and added the eastern wing to the north end of the house within six years. The house stayed in the Higgs family until 1901, when it was transferred to Ellen Inglis. Between 1941 and 1957, the house was restored to the Higgs family when it was purchased by Howard Roy Higgs. Its current owner, Delaey Robinson, acquired the property in 1982.

Until recently the approach to St. George's from Mullet Bay provided a preview of the town's Georgian splendour in **Wellington**, a classic two storey hip roofed house on the southern side of the road. A large and visually disruptive church was built at the street's edge and now blocks the view of the house.

The Secretary's Land on which Wellington stands was sold to merchant William Pearson Fleming in

daughter. Upon their deaths, Brown's executors were to sell all his properties and split the proceeds among his surviving children. This occurred in 1852, when Brown's heirs sold the property to Reverend Richard T. Tucker, who acquired the blacksmith's shop to the west three years later.

In 1854 The Armoury was an hotel, operated by a Mrs. Tucker, probably Reverend Tucker's wife. Twenty years later Tucker had moved to London and sold the property to Warwick merchant Samuel Chapman. Chapman died in 1883 and some years later his heirs sold to Lewis Pugh and S.S. Spurling, who in turn conveyed it to the Bermuda Volunteer Forces Association in 1922. For the next 51 years, the building was occupied by the Bermuda Volunteer Rifle Corps and acquired the name The Armoury. Drills were held on the top floor, while the middle floor was used for recreation and the ground floor for storing guns, ammunition and uniforms. During World War II, the BVRC entertained

visiting US servicemen there. The building was in a sorry state when the current owner, Robert Trew, acquired it from the Crown in 1973, but thanks to his care, this old St. George's landmark will survive into the 21st century.

Adam Brown built the cottage to the north of his house by cutting into the side of the hill. This building, **Armoury Cottage**, is known today as Top o' the Harbour, and is deceiving in appearance. Viewed from Duke of York Street, it is a modest structure which is more conservative in size than its neighbour to the south, with massive flanking chimneys on each end, one of which, sadly, has a window cut through its back. The triple keystones over the windows match those of The Armoury. There are two floors below the level of Duke of York Street, however, one of which used to open onto a much lower Duke of York Street. In 1865 the street was raised several feet, burying three doors, several windows and the garden wall of this building.

Wellington was once an austere but elegant suburban St. George's residence of very late Georgian proportions. These fine proportions have been almost obscured by a harsh renovation (c. 1980) which included the removal of its blinds, and the dark painting of the architraves.

November 1812, the first of those lots to be purchased. The following year Fleming built the house as it stands today along with a number of outbuildings and workshops. Fleming, who had emigrated to Bermuda from Montreal in 1810, married Georgiana Forbes Hinson in 1815, the daughter of St. George's merchant George Hinson. The following year, however, the young couple announced their intention to leave Bermuda and unsuccessfully offered to sell their "two-storey stone house, finished in the modern style, with cellars beneath, a large tank, kitchen, stable, and a wooden building near the water". In 1821 they once again advertised the house, now called Wellington after the Duke who thwarted Napoleon at Waterloo.

Although this second attempt to sell the house, then worth £1,000, also failed, the couple moved to New York anyway, where William died in 1824.

The house went to Fleming's executor, William Tucker, who rented it out for much of the 19th century. In 1848, for instance, Tucker offered to lease the cottage, garden, stables and carriage house at Wellington, lately occupied by the mail contractor. The

main house was presumably occupied by another tenant. Tucker himself lived in his house on Rose Hill. Wellington was acquired by Dr. Frederick A.S. Hunter in the 1870s after William Tucker's death and held by his heirs until 1922.

Today, it is part of the First Baptist Church complex, the church inconveniently situated near the fine old building.

The Georgian tradition in St. George's culminated in **Whitehall**, arguably the most imposing of all private residences in the town. (See photograph on page 86) It is set well back from Church Lane, separated by a broad expanse of lawn. The house was built by John Van Norden in 1815. He merged four early 18th century lots into one large property worthy of the house he envisaged. Originally from Bergen, New Jersey, John Van Norden sided with the Crown during the American Revolution and served as Lieutenant in the 3rd and 4th Battalions of Loyalist Volunteers who fought against George Washington's Continental Army from 1778 to 1782. After the war, he settled in Nova Scotia,

where he acquired considerable property in Windsor and became Master of English at King's College and a member of Freemason's Lodge 13 in that town.

In May 1796 he was posted to Bermuda as Naval Storekeeper and agent for naval prisoners of war. Van Norden was instrumental in chartering the first Masonic Lodge in St. George's and served as the town's Mayor from 1801-18. He was largely responsible for the construction of the Town Hall and Market Wharf (see chapter 2) and named the streets of the town, for the first time, after members of the Royal Family.

Van Norden, a civil engineer and the colony's Surveyor General, personally designed Whitehall and directly supervised its construction. He named the building after Whitehall in London, the administrative centre for the British Government. It is a model of Georgian symmetry, with its hip roof and perfectly balanced windows. Its corners are decorated with quoins, as are the gateposts on Duke of Clarence Street. The interior floor plan was likewise symmetrical, dominated by a grand staircase. It was enormous in

Eaves in St. George's

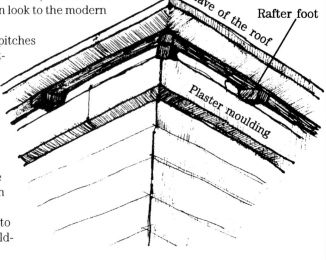

Until almost the end of the 18th century there were only two kinds of eaves anywhere in Bermuda. The common use was to have a rafter foot nailed or pegged to the end of the rafters to make it easier to hold the first tier of roof slate. This rafter foot gave a slight bell shape to the roof. Less common, and impractical with very steeply pitched roofs, was to omit the rafter feet altogether, giving the roof a slightly foreign look to the modern eye.

By the end of the 18th century gentler roof pitches made rafter feet less useful. The importation of outside decorative treatments and Portland cement with which to achieve them, led to the introduction of cornice mouldings. These almost always enclosed the eaves completely, but not in St. George's.

Here an unusual treatment became fashionable, perhaps because one of its earliest uses was at Durnford: the rafter feet still show above a simple, square cornice moulding. This style became popular throughout St. George's. An elaborate version might be doubled, but never rounded.

Sometimes it seems that the plaster was added to older rafter feet, changing the appearance of a building to conform to changing styles.

Labels on illustration: Eave of the roof — Rafter foot — Plaster moulding

---

size, rivalled only by Andrew Durnford's house on Stile Hill (see chapter 4). The coach house and stables to the north, the two storey buttery (or perhaps a watchtower) in the southeast corner of the property and the two storey house itself all apparently date to the initial building episode. Van Norden's Whitehall was a showpiece which displayed the Mayor's wealth, status and refinement to the community he presided over.

John Van Norden lived in Whitehall for eight years before he died suddenly in September 1823. His widow Magdalen sold a house on the northern part of the lot to Thomas Bascome, a free black carpenter, soon after John's death. She lived in Whitehall until 1838, when she advertised the property for sale in *The Royal Gazette*. She found a buyer in Daniel Seon, and left Bermuda for Nova Scotia to join her only daughter Sarah, the wife of Lieutenant Colonel John Bazalgette of the 49th Regiment.

Seon, a prominent St. George's merchant, lived in Whitehall until 1854, when he sold the property to Reverend Richard T. Tucker, rector of St. Peter's Church. Tucker apparently preferred his other residence, The Armoury, for he sold Whitehall just four

years later to Seth Harvey, the colony's Solicitor General.

The Harvey family was afflicted with tragedy. Seth Harvey and his wife Lucy had each lost a spouse before they married, and most of their children died prematurely. He buried no fewer than eight of his children before he died at Whitehall in 1870. Lucy followed four years later. In 1887 the house was purchased by merchant Thomas Ward Kelly for £1,500. He lived there until his own death in 1895.

Three years later, Whitehall once again became home to a Mayor of St. George's when Robert Harley James bought the property. James was responsible for erecting the fine wooden verandah and the wide entry stairs which grace the front of Whitehall and perhaps the less elegant parapet additions on the north side of the house. The James family fared no better than the Harveys. Robert's wife and five daughters predeceased him, so when he died in 1913, the property went to his son-in-law Ernest Evans and grandson Peter Evans.

In 1956 Frederick C. Outerbridge added Whitehall to his considerable holdings in St. George's. At present the large house is subdivided into a number of apartments

and is in a poor state of repair. Van Norden's grand staircase fell victim to this conversion and is no more.

The Georgian period of St. George's coincided with some of the most momentous events in the colony's history. The rapid expansion of Atlantic trade in the mid 18th century fuelled Bermuda's economy and, despite a decline in the town's commercial importance relative to the main island, there was still enough prosperity to initiate a wave of Georgian building.

The American Revolution disrupted the colony's traditional trading patterns, but offered new avenues towards wealth in the form of privateering. During and after the war Americans who had remained loyal to King George flocked to the town, bringing with them innovations in business, law and architecture.

The influence of British military officers and officials who arrived in the 1790s further reinforced the Georgian style as the most dominant mode of building, and the introduction of cement facilitated a greater degree of ornamentation in the town's Georgian edifices. By 1815 symmetry and decoration had become standard in Bermudian building practices.

CHAPTER SEVEN

St. George's Houses of the 19th and Early 20th Centuries

This c. 1910 photograph of Duke of York Street shows the Tower Building on the left and Arcadia looming over the town. The Police Station had not been built but the Perinchief Building and York House are on the right. (Courtesy Christopher M. Grimes.)

The 19th century was a period of great change for Bermuda. The colony's economy shifted from dispersed maritime trade, throughout the Atlantic and beyond, to agriculture and to service industries supporting the British garrison and Royal Naval Dockyard. This resulted in a narrowing of cultural influences. The architecture of the period reflects first a growing formalism in line and proportion and a later revolt against such formalism in the increasingly ornamental Victorian style, whose excesses are readily seen in the YMCA building (see chapter 3).

The introduction of concrete to Bermudian builders in the late Georgian period allowed them greater freedom of expression on a building's exterior. Pilasters increasingly displaced quoins on the corners of houses, and string courses and moulded cornices emphasised the

horizontal lines of a structure. Sidelights and fanlights around and over doors became increasingly common. Keystones continued to be added over windows and, for the most part, Georgian symmetry in floor plan and window placement prevailed. The smaller number of chimneys on these 19th century buildings tended to be situated where they were needed, rather than where they might balance the structure's layout. The buildings themselves ranged from grand houses erected by merchants who grew rich during the blockade running days of the American Civil War to the humble workmen's cottages constructed by former slaves.

Several became hotels or restaurants in the early 20th century to cater to visitors in the early years of Bermudian tourism.

St. George's 19th century buildings possess a unique style which readily sets them apart from the small ver-

nacular cottages and the regular Georgian houses which preceded them.

Nestled against the wall of the old Government Park on the northern edge of town is **Park Villa**, an impressive residence built in the 1820s. The original T-shaped core of this two storey hip roofed house belonged to sailmaker Thomas Wright who died in 1826. In his will he gave the house to his two daughters, Elizabeth Outerbridge and Susannah McCallan. They sold it in 1837 to Robert William Outerbridge. In describing the merits of the property, an advertisement in *The Royal Gazette* noted that the house had a large parlour, drawing room and two "extensive" chambers at each end of the building, with a brick paved kitchen, storeroom and wine cellar underneath. The two storey, four room adjoining house had also been built by 1837, although the rare and impressive three stack octagonal chim-

The triple chimney of Park Villa is unique in St. George's.

Ocean View Cottage. This tiny house may already have been standing on its Glebe lot when the property was bought by Stephen Benjamin Richardson from the estate of Bustern Bruce, another successful black St. Georgian, in 1847. It is so small and unornamented that it is difficult to date, but was probably built by Bruce between his purchase of the land in 1841 and his death in 1845. The simple chimney is unusually placed on the side of the northern wall and barely rises above the eaves. Richardson, a pilot by trade, was one of the most successful black Bermudians before Emancipation. He was born a slave in 1800, probably belonging to the white Richardson family of Mount Pleasant (see Wright Hall later in this chapter).

He was initially trained as a shipwright, but in his teenage years Richardson turned his attention towards learning the intricate reefs and channels at Bermuda's east end. During the 1820s he earned enough money to purchase his own freedom, and that of his wife Violet in 1831.

Until his death in 1879, Richardson followed the sea for his livelihood. He piloted countless vessels into and out of St. George's Harbour and, especially during the American Civil War, he was well paid for his services. He salvaged a number of wrecks and derelict vessels found on the northern reefs and in the late 1840s he ran a packet boat which shuttled between St. George's and Hamilton with, as he said in his advertisement,

ney at the west end was perhaps added at a later date.

Merchant Robert W. Outerbridge was a member of the Methodist Church and was a trustee for the building of the chapel in 1840. In his 70 years of life, he fathered seven children who lived to maturity and he outlived three wives, a considerable achievement when one considers that he married his third wife at the age of 67. After his death, the house was purchased by John R. Duerden, who served as a Member of Parliament for St. George's. In 1912, the St. George's Grammar School moved there from the Methodist Sunday School (see chapter 3) and occupied the building for a number of

years until a larger building was constructed immediately to the north of Park Villa.

The house has not changed substantially since the 1830s. The wooden verandah which afforded such a wonderful view of the town was replaced with a concrete one early in the 20th century and the long stable and coach house, built in 1854 to the west of the main house, has since been converted into an apartment. The house and grounds are much the same as they were when Robert W. Outerbridge lived there.

In total contrast, on Suffering Lane to the north of Fort George lies

Ocean View Cottage defies easy interpretation. Dating from the mid 19th century, its appearance suggests many restorations. The narrow buttresses were probably added to prevent the walls from spreading under the weight of a sagging roof, but they are so narrow that they would have been inadequate for the job. This would account for the late 19th or even 20th century roof, characterised by the raised moulding at the gable ends.

Melrose is an excellent example of a mid 19th century suburban house. Presently under restoration, the front of the house could not be photographed, but its classic proportion defined by white pilasters can be gleaned from this photograph. Its almost detached kitchen chimney with an extra flue for the bake oven clearly defines its position amongst the outbuildings.

"as much regularity as circumstances will admit".

Three of his sons became pilots and on one fateful afternoon in February 1876, all three set off in a storm to save a brigantine which parted her cable at Murray's Anchorage. The pilot's gig safely reached the vessel and put its captain on board but, while returning to Tobacco Bay, a large wave "hurled [the boat] bottoms up". James Richardson made it ashore after narrowly avoiding being dashed on the rocks, but his brother, George, drowned near land. The third brother, William, was hurled onto a rock just off shore by a large wave and was left there, torn and bruised.

A spectator, Royal Artilleryman George Dew, leapt into the raging sea and saved Richardson with the help of fellow soldiers. It is extraordinary that the Richardson family lost only one member to the sea when so many of them were pilots, a notoriously dangerous profession. After five genera-

tions, the Richardson family still own Ocean View Cottage which is surrounded by the later houses of other Richardsons.

Melrose, on the corner of Wellington Street and Khyber Pass Road, was built between 1848 and 1854 on land originally granted in 1767 by Governor George Bruere to his son William. Sandys Parish merchant Robert Tucker acquired the property early in the 19th century and his heirs subdivided it in 1845 into twelve 50-foot by 150-foot lots. The six northern lots were purchased by the Crown which erected a large new prison on the site the following year. John Davenport obtained four of the six southern lots but neglected to build on them. This land remained vacant until the early 20th century when the Grand Order of Odd Fellows erected a lodge, now known as the Somers Theatre or Somers Opera House.

The two lots on which Melrose

was built remained unsold as late as 1848, when they were auctioned. Although the deed for this sale was not recorded, it is likely that the purchaser was Reverend Richard T. Tucker. In 1854 a map shows that Tucker owned the lot and had built the main hip roof section of Melrose and the small shed roofed kitchen wing to the north.

By 1858 Tucker also owned Whitehall and The Armoury (see chapter 6) and preferred the latter as his residence. He sold Melrose to Agatha Harvey who lived there until she married and moved to Paget in 1863. In her will, written a decade later, she gave all future rents from the house to her goddaughter, Jane Bell, for her lifetime, and the actual property to trustee Reverend Landsdown Guilding. Bell and Guilding conveyed the property to Captain Robert Boggs for £450 and £27 a year to Bell for the rest of her life.

Boggs, a master mariner, was the son of Robert Sr., the governor of St.

Perfectly rectangular, the back of Poinciana House is strictly utilitarian, the chimney located for convenience, not symmetry, and sporting an off-centre military style chimney pot. The shed roofed building in the yard is also located for convenience not show.

George's Prison to the north. He died of heart failure at Melrose in 1890 after working for many years for William E. Meyer's shipping firm. The house was passed down through various Boggs descendants until 1994 when it was sold to current owner Donna Bell. Melrose is now in the process of a sensitive renovation.

Poinciana House, on the corner of Queen Street and Chapel Lane, was built by John Stephen Roberts in 1852 on an 18th century lot originally granted as a garden. The current building replaced a previous house erected by Irish architect Thomas Phelan in the early 1800s. Architecturally it is a transitional building between Georgian houses like Hillcrest and later buildings like Kent Lodge. It has a hip roof, symmetrical windows and floor plan, and one oddly placed chimney. There is heavy moulding on the corners and a string course. The house once had a wooden verandah on the south face but lacks the stocky pilasters and overly decorative keystones of later structures. A fine domed water tank abuts the house to the north.

In 1864 the Poinciana House that Roberts built was purchased by Dr. Frederick A.S. Hunter, who also acquired the neighbouring Old Rectory to augment the grounds of his house. He created the circular drive approaching the front of Poinciana House some time prior to 1875. Two years later, Hunter was living in Wellington (see chapter 6) when his son Joseph died, and Poinciana House was pre-

The Homestead is a good example of the many fine mid 19th century houses to be found in St. George's. The by-product of the infusion of wealth from American Civil War blockade running, they have an inward looking sense to them, typical of town houses of the period and quite different from the more village-like feel of the 18th century buildings in the town. A new sense of personal and family privacy was reflected in the architecture. The interesting verandah, projecting over the edge of the street on elegantly flared posts, elevates the household above the dust and dirt of the street below. The wall protects the garden from view.

sumably rented. During World War I the women of St. George's ran a home for soldiers and sailors in Poinciana House, supported by the rector, Canon Arthur Tucker. In the 1950s the St. George's Cricket Club met there. In 1957 the property passed out of the Hunter family when it was purchased by Pauline Cray.

The **Old Homestead** on the corner of Duke of York and Duke of Kent Streets has one of the best preserved wooden verandahs in Bermuda. This house was built on a lot originally granted as a garden for William Milbourne's now vanished house across the street on the site of the Toddings House. In 1816 there was a wooden house on the property when a lot to the south was granted to John Van Norden, on which the small coffee shop to the south of the main house was built. The present building with its graceful fanlight door, vertical moulding and top hung blinds, was erected by John Swainson in 1863 at the height of the American Civil War, when lodging was at a premium. The six-foot high barred railing in front of the house kept it safe from the many itinerant sailors who crowded the streets of St. George's during that war.

The Swainson family emigrated from Cumberland, England, in the late 1810s and occupied St. David's Lodge across the harbour. In addition to the Old Homestead, Swainson owned a bakery across the street on the corner

In the foreground is the older wing of Lemon Grove, with its steep pitched roof almost the only remaining sign of age. The shallow pitch, moulding and octagonal chimney in the background are 19th century.

sold the house to Ensign John McWillie in 1782 in return for ten guineas and her husband's discharge from the army. The following year McWillie sold the house to the garrison's doctor John Hutchison. From 1783 to 1805, Hutchison lived in the house and there is evidence to suggest that he rebuilt or substantially expanded Knapton's earlier structure. He was probably responsible for the symmetrical Georgian core of Lemon Grove, which has been spoiled by recent modifications.

In 1805 Hutchison sold Lemon Grove to Captain Andrew F. Evans of the Royal Navy for £1,100. Evans was the first naval superintendent and presided over the Royal Naval facilities in St. George's and Ireland Island. Although his duties required the captain to spend much of his time at Ireland Island, he preferred this home in the heart of St. George's to his official residence, an isolated cottage overlooking Ireland Cove, or the hulk *Tourterelle*, from which his broad pennant flew.

When Evans left the British North Atlantic Station, he sold Lemon Grove to Doctor Thomas Burch Tucker who gave the house its name, perhaps for the many lemon trees growing in his extensive garden. Tucker had a family medical practice in the town. The much loved doctor died suddenly at the top of Fort George Hill in May 1846, which he had climbed to see the beam of light from the newly erected Gibbs' Hill Lighthouse in Southampton.

Tucker's heirs sold the house to Postmaster James Thies in 1863. Thies was probably responsible for the present appearance of the main eastern portion of Lemon Grove. The octagonal chimneys and pilasters match that period. Throughout the 19th century, a front entry room, which has since been removed, projected east from the middle of the façade. Thies was part of a veritable postal dynasty. His uncle James Taylor was an earlier St. George's postmaster and his brother Thomas had also held that post before he died in 1860. After nearly two decades of prompt and reliable mail service, a London inspector found a number of discrepancies in Thies' accounts in 1879 which landed the St. George's postmaster in court. The shame of a guilty verdict and his sus-

of Pound Alley and Duke of York Street. This was built on the old 18th century Pound Lot, where stray animals were held until their owners could claim them. The yard surrounding the residence includes a garden to the north, formerly belonging to the Mitchell House, a well, privy and domed tank.

Lemon Grove is a building for all periods and thus defies easy classification. It could fit in any of the three residential chapters, but its 19th

century appearance has placed it here. The property was granted to mariner Moses Knapton in 1703, who had erected a house by July 1705. A portion of this ancient house, with its steeply pitched roof and narrow rooms, survives in the southern wing at the rear of the main building.

In 1745 Knapton's heirs sold the property to Jeremiah Higgs, whose daughter Elizabeth married John Green, one of the newly arrived British garrison soldiers, in 1779. Elizabeth

A fine 19th century door complete with fanlight and plain archivolt adorns the Wainwright house. What may have been glazed lights on either side of the doors, appear to have been subsequently removed for greater privacy.

The Basdens' granddaughter sold it to merchant George Wainwright in 1842. Wainwright enjoyed a modest prosperity in the 1840s and 1850s, but during the American Civil War he and his partner and son-in-law, Robert C. McCallan (see McCallan's Warehouse and Edgewater, chapter 4), made money renting space to the Confederate government to house the goods sent through the Union blockade. In 1865, after the war was over and St. George's returned to some semblance of order, George Wainwright levelled his antiquated house and built the grand, two room wide hip roof house which occupies the site today. While the symmetrical layout of Wainwright's new residence and the keystone decorated windows recall the Georgian style, the pilasters, string courses and the fanlight over the door are firmly mid 19th century features. The gateposts by the street and domed tank to the east probably predate the 1865 house. The front verandah originally had wooden balusters but these have been replaced recently with metal rails.

After his death in 1879, the house was briefly occupied by Wainwright's son Thomas, and then went to his daughter Mary E. McCallan. In 1922 her heirs sold the house to Frederick Robertson, well known for his drug store on Customs House Square, and it is currently owned by his daughter, Rita Rothwell.

Wellesley Lodge at the corner of Duke of York Street and Rose Hill Road is a well preserved example of mid 19th century architecture. The lot was part of a much larger grant extending from the Methodist Church to Khyber Pass Road, given in a blatant case of nepotism by Governor George Bruere to his son, William, in 1767. The property, along with Rose Hill, was acquired by Bruere's brother-in-law, President Henry Tucker, in the 1780s and sold by his widow Frances to John and Frances Lewis in 1810. As late as 1854 there was nothing on the lot, then owned by John Tudor Tucker and extending from the foot of Rose Hill to Duke of York Street.

In the 1860s the lots were subdivided. A house and a stable complex

pension from office prompted Thies to leave Bermuda forever, midway through his seventh term as Mayor of St. George's, to start a new life in Nova Scotia.

Samuel Chapman succeeded him as both Mayor and as owner of Lemon Grove, although he rented the property to others. John Tory Bourne, an entrepreneur of the blockade running period, died there in 1889. US Consul Edmund Willett also rented the house until his death in 1896. Sea captain Fred Virtue purchased Lemon Grove from Chapman's heirs in 1917 and spent his retirement reviving Thomas B. Tucker's earlier garden.

The house was extensively renovated in the 1980s, at which time eyebrows and other apparently older architectural features were grafted onto the building.

Wainwright House next door to Hillcrest (see chapter 6), is built on the site of a residence erected by Robert Burchall between 1699 and 1706. This earlier house was subsequently purchased by George Young in 1783 and was inherited by James and Mary Basden in the early 19th century.

One of a matched pair of buildings at the top of Duke of York Street, Wellesley Lodge was originally built without a verandah. It retains its fenestration, and its verandah (added after 1909) almost intact although the lower railings appear to have been replaced. A regular Georgian formality has survived well into the 19th century and the shutters enclosing either end of the upper verandah, once common, are now rare survivors.

were built to the north, now home to the Fire Station and the Corporation of St. George's workshops, while two nearly identical houses were built about 1865 at 1 and 3 Duke of York Street by John S. Hayward, perhaps with money earned during the boom days when the American Civil War blockade runners filled St. George's Harbour.

The two houses were L-shaped mirror images of each other. Although the second, Crofton, has endured some unfortunate modifications, particularly the enclosure of the ground floor verandah and both have had additions on the north, Wellesley Lodge has survived with fewer alterations. The building is simple in style, lacking the pilastered corners, keystones and string courses found on its contemporaries elsewhere in the town. Indeed, its sole original ornaments are the fanlights above the front door on each floor.

The verandah of Wellesley Lodge's twin at No 3 Duke of York Street has been altered, probably twice. The original wooden supports were replaced with concrete and then the verandah was filled in completely with particularly ugly sliding glass and masonry. Unsympathetic alterations like this are particularly harmful to a town which depends for its livelihood as much on its historic architecture as anything.

Rebecca Bruce purchased the house in 1887 from William H. Wilkinson, but had been running a boarding house or hotel there since at least 1876. Bruce apparently chris-

tened the house Wellesley Lodge, most likely named for the British family which gave the world the Duke of Wellington. To better provide for her lodgers, she added a wing on the northern side of the house, which gave it a rectangular footprint. About 1910, she also added the wooden verandah which graces the front of the building today, noteworthy for its decoratively-fretted Victorian balustrades. Rebecca Bruce died in the late 1910s and bequeathed the property to her nephew Edward B. Honeyborne, who converted it into a home.

Although not particularly old, the **Higgs Cottages** at 10 Old Maids Lane are unique in being a pair of semi-detached cottages. The lot was granted to Thomas Burt, who erected a house in 1702, but that building was gone by the time Hillcrest owner Richard Prudden bought the lot as an extension of his gardens across the

There are few "semi-detached" houses in Bermuda. Higgs Cottages are apparently unaltered examples from the 1870s. The building is simple, with a low roof and the plainest of pliasters continued into a cornice moulding under the eaves. Each half is symmetrical in itself and matches its partner exactly.

street to the north. Prudden's heirs sold it to Richard Minors Higgs in 1828, who left it fallow. In 1865 John Darrell Higgs bought the lot for £71 from his uncle Richard's estate. Two years later, he built the two-family dwelling as it stands today, a perfectly symmetrical building whose northern and southern halves mirror each other, right down to matching chimneys and privies in the back.

Higgs presumably rented the two sides of the building to tenants. In 1902 Higgs' heirs sold it to Postmaster Van Osdell Brown, who sold it to blacksmith John H. Corbin. Corbin ran a shop on Musson's Wharf near where his Dowling descendants' marine petrol station stands today.

Corbin gave the house to his daughter Edith Dowling in 1936 and she undertook a major renovation. While opening a blocked chimney, workmen found a small bag of gold

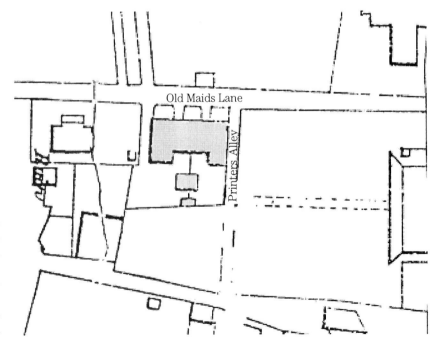

An 1876 plan shows the Higgs Cottages and their garden walls exactly as they are today. (Survey of the Island of St. George. Hurst and Watkins 1876. Bermuda Archives, Hamilton, Bermuda.)

The c. 1870 Toddings House is unusual in not facing Duke of Kent Street. It is a typical, rather austere, pilastered rectangular building with a string course and rather severe porch with crisp square cornice moulding, which is modestly repeated under the rafter feet in the characteristic St. George's style. The entrance is reached through a yard opening onto the street through solid gateposts. The chimney is hexagonal.

coins hidden by an unknown earlier occupant, and the money more than paid for the building costs. The house is now the residence of one of Edith Dowling's daughters.

The **Toddings House** on the corner of Duke of Kent Street and Featherbed Alley was formerly known as the Snow Plant Inn. Built in 1868 by Thomas Toddings, this "elegantly fitted up" house boasted two dining rooms, one on each floor, two large bedrooms and a parlour, with fire grates in each room for internal heating. In the early 20th century it was a popular tea room and restaurant. In the 1910s, visitors could get room and board for $4 a day.

An ornate verandah with cast iron railings projected out over Duke of Kent Street until at least the 1960s but it has since been removed.

Most of the decorations on this building are typical of the mid 19th century, wide string courses, vertical moulding and enclosed eaves, but the two hexagonal chimneys projecting from the hip roof are unusual and worthy of note.

The present building on this corner replaced an older house which belonged to Daniel Johnson at the beginning of the 18th century. He gave it to William Milbourne as a dowry when his daughter married Milbourne in 1709. The Milbourne family passed it to the Judkin family in the 1750s, who sold it to sailmaker Thomas Wright in 1784. By 1800 Wright owned virtually the entire block. A storehouse and sail loft to the south of his house have been incorporated into today's Somers Market.

After his death in 1814, the house was occupied by his daughter-in-law, Christian Wright, who sold it to Bustern Bruce, a black carpenter, in 1841. Bruce died in 1845 and two years later his widow sold the property to Nicholas C. McCallan. By this time the house was virtually a ruin. It was worth only £200 when McCallan sold it to Thomas Toddings in 1865.

Toddings erected a fine new house and bought up several adjoining properties, going heavily into debt to do so. He mortgaged the house to baker John R. Swainson, who owned the Old Homestead across the street. By 1884 Toddings was more than £900 in debt so Swainson was forced to foreclose.

The Swainson family later rented it to John Gillberg, the proprietor of the Snow Plant Inn. In 1963 Frederick C. Outerbridge purchased it and converted the building into apartments.

Whitehall Cottage, immediately to the north of Van Norden's Whitehall on Duke of Clarence Street, was built in 1875. The history of the lot goes back to 1709 when it was granted to Rebecca Jenour, a widow who lived in a house which was demolished to make way for Whitehall. Jenour married Reverend Andrew Auchinleck and had a daughter, Rebecca, who married a young Scot named Robert Dinwiddie. After

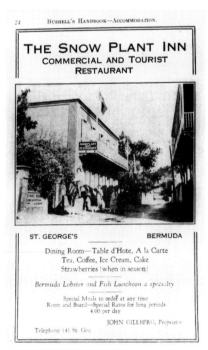

On the left is the Toddings House when it housed the Snow Plant Inn. The wrought iron cantilevered balcony has since been removed, but the wooden one on The Homestead across Duke of Kent Street survives. (Bushell's Handbook 1930.)

Whitehall Cottage dates from the late 19th century and is distinguished by pilasters with simple capitals, plain eave mouldings, a fanlight adorned front door and short keystones. The lateral steps adapt to the proximity of the street. The louvred basement window is an all too common modern blemish.

Chapman, perhaps on speculation, between 1879 and 1882, and sold to Englishman John Alderman. In 1920 John Kirby Outerbridge purchased Kent Lodge from the late Alderman's daughter. His granddaughter occupies the house today.

Tower House on Duke of York Street was built in 1883 on the site of gunsmith George Tourgouse's early 18th century homestead. In the 1820s James Forbes, a free black pilot, lived in a house set right against an earlier, narrower Duke of York Street. Forbes had an impressive career. Born in 1770, he had earned his freedom and purchased his house by 1819. In 1825 he survived three weeks on the open ocean after his pilot boat was blown out to sea in a gale. Even before Emancipation, Forbes was named Warden of the King's Pilots, a post that recognised his superlative knowledge of the island's reefs and channels. He died in July 1842 at the age of 72 after long and distinguished service to the colony.

The house was bought by Catherine Tucker, the widow of Benjamin Tucker, who lived there until it was demolished in the 1870s to widen Duke of York Street.

Tower House was built by mer-

serving as Collector and councillor in Bermuda, Dinwiddie was promoted to Customs Surveyor of all of Britain's southern and West Indian colonies, a post which required him to leave Bermuda. The couple moved to Virginia and he eventually became Governor of that colony from 1751 to 1758.

Two years later, the Dinwiddies were living in London when they gave the lot to their Godsons Christopher and Thomas Smith. John Van Norden purchased the lot from them and it was regranted in 1815 as part of the Whitehall lot. Within a year of his death, Van Norden's son-in-law sold it to Thomas Bascome, a free black carpenter who lived in the two storey house at 8 Duke of Clarence Street to the north. Bascome died in 1854 and his widow followed him to the grave a decade later. The property was divided among his heirs in 1867. John C. Bascome subdivided his share in 1875 and, a year later, a military map shows

that the present Whitehall Cottage had been built on the lot. The building is typical of the period and is remarkably well preserved, with pilasters on the corners, a fanlight over the front door, keystones over the windows and attractive pedestal gateposts.

Built about 1881, **Kent Lodge** is a relative newcomer to St. George's. Its stocky pilasters, heavy string course and large symmetrical windows are typical of late 19th century construction techniques. The house has decorative keystones above its windows and top hung blinds on the upper floor. Elsewhere on the property is a two-horse stable, a tank and privy. The wall surrounding Kent Lodge may predate the building and date from the time the lot was a garden for the now ruined Longford (see chapter 5) across the street. The house was built by Warwick merchant Samuel

Kent Lodge demonstrates the fundamental simplicity of mid-Victorian houses built in St. George's. Austere pilasters, string course, cornice moulding and keystones over the windows emphasise the severity of the design.

chant Frederick Jones a year after he purchased the property in 1882. It is thought that the decorative, enclosed wooden verandah and the stocky two storey tower which make the house so striking were added in 1888. Early 20th century photographs of the building show signs advertising seed and other wares. The house behind this eye-catching façade is an ordinary hip roofed building with two asymmetrically placed internal chimneys.

Tucked between the northern side of Wellington Slip Road and and what was once the easternmost cove of Mullet Bay, now filled in and used as a park, is **Francis Cottage**. Built on land originally allotted to the Colonial Secretary, this property was granted in 1815 to William A. Morse but it reverted to Secretary Robert Kennedy in 1845 after Morse's heirs stopped paying their quitrent. This lot and many others remained untenanted for the next 40 years. In 1884 the land was subdivided into smaller lots. Although this subdivision initiated an explosion of house building to the north of Mullet Bay Road, few buyers could be found for the lots at Lower Wellington. The cottage was built between 1884 and 1898 by an unknown tenant of the Kennedy family. In 1913 Richard Probyn Francis purchased the house and land, then worth £200.

The building is typical of the late 19th century, with pilasters, enclosed eaves, heavily moulded cornices, and keystones over the windows as deco-

Francis Cottage, a late 19th century cottage on Wellington Slip Road, has retained its original form except for an added basement apartment. It is a good example of a workman's cottage of the era and may have housed someone employed by the St. George's Marine Slip Co.

Tower House, an unusual late 19th century residential and commercial building on Duke of York Street, has this bold tower at its corner. The tower was added to the plain pilastered rectangular building behind it as was the verandah.

The James Burch House on Shinbone Alley was rebuilt in 1903 after its predecessor had decayed beyond repair. It has a simple if dominant cornice moulding, pilasters, and string course. The keystone decoration over the windows is carried right up to the moulding above. Little room was left for the verandah, which was, however, essential to reach the living quarters on the upper floor.

ration. The wood panelled front door is almost certainly original, as is the small privy downhill to the west. It is an outstanding, virtually unaltered example of a modest workingman's cottage.

The **James Burch House**, on the garden side of Shinbone Alley, is noteworthy for its fine, narrow ve-

randah. An earlier house worth £150 was standing on the site in 1827, built by William A. Astwood, a free black man. He subsequently died and his widow Phoebe occupied the house for another 40 years. Substantial work was done to the building in 1865 when it was either rebuilt or extensively modified. Astwood's house was in a dilapidated condition by 1898, when it was

demolished to widen Shinbone Alley.

In 1903 James Burch erected the present building and incorporated the ornamental motifs and style of the mid 19th century, keystones, pilasters and enclosed eaves, into the design. Burch also built the double wooden verandah, unusual for its exterior staircase which provided a separate outside entrance to the top floor. This

Echo Heights stands bleakly on its treeless hill, Gothic novel style, and dominates the skyline from Mullet Bay. In the severest of late Victorian styles, the house was built in about 1904. It appears to be completely unaltered, retaining its unpainted plaster finish with striation to imitate stone construction, original four-over-four fenestration, and heavy cornice and gable mouldings. The chimneys have British chimney pots.

suggests that the building was either rented to two separate tenants or, perhaps, that the Burch family household was multi-generational or extended, and that the exterior staircase and separate entrance afforded relatives living above some degree of privacy.

Echo Heights, perched high above Mullet Bay, is a windswept house built in 1904 by Alexander F.B. Spurling. Unusual for its unpainted plaster walls, the house has two three-sided bays which look out over Ferry Road and Mullet Bay. When built, Echo Heights was surrounded by 20 acres of land.

In 1930 the family divided the land after Alexander Spurling's death, and today there are five houses occupied by his descendants on the original property.

To the west of Echo Heights lies Wright Hall in the sprawling complex of the **Bermuda Biological Station for Research**. This 14-acre tract was granted in 1758 to Samuel Trott and John Slater, who failed to develop the land. In 1794 the property was regranted to Major Thomas Hare of the Royal Artillery, who, within the next two years, erected a residence which he christened Mount Pleasant. The cluster of houses near the eastern shore of Richardson's Bay is probably Hare's homestead. After he died in 1796, the house was occupied by his mistress but it reverted to the Crown

when she failed to pay the quitrent.

In 1800 it was purchased by Robert Richardson, whose family and descendants occupied Mount Pleasant for the next 80 years. In the 1880s the house and land went to Henry Hilgrove

Wright Hall owes little to Bermuda's architectural tradition but follows its contemporaries in the United States. Its austerity was relieved by a substantial double verandah.

Hollis, a Bailey's Bay ship's captain who ran the blockade into Texas during the American Civil War.

In 1911 Hollis' son, Dr. Austin Hollis, built Wright Hall, the large building easily seen from Ferry Reach, as a sanitorium where patients might recuperate from lingering illnesses or stress. New York architect Frederick Lansing designed the building. Unfortunately for Hollis, few invalids used his facility. In 1927 it was transformed into the Shore Hills Golf and Country

Club, "The Garden Spot of Bermuda", with a nine-hole golf course and tennis courts on the property. The venture proved short-lived. Dr. Hollis' widow sold the resort in 1931 to the trustees of the Bermuda Biological Station, who had been looking for a suitable base. Using a generous gift from the Rockefeller Foundation, the Biological Station built a number of new facilities and converted many of the older buildings on the site into living quarters. Since the 1930s the Bio Station has used the wharf, laboratories and libraries at Mount Pleasant to further scientific understanding of Bermuda and the Atlantic.

In 1933 millionaire William Vincent Astor admired the placid waters of Ferry Reach and decided to build a "cottage" there to serve as a refuge from the bustle of New York City.

Astor purchased land from the old Underwood estate, owned by the Packwood family since 1846, when exslave Robert Packwood purchased the

A 1930 advertisement for Shore Hills Hotel taken from Bushell's Handbook.

The Astor House was vernacular revival on a large scale. The attempt was generally extraordinarily successful, but occasional details, such as the purely decorative eyebrow, are both overweight and unnecessary.

to fetch the newspaper.

During World War II, Astor served in the US Navy, and when he returned to Bermuda in 1946, he found that his wonderful view of Ferry Reach was marred by the airfield which the US Government had created out of Longbird Island. He feigned indifference but sold the house in 1952.

Today, the grand house has been divided into 13 apartments. The electric locomotive lies neglected and rusting and the tracks which led to the Bermuda Railway line are being reclaimed by nature. This spur, incidentally, is the only railway track remaining in Bermuda since the main line was dismantled and sold to British Guiana in 1948. The sprawling "cottage" remains an important landmark and is usually the first house in St. George's Parish seen when approaching the island on Kindley Field Road.

By the early 20th century, Bermudian architecture had come full circle. The rise of tourism focused many St. Georgians on the town's most valuable asset for attracting visitors, its deep and rich history. Houses like Astor's demonstrate how the elite visitors who flocked to Ber-

65-acre tract at auction for £604. The house that Astor built was large by Bermudian standards, a blend of traditional Bermudian vernacular elements which created a residence much older in appearance. He named it **Ferry Reach**, though most Bermudians call it the Astor Estate after the man who built it, or the Bierman Estate after the present owners. Architect N.W. Hutchings and consultant builder Edward Winiger undoubtedly studied many old Bermuda buildings before committing their design to paper. Astor's long house stretches along Ferry Reach to give every room a view of the water. The house was lavishly furnished with antiques from the Astor family collection. The lower level had a movie theatre with a French leather screen and large aquarium tanks where specimens Astor collected in the Galapagos Islands while yachting were displayed.

Outside, there was a croquet lawn and swimming pool for the diversion of Astor's guests. When com-

pleted, the house was worth £27,000, an astounding sum for the period. Astor purchased ten acres to the north in 1939 and built a private railway spur which connected his house with the Bermuda Railway track. He sent a servant to the North Shore each morning in his private electric locomotive

Decorative elements on the Astor House have been exaggerated in an attempt to balance the scale. Here the Flemish gables are over elaborated, their feel almost oriental, and the chimney stepped too quickly for the width at the base.

A domed tank is the clever inspiration for this tool shed. It sustains a cottage that might have been built two centuries earlier.

muda sought out the old and the unique in Bermuda's past, as part of their escape from the formal and modern world they had left in America. The once spurned and hopelessly old fashioned early 18th century vernacular cottages now came under the close scrutiny of architects rebelling against modernity. The vernacular revival launched in houses like Ferry Reach found more expression in the Tucker's Town buildings of the 1940s and 1950s.

Chimneys as a Dating Tool

The chimney is one of the best ways of determining the age of a Bermudian building, and in St. George's there is a particularly wonderful selection to view.

The oldest chimneys are characterised by separation from the gable roofs they adjoin. This is believed to be because the roofs were originally thatched or of wooden shingles. The thatch would have tended to protrude beyond the house wall, and because of the danger of fire the chimney had to be further out. A good example is the one at the eastern end of the Old Rectory.

Most typical of the 18th century are the huge chimneys at the gable end of so many houses. St. George's abounds with them, and throughout Bermuda they stand out. Sometimes the only remaining sign of age in a building is a massive chimney. Their shape in section is what characterises them most clearly - they are much longer than they are wide. The blocks of stone used must have been thin, but they are of enormous strength, as proved by their durability. All chimneys of this period had stepped shoulders. The earliest ones had a simple band of necking at the very top.

Such chimneys always had two flues, normally one serving a fireplace in each storey. Usually the space between the flues was filled in, though sometimes a faint indentation shows between the two. But at Bridge House a gap has actually been left between the two flues, even though there is a common top.

As time progressed the necking at the top of the chimney tended to get more elaborate. First there were two rings of necking, one at the very top, the lower one a few inches below. Chimneys built later might have had several rows of necking, or necking rows further apart, or even dentil moulding or other decorative details at the top.

During this period single flued chimneys were also built. These followed the general pattern of their larger contemporaries but are far less characteristic. As time progressed, and St. George's developed as a town providing services first for administrators and seafarers, then for the British military forces, many small chimneys were built all over the town. These are mostly short, with many different styles of top. Some have a British military style clay chimney pot inserted in the top of a traditional Bermuda chimney.

They have all different styles of shoulder. Sometimes they are clustered two or three together on a building. Along the northern part of the Taylor House is a wonderful collection of these little chimneys. Nearby Stewart Hall has no fewer than seven chimneys.

Latest of all came the hexagonal and octagonal chimneys of the late 19th century.

Garrison Town

A rare photograph of Ordnance Island taken about 1868 shows in the background the Esten and Dickinson Houses on King's Square and some of the buildings of Water Street west. (Green Album: Bermuda Archives Collection, Hamilton, Bermuda.)

The British military has been absent from St. George's for many years, but buildings scattered around the town and parish evoke nearly two centuries of military presence. The colony's founders were sailors and many of the early settlers were soldiers, veterans of wars in Ireland and the Low Countries. They established England's second foothold in the New World on an island which, though uninhabited, had been claimed by the Spanish Crown for a century. The first Bermudians fully expected an enemy attack and fortified their home accordingly. Throughout the 17th century, every able-bodied man between the ages of 16 and 60 was a militiaman, regularly drilled to fight and ready to repel Spanish, Dutch or pirate invaders.

The change to maritime pursuits after the Company period took many of the colony's male population from the island for extended periods, which weakened Bermuda's defences. To remedy this shortcoming, in 1701 the Crown dispatched His Majesty's Independent Company, a troop of 50 soldiers, as the first permanent British garrison. They arrived with Governor Benjamin Bennett, himself an old soldier who had commanded a company in Ireland.

As a group they left much to be desired. One early commander was a thief and counterfeiter, and only the pleas of his wife saved him from the gallows. They lived in barracks dispersed around the town, usually private dwellings or storehouses rented by the government. The company was transferred to the Bahamas in 1727, but returned to Bermuda after fear of a slave uprising in 1730 prompted London merchants trading with Bermuda to petition the Crown.

Soldiers in the Independent Company were rarely replaced, prompting one governor to assert that their "number is pretty well, but not ten of them fitt for anything, a parcel of poor old sickly wretches...as for their arms, there is not one of them they dare venture to fire". On the eve of the disbanding of the Somers Island Company in 1672, another governor declared, "they seem to be more fit for an hospital than to defend the country".

The island's forts often matched the unfit state of the garrison. They were invariably out of repair and often lacked operational cannon, tools and gunpowder.

All this changed with the American Revolution. Bermuda assumed immense strategic value in relation to the rebellious colonies, and was used by the Royal Navy and loyalist privateers throughout the war. Several detachments of British troops were posted to the colony to repel any attempted American invasion.

After the war, Bermuda became the bridge between Britain's Canadian and West Indian possessions, a vital stepping stone in the Atlantic.

Britain desperately needed to keep Bermuda out of enemy hands for the island lay astride the main shipping lane between the Caribbean and Europe. A hostile power in Bermuda would cut off Great Britain's trade with its valuable West Indies colonies.

Captain Andrew Durnford of the Royal Engineers reviewed the colony's inadequate defences during a visit in 1783 and pleaded with the Crown to make Bermuda the "Gibraltar of the West". His advice was taken. He and Lieutenant Thomas Hurd of the Royal Navy accompanied Governor Henry Hamilton to Bermuda in 1788 and set to work fortifying the island and mapping its channels and reefs. Their efforts led to the establishment of a Royal Naval base about 1808 in the colony, culminating in the construction of the massive Dockyard on Ireland Island.

Throughout the 19th century dozens of regiments were posted to Bermuda to man the forts which guarded the approach to the Dockyard. The majority of these forts were in St. George's.

Starting with the arrival of the 47th Regiment in 1797 and ending in 1953, there was an unbroken chain of British Army units guarding Bermuda from the Empire's enemies.

The early fortifications of St. George's have been described in chapter 2. The King's Castle and a few others continued to be used, strengthened and updated by Andrew Durnford and his successors, but the British military constructed a new series of fortifications to match the changing needs of warfare. Bermuda's 19th century forts were at the cutting edge of military architecture, built by gifted officers of the Royal Engineers who cleverly adapted the island's building materials and landscape to their tactical needs.

St. George's, the gateway to the colony, was guarded by a string of new forts designed to reinforce and cover each other. The first line of defence was **Upper Paget Fort** and its successor, **Fort Cunningham**, built on Paget Island on the hill above old Paget Fort. Its long range guns, placed on higher ground, covered both the entrance to St. George's Harbour and the channel leading to Murray's Anchorage and the Dockyard, making obsolete Fort Popple, Smith's Fort, the Town Cut Battery and Paget Fort. The moat and lower masonry of Fort Cunningham were completed in 1823 and named for Captain Thomas Cunningham, RE. In the 1870s, the upper part of Fort Cunningham was removed to build a state-of-the-art iron skin fort, with four layers of five-inch-thick iron plate protecting two 38-ton rifled muzzle loaded cannon and a number of slightly smaller guns. A 1991 archaeological excavation discovered these massive guns and also found traces of camouflage on the fort's exterior walls, the earliest documented use discovered to date.

After Fort Cunningham, **Fort Victoria** and **Fort Albert** were positioned to bring their guns to bear on vessels heading for the Dockyard.

These forts, carved into Retreat Hill, commanded the channel along the eastern coast of St. George's Island.

Fort Victoria is the most complex fortification outside the Dockyard, with an inner and outer moat and two detached ravelins. It was completed by 1842 and armed with eighteen 32-pound cannon. The outer moats and ravelins are well preserved, but the inner keep was drastically altered when the adjoining hotel was built in the late 1960s.

Fort Albert to the east is a pentagonal moated redoubt, completed shortly after 1842, with a small interior keep. Although its moat is heavily overgrown and later batteries have been added, the fort is in good condition. The American spy Albert Fitz wrote in 1842 that these were "works of the first class, and [of] great strength".

Fort St. Catherine, on the northern tip of St. George's Island, was perfectly situated to dispatch any enemy which weathered the fire of the first three forts. Just offshore, the Narrows Channel turns abruptly, forcing vessels to slow down to manoeuvre or risk running onto the reefs. The gunners at Fort St. Catherine could fire point-blank at their foe.

The present fort, begun in the 1830s, replaced a pair of batteries erected by Andrew Durnford in 1793. It had a shot furnace to heat cannon balls which would set wooden warships aflame. The keep and dry moat are much as they were when built in the 1830s, but later works overlay the original gun platform. Today, the fort

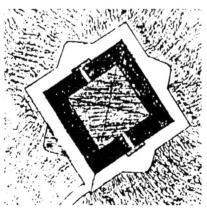

Fort George

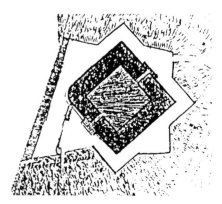

Fort William (Western Redoubt)

Fort Victoria

Details from a plan of St. George's and its environs made by Surveyor General N.J. Darrell in 1854. (Public Records Office, CO/37, London, England.)

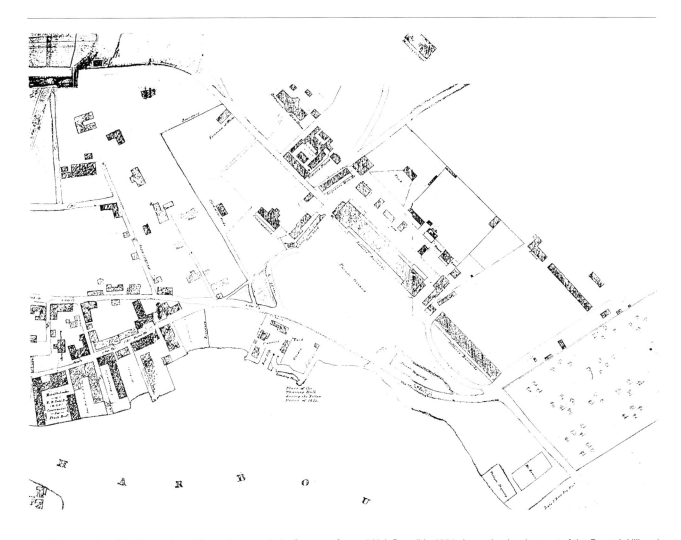

Detail from a plan of St. George's and its environs made by Surveyor General N.J. Darrell in 1854 shows the development of the Barrack Hill and Top Square areas. (Public Records Office, CO/37, London, England.)

houses a museum devoted to the history of Bermuda's fortifications.

Fort George and **Fort William** were built to guard the "back door" into St. George's from the Ferry and North Shore. Fort George replaced an earlier redoubt built by Andrew Durnford on the site of The Mount, Governor Moore's 1613 tower. Completed in the mid 1840s, this redoubt was built in the shape of an eight pointed star surrounded by an inner keep reached by drawbridges spanning a dry moat. Throughout the 19th century, the signal station at this fort relayed messages to Hamilton, Gibbs Hill and Dockyard and was a vital link in the military communication network. Today the Bermuda Harbour Radio station broadcasts from the roof of the keep. The "eye of the island" first envisioned by Richard Moore nearly four centuries ago is now technologically advanced.

Fort William, near the 18th century Government House, was similar in plan to Fort George. It was built on the site of Moore's Warwick Castle. The fort was begun in the 1830s but not finished until 1853. Like Fort George, it had a three storey inner keep surrounded by a redoubt. By the time it was completed, however, artillery had advanced to such a degree that the work was obsolete.

In the late 1880s the fortification was converted into a huge powder magazine when the dry moat was roofed over, creating a series of long, cavernous rooms.

Late 19th century fortifications include **Alexandra Battery**, built in 1863 and expanded in 1869 and again in 1900, at Buildings Bay, and **St. David's Battery**, built before 1910 at Great Head on St. David's Island. These round out the seaward defences in St. George's.

Members of the British garrison who manned the forts of St. George's lived in or near the town and played an important role in the local economy and community. In 1778, during the American Revolution, two companies of the 55th Regiment occupied several private houses in the town, as well as the State House and old gaol (see chapter 2). Suspicion about the loyalty of many Bermudians caused strife between the soldiers and the people.

The arrival in 1780 of 600 infantrymen from New York, many of them recovering invalids, and another 81 shipwrecked Royal Artillerymen, prompted the garrison commander, Major William Sutherland, to complain about the poor quarters his troops occupied, "more fitt for hoggs than men".

In February 1780, work commenced on a barracks for 100 soldiers on a hill to the east of town, the first

Surviving almost intact is this fine example of a barracks building from the late 19th century, a time when basic accommodation, often tented, for ordinary soldiers was giving way to something less harsh. Most of the fenestration (eight-over-eight-over-eight) survives. The roof would originally have been of impractical Welsh slate, regularly removed by hurricanes and as regularly replaced by the military.

of many on Barrack Hill. One year later, a military hospital was added.

The size of the permanent garrison establishment in 1797 varied between 300 and 1,300 but averaged about 500 soldiers. The cluster of buildings on Barrack Hill grew in number and became diversified in function. In addition to the Royal Barracks, a long and massive building for enlisted men was built. By 1854 there were also officers' barracks, a sergeants' mess, a canteen, a quartermaster's store, a district military prison, a hospital, a gun shed and guard house.

The site was even more complex and crowded by 1876 after three new barracks and married officers' quarters were added, along with a cluster of workshops, bakeries and stables, and a whole new barracks complex for artillery and engineers next to Fort Victoria.

Although the Royal Barracks fronting on the military parade ground has been demolished and replaced by modern housing, several of the 1870s barracks have survived. C block and D block have been refurbished and are used by a variety of businesses. These long buildings housed the hundreds of enlisted men who manned the forts. Although the dimensions, floor plan and design of the barracks were the same throughout the British Empire, their construction here is uniquely Bermudian. There is a blend of standard issue imported materials such as cast iron pillars, slate for roofing and tall, vertical windows, with Bermudian stone and colourwashed plaster. They were well ventilated, a vital consideration on a station periodically racked by yellow fever, and provided better living conditions than most stations.

The British army hierarchy was rigid, reflecting the class structure of 19th century British society. The officers came mostly from the gentry and upper class, while the rank and file were recruited from the working classes and poor of the English shires, Scotland, Ireland and elsewhere in the Empire. The officers of the various service branches stationed in Bermuda had messes and housing separate from the men they commanded.

In the early years of the garrison, regimental officers rented privately owned dwellings from the citizens of St. George's, but by the early 19th century, the War Department purchased or built houses on Barrack Hill for the regimental commander, the senior officers of the Royal Artillery, Royal Engineers, Ordnance Corps and the Clerk of the Works, as well as mess buildings for their use. Most of these buildings survive today but have been converted into apartments. Their exterior grandeur is still apparent, but internal configurations have been drastically altered.

Sandhurst is the oldest and grandest of the complex of officers' housing. The main octagonal core is possibly the first garrison hospital, whose construction was prompted by

"A View taken from the Wooden House" by Thomas Driver, identifies Sandhurst as William Gray's House. The painting is not dated but from other evidence it was probably painted between 1816 and 1818. Sandhurst may be roofless because it was being rebuilt or reroofed. The curved entrance to the grounds survives to this day. (Courtesy Fay and Geoffrey Elliott Collection: Bermuda Archives, Hamilton, Bermuda.)

Dr. Richard Bell. By October 1780 the "malignant bilious fever" which originated in the town's overcrowded gaol had spread to the garrison soldiers quartered in the town.

Dr. Bell petitioned the House of Assembly for a hospital 50 feet long, divided into three wards, and his request was readily granted. The Assemblymen, many of whom had members of their families living in the town, were in favor of removing the sick soldiers who might spread the infection to townspeople. The hospital was completed by February 1781, but by then Dr. Bell had other problems to contend with. Wily St. Georgians were selling rum to his patients, "highly pernicious to our good old men's health", so he requested that a guard house be built on the grounds to halt the practice.

By 1785 a new hospital at the top of Old Maids Lane was leased for 21 years and the hospital at Sandhurst fell out of use.

Naval Commander Francis Pender owned Sandhurst in 1797 and three years later sold it to Humphrey

Dalrymple Bland, who may have completely rebuilt the structure. St. George's merchant William Gray purchased the house and surrounding ten acres in 1810 and apparently added the two flanking wings to the octagonal core. A watercolour by Thomas Driver, probably painted between 1816 and 1818, shows a roofless house with these extensions, so perhaps the additions were being built at that time.

The front door, capped with a pediment, gave entry to a quoin edged porch which projected south from the octagonal core building, whose cornice was decorated with dentil moulding. Fine old exterior chimneys were symmetrically situated midway along the walls of the additions.

In 1818 Gray sold the house for £1,500 to the War Department, which converted it from a private dwelling into the mess for the officers of the Royal Artillery and Ordnance Department. A sketch of the house, made by Gaspard Le Marchant Tupper about 1857, shows that the dual side staircase, lined with imported Yorkshire

flagstones, had been added. The formal symmetrical landscaping of the foreground of the building is captured in that painting and in a military map

Sandhurst is a fascinating example of the steady growth of the military establishment applied to a house in traditional Bermudian style. The original building, dating from 1781 was probably unadorned. The strong dentil moulding around the eaves was probably put on when William Gray added the wings to the elongated octagonal central building in 1808. This elegant Regency structure was subsequently completely engulfed by piecemeal additions. Only the entrance porch room and flanking verandahs attempted the dignity and style of the original. The final insult is the 1898 addition on the right, defined by its cheap construction and an ugly basement arch which pioneered the arcomania of our own times.

"Royal Artillery Mess House" painted by G. Le M. Tupper c. 1857/8 shows Sandhurst at its grandest period. (Courtesy Fay and Geoffrey Elliott Collection: Bermuda Archives, Hamilton, Bermuda.)

made in 1876, by which time the mess was shared by the officers of the Royal Artillery and Royal Engineers. The curved entrance to the property survives to this day.

The map also reveals that the tank and catchment to the northwest of the mess had been added by this date, as well as a now vanished detached kitchen to the east. The addition on the far west, as well as the concrete verandah in front, were added in 1898-99 at a cost of £853. This last unfortunate phase of construction did much to spoil the well proportioned façade of the early building. The elegance of the verandah's pillars does not make up for the fact that the front of the original building is now hidden in shadow.

The substantial lower storey is cut into bedrock. This is completely exposed from the north side. While the front of the building abounds with quoins and decorative moulding, the rear is strictly utilitarian in appearance.

Exactly when the building acquired the name Sandhurst remains

unclear, but it serves as a reminder of the elite officers' training school in Surrey, England, through which most British army officers passed on their way to their commissions.

Mount Pleasant, to the north of Sandhurst, is more secluded and therefore retains more privacy. The hip roof core of the house was built in 1825 by Scottish merchant John Barr, who christened it "Ben Lomond". In 1837 he sold the house and ten acres to the War Department for £3,000, a considerable sum. It became the residence of the commanding officer of the Royal Engineers, who was responsible for the ongoing fortification of the island.

The wide verandah and two additions were built between 1854 and 1876, as were two symmetrical outbuildings in the rear, perhaps when the Royal Engineers commander moved out and the building became general field officers' quarters. The house remains virtually the same as it was in 1876.

Across the street from Sandhurst stood **The Bungalow** until it was

demolished in the 1980s. John Van Norden built it in the late 1810s. His widow sold it to Stephen Egan in 1824, who in turn sold it in 1829 to the British military for £500. In the 1850s it was the home of the Foreman of the Works who was in charge of fort construction. For the rest of the century it was a general officers' quarters.

Unlike The Bungalow, **Paradise Cottage** next door still stands. The main core, now nearly overwhelmed by later additions, was built before 1817. It was the home of schoolmaster John Darrell before he lost it through foreclosure. From 1825 until 1830, the house was owned by the Clerk of the Works, George Joynes, who sold it to the War Department for £500 when he returned to his native Scotland. Several additions were made when the building became Royal Artillery officers' quarters in the 1870s, but the two old chimneys of the original house survive and can be seen projecting from the much altered roof.

Arcadia, to the south, presides over St. George's from the top of Barrack Hill, a familiar landmark of the

The most impressive of the military buildings dominating the hill above the east end of St. George's, Arcadia actually has little to lend it distinction beyond mass, its long verandah and the pediments on the tower windows. Its great size and elevated position gave it what the British required, visual dominance of the colonial town.

town. John Van Norden purchased and consolidated two earlier grants in 1811 and built a substantial house the following year. He sold the house to William Gray in 1813, who sold the house and lot to the War Department five years later for £2,500.

A large building with a long verandah facing the town appears on an 1854 map as the garrison commander's residence, which became a general field officers' quarters by the 1870s. This earlier structure was demolished before 1891 and the present building was erected between 1898 and 1900 at a cost of more than £3,000. It was meticulously planned, right down to the window mouldings, and was built as it stands today in one episode.

The high tower was intended to dominate the town's skyline. The verandah provided a pleasant promenade for the residents. In the plans

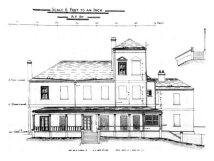

The Record Plan for Arcadia was drawn in 1901, after the building had been completed. (Bermuda Archives, Hamilton, Bermuda.)

it was designated OCRA, probably for "officer commanding the Royal Artillery", but it had acquired the name Arcadia by the 1920s. The building remains virtually untouched as it approaches its 100th birthday.

While Arcadia commands a magnificent view of the town, **Boeotia** has an equally fine view of the harbour on Cut Road. It is perched on a cliff over-

The arched entrance porch of Arcadia is designed to impress. Solid, with classically inspired pilasters, entablature and pediment, there could be no doubt that this was the entrance to a place of social importance.

Boeotia is another skyline building designed to dominate by its size and position. In a severely plain classical tradition, its concrete wrap-around verandah lends this otherwise relatively insignificant building the social importance sought by its designers.

looking Convict Bay. Francis Forbes Hinson built a predecessor to Boeotia on the site in 1828, which he called Troglodyte. It was later the home of merchant John Barr. The British military acquired the land in 1877 and razed the earlier structure. In July 1899 the Royal Engineers commenced work on a new field officers' quarters and completed the building in 1901 at a cost of £1,891. It was christened Boeotia by the military.

The rather plain residence has good proportions, with a moulded cornice below its shallow hip roof. It has a wide verandah on which officers might have lounged and observed the shipping activity in the harbour.

This fine building and its grounds have been neglected, but new owners are about to start to work on the house.

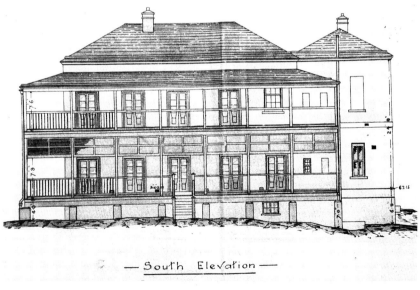

— South Elevation —

Boeotia was recorded after completion by draughtsmen of the Royal Engineers. 1904 drawing. (Bermuda Archives, Hamilton, Bermuda.)

A photogravure of the Military Hospital when it had wooden wings and a wooden verandah. The joins in the roof are clearly visible. (Courtesy St. George's Historical Society Collection: Bermuda Archives, Hamilton, Bermuda.)

To the east of the garrison barracks complex, near the shore of St. George's Island, stands the former **Garrison Hospital**. The building was deliberately set apart to prevent the spread of contagious diseases, as well as to take full advantage of sea breezes thought to be essential to the recovery of invalids. This hospital was actually the fourth in a series. The first was Sandhurst on this site. A second, at the north end of Old Maids Lane, was rented from John Smith for 21 years. The third hospital was run by the Ordnance Department in a building rented from John Davenport. This structure, later known as Sunnybank, was demolished by the Corporation of St. George's to build the wharf at Tiger Bay. The Garrison Hospital is the largest and best preserved of the four.

The Garrison Hospital was built, probably in 1819, on land purchased from Joseph Hutchison in 1818. It was intended to cope with a yellow fever epidemic which was particularly devastating to the garrison. It is an imposing two storey building with a wide central pediment and an imposing entry porch. The two wings on either side have military style cast iron verandahs

A fine example of the mid 19th century Imperial style, the Garrison Hospital has a central pediment and classic revival entrance with recessed columns and entablature. The symmetrical lateral wings, once much extended by wooden additions, are shaded by verandahs in classic military style.

on which patients could "take the air" to speed their recovery. At the rear of the building a walled enclosure contains a variety of detached outbuildings, including the former cook room and bakery, privies, guard room, pump house and "dead room" or morgue.

By 1873 the hospital had been expanded with further additions to the wings. In a photograph of the building taken about 1910, it can clearly be

seen by looking at the roof where the original hospital ended and the additions began.

In the 1950s, the additions were removed, restoring the hospital to its original early 19th century size. Many of the old walls and outbuildings surrounding the hospital survive in various states of disrepair. It is now Chelsea Apartments, a name reminiscent of the royal hospital in London which

The Garrison Chapel (now the Ethiopian Orthodox Cathedral) is another fine example of an "issue" military chapel adapted to the local materials. Similar structures may be found anywhere in the erstwhile British Empire, but few will have the solidity derived from the Bermuda stone construction. A stone roof and a change from casement windows would translate it into a Bermudian church of 19th century Gothic inspiration.

Point was supplemented, first in the 1810s with the construction of the fort on Ferry Island, and in the 1820s by the **Martello Tower.**

The latter was begun by Major Thomas Blanshard of the Royal Engineers in 1823 and bears this date above its entrance. Originally of French design, the British adopted this simple yet effective defensive work and built a string of them across the south of England and in many colonies. The single cannon on the tower commanded a 360 degree arc of fire. The walls are asymmetrical, with the thickest part facing the gap between Ferry Point and Coney Island, the most likely direction of attack. The tower is the only example of this type of fortification in Bermuda. Another tower was planned for the Dockyard but was, apparently, never built. In 1828 Blanshard also built a substantial magazine nearby to store gunpowder for the forts. Its thick stone walls are supported by massive stone buttresses.

The two storey L-shaped gable roof house commonly called **Ferry Point Cottage** is either a barrack constructed in 1781, or a considerable expansion of the last of a series of ferry keepers' houses dating back to the earliest days of the colony. During the American Revolution, the House of Assembly provided funds to build quarters for some of the garrison troops then lodging in town. This rather plain building is dug into the side of a hill and has a massive chimney on its north side, no doubt used

Bermuda's only Martello Tower was built in the 1820s and stands in its deep ditch in lonely isolation guarding the back door to St. George's Harbour at Ferry Reach. It is an almost round oval, solidly built of the harder local stone. The ground floor held a water tank and stored powder, the upper housed soldiers, and the roof level mounted a single gun.

Charles II commissioned Sir Christopher Wren to build in 1682.

The former **Garrison Chapel** is another survivor from the former garrison. It was built in the 1840s to hold services for the garrison troops and to alleviate the overcrowding of St. Peter's Church (see chapter 3). It is a fine example of virtually unaltered ecclesiastical military architecture executed in Bermudian building materials. The entry porch and side walls have pleasing exterior buttresses and the doors and arched windows of the building are all capped with eyebrows. The northern end of the gable roof houses the church bell, suspended within a stone arch. Years after the garrison closed, the chapel was designated the Cathedral of the Ethiopian Orthodox Church in Bermuda.

To the northeast of the Garrison Chapel lies the military burial ground, first consecrated in 1806. The cemetery was a gift from the parish vestry, which felt that the size of the town's churchyard was "inadequate to the increased mortality which prevails among the military". The gravestones bear testimony to the deadly waves of yellow fever which periodically swept through the garrison, as well as to the many accidents accompanying the building of the island's fortifications and the dangers of drilling with cannon and small arms. Today, it is a peaceful resting place overlooking Hurd Channel to the east.

In addition to the main garrison on Barrack Hill, there was usually a detachment of troops at Ferry Reach to defend St. George's Island from a landward invasion. The old fort at Burnt

Ferry Point Cottage is in the traditional 18th century hillside style with the living quarters above a substantial basement. Its chimneys, however, are unusual, one being on the side of the house rather than supporting a gable and the other being placed to the side of its gable. The steps on the right reached a now blocked door.

by the soldiers to prepare their meals. The catchment and tank to the west also date to that period. The walled enclosure in front of the building originally held horses and livestock while their owners were on the main island, and was the site of a cockfight in 1785 when St. Georgians pitted their roosters against those from the main island. The troops used it as a cemetery in the early 19th century, but by 1850 it had been converted into a garden.

In 1846 the War Department in London bought, by Act of Assembly, the western 30 acres of St. George's Island, including the barracks, magazine, "Ferry Tower", two walled gardens, a lime kiln and the two ruined forts, but had to grant a right of way to the ferry dock. Until The Causeway from the main island to Longbird Island was completed in 1871, the Ferry Road was the main thoroughfare be-

This shows the L-shape of the Ferry Keeper's house. This is the uphill side of the house and the living level can be reached by a low flight of steps.

tween the Town of St. George and the rest of Bermuda. After the deadly yellow fever epidemic of 1854, the British garrison made it standard practice to quarter at least half of their force in tents at Ferry Point.

The land was sold back to the Bermuda Government in 1928 for £1,090 on the condition that they main-

tain the cemetery for the yellow fever victims of the 56th Regiment. The barracks was used as a quarantine station after it was abandoned by the military. Ferry Point is now a park.

Although the workshops, barracks, forts and quarters of the British Army were extensive, the facilities of the Royal Navy, Commissariat and Ordnance Departments, and the convict establishment, were no less impressive, though fewer in number.

The supplies needed by the garrison were considerable, ranging from cannon, gunpowder and shells to supply the forts to provisions and uniforms to feed and clothe the troops. Initially, private merchants were contracted for supplies and storage space but they proved unequal to the demands of a fully established garrison. The British military needed its own wharves and storehouses. The War

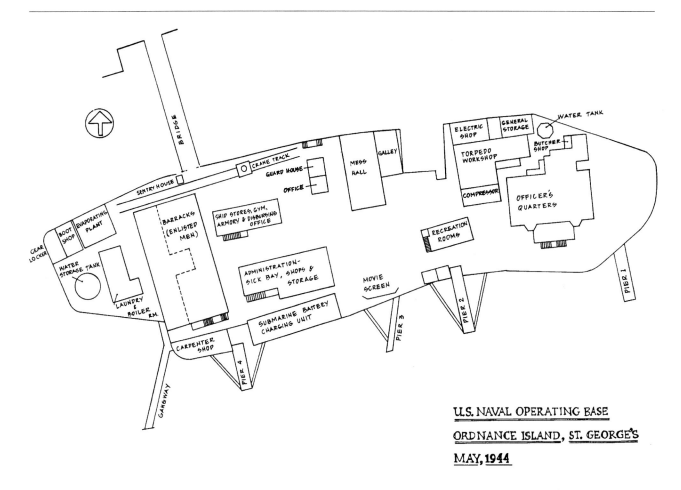

U.S. NAVAL OPERATING BASE

ORDNANCE ISLAND, ST. GEORGE'S

MAY, 1944

Map of Ordnance Island in 1944. All buildings other than the Officer's Quarters (formerly the Storekeeper's House) and the Torpedo Workshop (now the Customs and Marine Police) have been demolished. Copied by Barbara Finsness from a plan in the Corporation of St. George's deeds. (Courtesy the Corporation of St. George's.)

Department responded by purchasing or building facilities in and around the town. Until the Dockyard was built at Ireland Island, the Royal Navy was supplied as well.

Of the three military wharf complexes, **Ordnance Island** is the most impressive, with a long history of use as a storage facility.

In January 1621 Governor Nathaniel Butler built a large storehouse of framed cedar in a "smale Island lieing nere unto the towneswarfe" for receiving English supplies. This Company-owned public storehouse was erected on an island later named Ducking Stool Island, where liars, gossips and scolds were ducked in the harbour as punishment. To the east, roughly in line with Block House, was Gallows Island, where 17th and 18th century felons met their end in full view of the crowds assembled on nearby King's Square. As early as 1670, there was an attempt to connect the

two islands with a causeway to serve as a breakwater for the safer mooring of vessels near the Town Dock, but this project evidently failed. More than a century later, Henry Tucker obtained Ducking Stool Island in 1781 and Nathaniel Butterfield acquired Gallows Island four years later.

By 1795 both islands had been purchased by Ordnance Commissary Simon Fraser for a combined price of £100. Fraser, a Scotsman, arrived in Bermuda in 1783 to oversee the cannon, shot and gunpowder belonging to the Royal Navy and issued to the island's forts. He had ambitious plans for the two islands off Market Wharf. In 1799 he successfully petitioned the newly formed Corporation of St. George's for permission to connect the two islands by means of a wharf and create one large island just off King's Square. By 1804 a map of the harbour reveals that the two islands had been connected, forming the single island of today. The progress of Fraser's work

is reflected in his parish assessments, which went from £1,600 in 1800 to £2,000 in 1808, and then from £3,000 in 1810 to £3,500 the following year.

In 1814 Fraser sold Ordnance Island, as well as Hen Island in the middle of St. George's Harbour, and several buildings, to the War Department for the incredible sum of £14,193. The wily Scotsman returned home with his fortune and died in Edinburgh in 1819. Fraser had spent a considerable sum building the wharf and storehouses, but the sale price by far exceeded his expenses: purchased for £100 and sold for over £14,000. During the War of 1812 Fraser was a British agent in Connecticut and thought to be a spy. Perhaps the price had an element of reward.

Under the tenure of the Ordnance Department, the island became crowded with buildings. The west end was dominated by Fraser's former residence, which by the 1850s was converted into the offices of the Royal

The Storekeeper's House on Ordnance Island is a large U-shaped building in the late Georgian tradition with simple pilasters of two storeys over a substantial basement level. The inside of the U has subsequently been filled in under a shed roof. The south façade has two half hexagon bays between which an ugly concrete verandah with lateral steps has been added. Some surviving wooden moulding hides in the eaves. The house is the last survivor of the many military buildings on the island and deserves a better fate than its current neglect.

building faced the town square to the north. The space between the two northern wings was filled in with a flat roofed addition in the late 19th century, and the main entrance was moved to the southern side of the building. This house was the residence of William Penno's family in the 1840s, before his wife inherited Durnford in 1857 from her father. In addition to the Royal Engineers' office and the Ordnance Storekeeper's house, by 1854 there were also several ordnance storehouses, a boat house, fish pond, coal shed and guard room on the island. Twenty years later, the Ordnance Department had added blacksmith's and carpenter's shops, a crane and several tanks.

In 1932 the War Department sold Ordnance Island to the Corporation of St. George's for £4,500, less than one third the sum they had paid for it over a century earlier. The Corporation leased various stores to local companies, including Gosling Brothers, J.E. Lightbourn, John F. Burrows and Furness, Withy & Co.

During World War II, Ordnance Island was occupied by the US military, which turned it into a submarine outfitting base by building a series of piers along the southern wharf and constructing a submarine battery recharger near the wharf's edge. In February 1944 the island was connected to the mainland when the US Army Corps of Engineers built a wooden bridge.

Engineers. This long building had an ornate porch, with an entryway decorated with a fanlight and sidelights. Wooden verandahs flanked both sides of the porch, and the whole building was surrounded by a stone wall.

While cannon barrels and piles of shot lay clustered around the house, gunpowder was stored at Hen Island, which had accompanied Fraser's sale of Ordnance Island. This safety precaution was taken during Fraser's time when a bolt of lightning struck the Hen Island magazine on November 1, 1812, igniting 400 barrels of gunpowder. Miraculously the caretaker and his family escaped unhurt.

The three storey Ordnance **Storekeeper's House**, built by 1816, lies at the east end of Ordnance Island. Originally U-shaped, this hip roof

Most of the buildings shown in this World War II photograph of Ordnance Island have since been demolished. The Storekeeper's House, which still survives, can be seen at the right. (US Bases Collection: Bermuda Archives, Hamilton, Bermuda.)

Ordnance Island showing the Simon Fraser House unsigned and undated but c. 1814. (Bermuda National Trust Collection: Bermuda Archives, Hamilton, Bermuda.)

Simon Fraser's old house was more than doubled in size to create a barracks for enlisted personnel, while the officers occupied the Ordnance Storekeeper's House at the other end of the island. Other storehouses were converted into a galley and mess hall, laundry, machine shop, sick bay, torpedo workshop and recreation room. In 1946 most of the island was returned to civilian use but the USO continued to run a club for US servicemen.

One by one, the old Ordnance Department buildings were torn down in the late 1970s and 1980s. The guardhouse and one old storehouse were demolished to prepare the site

Detail from Thomas Driver's 1822 painting from Signal Hill. It shows the Simon Fraser House on Ordnance Island and the Store-keeper's House. (Bermuda Archives Collection, Hamilton, Bermuda.)

The Simon Fraser House on Ordnance Island and the later buildings in the foreground have all been demolished since this photograph was taken in 1941. (US Bases Collection: Bermuda Archives, Hamilton, Bermuda.)

for the reconstruction of the *Deliverance*. Fraser's early 19th century house and the 1940s barracks which were added to it were razed in the mid 1980s after a fire.

Today, only the Ordnance Store-keeper's House, an elegant dome topped tank and a nearby storehouse, the torpedo workshop during World War II, survive. The former is in poor condition and unoccupied. The west end of Ordnance Island remains lively, with visitors passing to and from their cruise ships. The east end of the is-

land is solemn and desolate.

Commissariat Wharf on Water Street West was built by merchant John Fisher, a loyalist who fled South Carolina during the American Revolution. Fisher was the first commercial agent to supply the garrison's needs. Between 1792 and 1796, he bought three early 18th century water lots and combined them into a single large wharf capable of handling the supplies necessary to feed, clothe and equip the 500 or more troops of the 47th Regiment.

Fisher built a large store for general supplies, since replaced by the brick Carriage House Museum building and also erected a row of cattle stalls along the western edge of the property. In 1812, he sold the whole complex to George Damerum, the Assistant Deputy Commissary of Bermuda, for the enormous sum of £5,000. In 1837 the Commissary Department added to their facilities by purchasing an empty water lot to the east from Joseph Wood Judkin for £600. Shortly thereafter, the Crown erected a warehouse, now home to the **Carriage House Restaurant**, using yellow bricks imported from England. In 1876

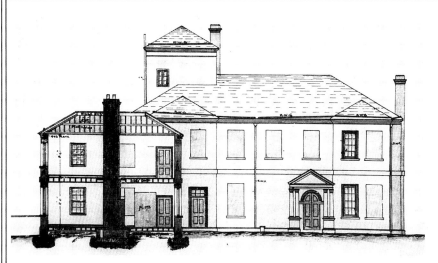

Military Architecture

The two most obvious aspects of military architecture were iron verandah columns and railings and Welsh slate roofs. Neither were very practical in Bermuda, the first requiring constant painting, the second replacement after almost every hurricane. Because of this impracticality, they were rarely copied in local building, and then only by the most pretentious.

Ventilation was something of a fixation with the military, perhaps because the ordinary soldier wasn't prone to frequent bathing. Two kinds of roof ventilators arrived with the military. One was a small penthouse arrangement at the crown of the roof, rather more efficient, if less graceful than the usual Bermuda slits between rows of slates. The other was a small louvred gable projection often used over verandahs. The rooftop ventilators were also added to existing local stone roofs of houses occupied by the military and were also copied, particularly in St. George's.

Perhaps because they had failed to impress the locals with their buildings, at the turn of the 20th century the military built several grand officers houses using Bermuda materials. The grandest and most imposing was Arcadia, a clearly English house design which still dominates St. George's from its Barrack Hill site. Both Arcadia and, to a lesser extent, Boeotia had imposing entrance porches.

The only other military detail to

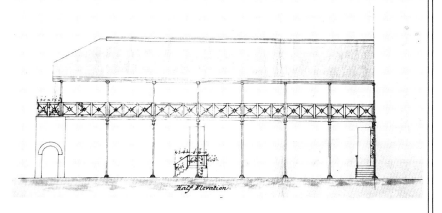

BERMUDA, St GEORGES,
SOLDIERS' BARRACKS,
Details of Ironwork to Verandah &c.

Half Elevation.

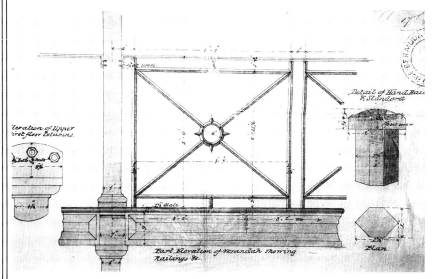

Detail of Hand Rail & Standard

Iteration of Upper first floor Columns.

Part Elevation of Verandah showing Railings &c.

Plan.

find its way into use in Bermuda was the ceramic chimney pot. These may have worked more effectively with the small coal grates of the time by creating an improved draft; no one could have thought they improved the appearance of a Bermuda chimney.

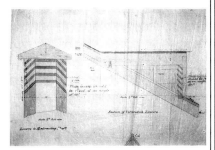

This prominent brick building dates from the first half of the 19th century and was built by the British military as a warehouse for their stores. The upper floors are now a Carriage Museum, while the ground floor has been sympathetically enlarged and today houses an architecturally pleasing restaurant with warm, heavy brick arches.

a small building on the north served as the Commissariat Department offices, while the area which is now the restaurant was the "pork stores" crammed with barrels of salt pork, a staple of the soldiers' weekly rations. Elsewhere on the property were workshops and a slip and boathouse for lighters.

In 1930 the Crown sold the property to H. Bernard Wilkinson for £2,850, less than half the purchase price of a century earlier. In 1975, the Wilkinson Trust undertook a major redevelopment of the property, building the Carriage Museum on the site of the old General Stores and turning the brick warehouse into the Carriage House Restaurant, and demolishing the old Commissary Department office to create a new entrance to the restaurant.

To double the size of the restaurant, the Wilkinson Trust built a one storey extension to the west which mirrored the layout of the original

brick structure. Sharp eyed diners notice the difference between the rounded edged yellow bricks in the old room and the new, reproduction cast brick stucco in the addition.

Convict Bay is by far the most changed of the three military support facilities, since most of its buildings were levelled in the 1980s to make way for condominiums. The area is named for the relatively short period between 1833 and 1854 when convicts from Great Britain were kept in hulks moored nearby. Prior to this, the bay was entirely lacking in wharves or storehouses and was used principally for shipbuilding and careening vessels.

The first convicts arrived in Bermuda in 1825 to work on fortifications and construction of the Dockyard. The hulk *Antelope* arrived in St. George's late in 1832 with about 400 prisoners. Each day the convicts were ferried ashore from their hulk to quarry rock or to help build the forts and military storehouses of St. George's and were

returned to their floating prison at night. To facilitate their daily landing, the Royal Engineers constructed a wharf, boat slip, garden and cluster of buildings at the east end of town.

The convicts were paid for their nine hours of daily labour and actually received more and better provisions than the soldiers who guarded them. By the 1850s the Crown was spending over £100,000 a year to maintain the convict establishment. In 1853, however, yellow fever took hold in the St. George's garrison and in the convict hulk *Thames* with devastating mortality. The epidemic claimed 345 soldiers, one quarter of the garrison, and 152 convicts, one third of the hulk population, along with 85 St. Georgians. In the wake of this tragedy, the practice of employing convicts in St. George's was discontinued. A decade later, the convict establishment at Ireland Island was also abolished.

After the convict hulks left, the wharf complex reverted to the Royal

Detail from Thomas Driver's 1833 painting shows one of the hulks at Convict Bay. (Courtesy Fay and Geoffrey Elliott Collection: Bermuda Archives, Hamilton, Bermuda.)

Engineers who expanded it considerably. By 1876 the whole area between Water Street and the cliffs below Boeotia had been purchased by the War Department and "wharfed over" for landing and storing the equipment needed to construct or improve Forts Victoria, Albert, George, William and St. Catherine, as well as the battery at Buildings Bay. The complex of buildings included general storehouses, coal yards, a torpedo shed, cement store and workshops, with storage space for gun cotton and other goods carved out of the cliff to the north.

Additional piers and cranes were later added to aid in unloading the massive muzzle-loaded cannon installed in several of the forts in the 1870s. All the Royal Engineers' buildings were demolished to construct the condominium complex on the site.

The British military had a profound effect on the culture and commerce of Bermuda in general and St. George's in particular. Throughout the 19th century, Bermuda's economy was heavily subsidised by Crown spending to support the garrison troops, with many lucrative contracts going to local merchants. The British government spent as much as £100,000 a year on the convict establishment alone. Add to this the many soldiers who spent their pay in the town's grog shops, taverns, dance halls and grocery stores and one begins to appreciate the importance of the garrison.

It is more difficult to measure the cultural intermixing between St. Georgians and the military. Bermuda had developed its own distinctive styles of speech, architecture, dress and manners over the course of nearly

two centuries. With the arrival of the Royal Navy and the garrison, Bermudians were brought into contact with the very latest trends in London, creating a revolution in taste and fashion. The presence of the garrison also corrected the gender imbalance in the town. Women once destined for spinsterhood found ready matches on Barrack Hill. No regiment was without its band, which played at the dances and balls which brought soldiers and the town's women together.

The officers of the British army and Royal Navy formed a rival elite to the town's merchants and politicians. Some Bermudian women married brevet-majors or post-captains and departed Bermuda for a life abroad.

The military also brought with them British sports and hobbies. Cricket loomed large in importance, and the match played between the

James B. Heyl's photograph shows clearly the buildings at Convict Bay and along the eastern end of Water Street. (Bermuda Through the Camera of James B. Heyl 1868-1897.)

Royal Navy fleet team and the garrison regimental team was a major event on St. George's social calendar. Throughout the 19th century, the games were played on the military parade grounds in front of the Royal Barracks overlooking the town before a lively crowd of soldiers, sailors and civilians. The Bermuda Cricket Club was founded in St. George's in 1845 and played its first game against the garrison.

Horse racing was another popular entertainment eagerly pursued by the British military, who had a near monopoly on the island's fastest riding horses. The St. George Stakes was held on January 28, 1846, and featured ten horses and riders racing in sprints and hurdles. The Governor attended the races and the ball which followed.

Garrison and Royal Navy officers were also active yachtsmen, and it was not an uncommon sight to see sailboats racing in St. George's Har-

bour. Indeed, the British military were instrumental in founding the Royal Bermuda Yacht Club, which met first in St. George's and only later moved to Hamilton. In 1845 Lord Mark Kerr, a captain in the 20th Regiment, was elected the RBYC's first commodore.

Theatre and music were other diversions for the officers and men. In addition to their bands, most regiments had a dedicated group of actors who put on amateur dramatics wherever they were stationed. The more permanent corps of Royal Engineers built themselves a theatre in 1864. The regimental bands entertained both the garrison and the town's civilian inhabitants at public concerts in King's Square or played more exclusive venues in private homes. They introduced Bermudians to a wide range of music and kept them current with the latest pieces from Britain. Individual musicians also imparted their skills to St. Georgians through instruction. Band-

master of the 42nd Regiment Christian Loeblin, for instance, offered to teach pianoforte, guitar, violin, organ and flute to interested Bermudians in 1847.

A fox hunt was held in St. George's in October 1845. The officers of the 20th Regiment brought several foxes and packs of hounds to Bermuda. But the short supply of foxes and the expense of keeping hounds prevented these hunts from becoming regular events.

The history of the colony's defences has come full circle. In the post Cold War age of missiles, "smart bombs" and satellites, Bermuda's strategic importance has faded. Great Britain, Canada and the United States have closed their military outposts and left the island's defence to the Bermuda Regiment. Although the British military has departed, it has left an important architectural and cultural legacy in many familiar buildings and institutions.

CHAPTER NINE

St. David's and Tucker's Town

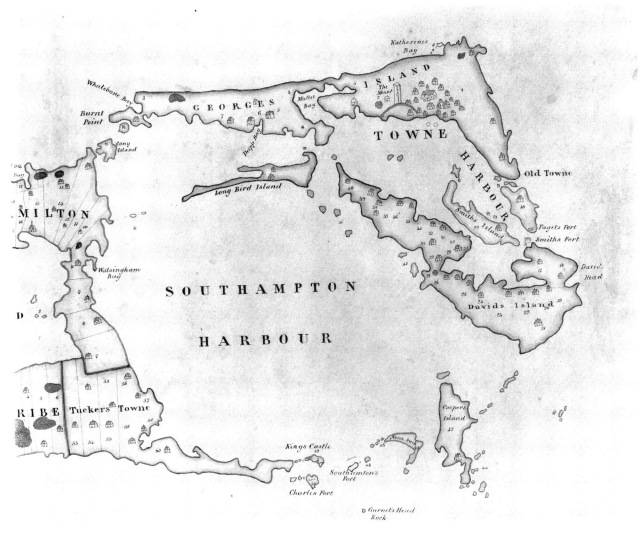

Detail from Gabriel Mathias' 1739 copy of Richard Norwood's 1663 map. ("Map of Summer Islands called Bermudas", Bermuda Archives Collection, Hamilton, Bermuda.)

St. David's Island and Tucker's Town, while part of St. George's Parish, have always been distinctly different from the town across the harbour. They were both settled very early, before the eight parishes to the west. The eastern half of St. David's and all of Tucker's Town were set aside early as public land, mostly for the use of the commanders of the nearby forts. The western half of St. David's Island was divided into 40 lots of five acres each, which were awarded to the shareholders of Hamilton Parish in 1619 to compensate them for the poor quality of their land. These small lots were usually subleased or sold to St. David's islanders who lived on the land.

Situated between Bermuda's two early harbours, St. David's was a hive of activity for much of the 17th century. The local economy existed on tobacco growing and livestock raising.

Tucker's Town, established by Bermuda's second Governor, Daniel Tucker, was intended to be a port to rival St. George's in size, but was far more exposed to the weather and failed to attract many settlers. From its founding, it was a town only in name. After the transition from to-bacco growing to shipbuilding and trade, St. David's islanders readily embraced maritime pursuits ranging from fishing, turtling and whaling to piloting, navigating and shipbuilding.

As trade shifted to the western parishes, St. David's became more isolated and insular, having little in common with the mercantile and bureaucratic activity at the capital. Due to the lack of adequate roads, boats were almost exclusively used to get from place to place within St. David's. The 40 or so families who lived there in the 18th century formed close bonds and overlapping kinship ties until most of

Fishponds

For centuries, St. David's islanders have looked to the sea for their livelihood. While whaling provided an exciting if infrequent source of profit, fishing was the mainstay of the local economy. In an age without refrigeration, fish had to be either eaten quickly before they spoiled, or preserved with salt. The fishpond offered an alternative means of keeping fish alive in captivity until they were needed in the kitchen.

Bermuda's first fishponds were natural lagoons such as those at The Crawl and Devil's Hole. It is thought that the concept was introduced by Bermuda's first black slaves, who had used similar "kraals" in West Africa. The "Craule" in Hamilton Parish had acquired that name by 1623.

In the early 20th century, E.A. McCallan remembered that "on the shores of St. David's were forty-odd fishponds, most of them on the north shore. The majority were built of squared masonry laid in mortar [although] one or two were caves." The fishponds were built astride currents so the water remained fresh to keep the fish alive.

The confined fish were regularly fed and fattened in much the same way as hogs or cattle, and often fetched double the price per pound of those caught on the reefs. Today few if any fishponds are in active use, but almost every coastal house once had one.

The ruins of artificial fishponds cut into the rocky foreshore are a common sight along the north side of St. David's Island and much of the North Shore.

---

the islanders were related to some degree.

The 1758 granting episode sponsored by Governor William Popple had a disruptive effect on the tight-knit group. Tenure of the eastern 12 public shares was auctioned, and only two St. David's islanders purchased the right to the land they occupied. The rest were either turned off their land or became sub-tenants of those who bought the use of the land. In some cases, the new owners built substantial new houses (see St. David's Lodge below) while others simply used the land to grow cedar trees for shipbuilding. This choice of land use further reinforced local reliance on the sea for livelihood—land being used for growing timber was not available for cultivation or pasture.

In response to the government sponsored agricultural revival in the late 18th and 19th centuries, a few St. David's islanders abandoned their maritime pursuits and farmed the land. Planters in St. David's grew Bermuda's best arrowroot, while farmers in Tucker's Town had short-lived success cultivating cotton. Later in the 19th century, St. David's fields yielded bountiful crops of onions and potatoes, while in the early 20th century, Easter

lilies became a lucrative cash crop. The improvement of fields did not have a corresponding effect on the inadequate road system, and as late as 1885 there was only a single-width track across the island. In many places this was too steep or rocky to be of much service. St. David's, with the completion of the Severn Bridge in 1934, was the last large island to be connected to the rest of Bermuda, more than 50 years after the completion of The Causeway.

The island was fundamentally changed in World War II. The British government leased bases to the United States for 99 years. After considering sites in Warwick and Southampton, the US military chose St. David's Island as the site for an airfield and major strategic base. Almost the entire western half of St. David's Island was needed. The island was to be widened in an ambitious scheme to create 750 acres of new land, more than double the acreage of the leased land, by dredging and filling in Castle Harbour. Nearly 20 million cubic yards of fill were dredged to form the new base, which by the end of 1943 had cost the US government $42,000,000. When finished, the base was named Kindley Field for Captain Field E.

Kindley, a World War I flying ace.

The summer of 1941 was a tense time on St. David's, as houses were selected for demolition and compensation was haggled over. Awards usually amounted to about two-thirds the value claimed by those displaced. In the end, nearly 100 houses and 113 properties totalling more than 200 acres fell victim to the bulldozers in 1941, the ultimate sacrifice on the part of St. David's islanders towards the war effort. Much of the compensation was taken up by reconstruction of new houses. A few of the old houses were spared and left in their original state as part of an elaborate camouflage scheme for the base. New military buildings were mottled with cedar and palm coloured greens to blend into the foliage, so the white-roofed original cottages would appear to be sparsely strewn about a rural and untouched island.

Although they kept their property, the new base had an equally profound effect on people at the east end of St. David's. Many of those displaced crowded into the remaining half of the island, increasing the density of housing. Added to the relocation was the challenge of coming to terms with about 4,000 new neighbours. A lucra-

St. David's Lodge, once a tall narrow building with gables and chimneys, has now been surrounded by extensions and a verandah, subsequently itself enclosed.

tive rental market developed to cater to US military personnel who chose to live off-base.

The US base was of strategic importance in both World War II and the Cold War and made major contributions to Bermuda. The campaign against the German Atlantic U-boat fleet depended on the island's central location. During the Cuban Missile Crisis in 1962, Bermuda's base went on red alert as John F. Kennedy, the Russians and Fidel Castro brought the world to the edge of nuclear war. Throughout the 1960s the NASA station on Cooper's Island played a major role in space exploration. The new airport ushered in a postwar civilian tourist boom, and the base provided Bermuda's first television transmission. After the collapse of the Soviet Union, Kindley Field fell victim to the base closure movement as the US defence budget constricted. In 1995 the considerably enlarged tract acquired from

St. David's islanders more than a half-century earlier was returned to the Bermuda government.

The vernacular architecture of St. David's was more conservative and differed from that of the town buildings of St. George's, partly due to the island's isolation and rural character. Most old buildings were one room wide and they rarely exceeded 15 feet in width. Because the older style of using gable roofs persisted, hip roofs were relatively uncommon in the 18th century. While homes on St. David's possessed the same high tray ceilings as houses elsewhere, they were usually boarded rather than lathe and plastered, reflecting the fact that their builders were more often shipwrights than masons. Architraves over windows and doors were rarely found, and the windows themselves were generally set flush to the outside wall. E.A. McCallan in *Life on Old St. David's* remembered seeing remnants of tim-

ber frame buildings, with wall plates supported by studs stepped on sills and masonry infill in the spaces between the uprights. Many of the buildings he knew disappeared when the base came, but even now, scattered among the many 20th century houses, are a few old homesteads of considerable antiquity.

Surrounded by water and 100 acres of land, **St. David's Lodge** (now sometimes called the **Old Pilot Station**) was St. David's grandest estate in the 18th century. Then almost an island at the tip of the northeastern peninsula, the land was granted to Dr. George Forbes in 1758. By 1789 John Esten had purchased it from Forbes' heirs and erected the core of the house of today, then worth £333. The steeply pitched roof and two large chimneys flanking the gable ends of the northern portion of the building clearly date to the late 18th century.

Compared with the lofty elegance of Gibbs Hill, the St. David's light is a sturdy, utilitarian octagonal building characterised by its band of dark red paint. The keeper's house is a typical Bermudian plain two storey house while the adjacent outbuildings suggest a British military provenance and sport decorative pilasters and moulded parapets.

While she lived there, arrowroot was cultivated on the land surrounding the house. An 1867 division of her mother's estate lists "arrowroot mills" among her assets, and the tanks surrounding the dwelling would have aided the processing of the pulp.

The island was requisitioned from farmer Malcolm J.G. Hollis in 1922 as a potential site for a leper asylum. There were only eight cases of leprosy in Bermuda, four of them St. David's islanders, but the 600 residents of St. David's unanimously protested against using their island to quarter lepers and threatened to burn the house down if the project went ahead. In the face of this united opposition, the government moved the location of the leprosarium to Devonshire and the St. David's house was converted into quarters for Bermuda's pilots.

The flat roofed section, between the old core and a gable roof addition to the south, still has the platform from which the pilots kept a lookout for incoming vessels. The pilot station was moved in the early 1970s and the complex was annexed to St. David's Primary School to the south, built on the edge of landfill which created a sports field.

The most striking feature of the island is **St. David's Lighthouse** which, for more than 100 years, has warned approaching ships of Bermuda's treacherous reefs. It towers above Mount Hill where in earlier years Bermuda's first colonists lit bonfires to signal inbound vessels and alert the rest of the island that a new sail had appeared on the horizon. In the 1660s the house of planter William Allen stood where the lighthouse and keeper's house are today.

The lighthouse was the creation of Joseph Ming Hayward, who fought long and hard in the House of Assembly to realise his goal. Despite the construction of Gibbs Hill Lighthouse, vessels continued to be wrecked at the east end because intervening hills blocked the Southampton light for part of its arc. Between 1873 and 1878, 42 vessels struck the reefs and five were total wrecks. In response, Hayward lobbied for and personally oversaw the construction of the new lighthouse, from 1876 until its completion in 1879.

The parallel gable roof wing just to the south may also date to this period, but it has been raised and re-roofed. The roof has a shallow pitch and the eastern chimney has been nearly buried by the modification.

Like the Forbes House on Smith's Island, the Estens may have used St. David's Lodge as a summer retreat or as a safe haven from epidemics. In his 1803 will John Esten left the property to his two sons, John Esten, a doctor, and James Christie Esten. The brothers tried several times to sell the property. In 1805 John advertised in the *Bermuda Gazette,* boasting that the 100-acre tract offered ripe timber, two comfortable houses and was good "limestone land"

for quarrying. Fourteen years later, James Christie Esten was apparently living there when he offered to sell his commodious home, St. David's Lodge, which was "too well known to require a more particular description".

In 1837 Esten finally found a buyer in the widow and children of the late Samuel Trott of Verdmont in Smith's Parish. St. David's Lodge became the residence of Catherine P. Trott. Legend has it that she was engaged to marry a Trimingham sea captain. On the eve of her marriage she sighted his ship from the hill, but a hurricane drove it from the coast and it was lost with all hands. She died unwed at the age of 84 in St. David's Lodge in 1895.

The wooden Hureka House on Lighthouse Hill typifies an unusual form of building, probably introduced from the West Indies about the turn of the 20th century along with the large number of immigrants from the islands brought in to work on the Dockyard and other military projects. Because in Bermuda wooden houses were usually set on stone foundations rather than on the characteristic wooden stilts seen in the islands, they have adapted well to traditional Bermuda proportions.

The octagonal lighthouse differs from the one at Gibbs Hill in that it is made of Bermuda stone and, at 55 feet from base to lantern, is considerably shorter than its Southampton counterpart. Its fixed kerosene lamp was first lit on November 3, 1879, by Hayward's wife. In 1922 the original 3,000 candle power light was replaced by one ten times as bright, and at about the same time the unpainted exterior received the distinctive dark red band which identifies it today. In 1961 the kerosene light was replaced by an electric beam and four years later an automatic light was installed, eliminating the need for a keeper, a post that St. David's islanders had held for nearly a century.

On Lighthouse Hill, below the lighthouse, stands **Hureka House**, one of Bermuda's few wooden houses. The age of the timber sided building is uncertain, but the land on which it stands was acquired by Tom Fox, a free black man, in 1803. By 1826, Fox had acquired two adjoining lots totalling 35 acres, worth £700, and a house worth another £200. His assortment of gigs, sailboats and whaleboats attest to his maritime pursuits.

In his 1838 will Fox left his house and 15 acres on Mount Hill to his grandson Anthony Minors on the condition that he never marry Frances Burchall, the woman with whom he was living. His land to the north was inherited by Fox's other grandson, James Minors, who passed it on to his son, Jacob W. Minors, in the 1870s.

The core of the wooden house is said to have been built early in this century, and certainly a 1912 plan, a copy of an earlier plan, shows a wooden house owned by George T. Richardson on the site. Norwood and Jimmy Minors may have used the building as a club house in the 1920s. At that time it is said to have been called The Academy.

In 1950 Charles Paynter bought the house and considerably expanded it by adding a kitchen, bedroom and verandah. The additions have been so carefully made that it would be difficult to tell which is the original part of the house. It is at present owned by Charles Paynter's granddaughter, Lucinda O'Brien.

Nearby **St. Luke's AME Church** also started as a woden building. The church's first preacher, Reverend Austin Richardson, initially preached on the public dock under a canvas awning, but inclement weather pressed the new congregation to seek a more permanent and sheltered venue. In 1888 John Fox donated the land and materials to build a wooden mission house and chapel, and the shipwrights and carpenters in the congregation slowly erected the new hall over the course of the year. The building was officially opened on February

St. Luke's AME Church, perhaps in a conscious bid to outshine the austere Anglican Chapel of Ease, went in for the full complement of late Victorian embellishment, despite having to contend with a steep and awkward site.

6, 1889, and for the next half century St. David's Primary School met there on weekdays.

In 1924 the congregation made plans to build a stone church next door, a smaller version of a church which one parishioner had seen in Europe. The shipwrights, masons and craftsmen, led by their shipwright minister John DeShields, made substantial progress building the new place of worship before a terrible hurricane ravaged the island in October 1926. The storm cracked the walls, tore down the gable ends and damaged the bell tower. But the roof held firm, a testament to the skill of the workmen. The interior is framed with distinctive curves like the inverted hull of the ships they were used to building. Repairs and the remaining construction were finished in 1928, and St. Luke's has served the community since then. The older wooden mission house was torn down in 1965 to be replaced by a stone church hall. The fabric of St. Luke's Church demonstrates the ability of the island's shipwrights, while its

very existence testifies to the strong sense of community and commitment on the part of the congregation.

Cocoa Bay Cottage, once **Pride of India Cottage**, sits on the shore of Dolly's Bay by the spot long known to St. David's islanders as Cocoa Hole. An added lattice porch adorns the 18th century portion of the house. Originally probably only two rooms, the tiny cottage has a gable roof and large chimney, and was almost certainly built in the 1760s by David Sears. From Smith's Island, Sears obtained a half share grant in 1758 for the land on which the cottage stands. He died about 1780 and the land was occupied by Eliza Sears, probably his widow. In 1789, she was assessed £100 for a house that is almost certainly the core of the present cottage. She sold the property to Jonathan Fox in 1796 and it remained in the Fox family for the entire 19th century.

After the American Civil War, the house belonged to carpenter Charles Stiles Fox, who left it to his five children by Charlotte Rebecca Hayward.

By 1888, pilot Aubrey Copeland Fox had bought his siblings' shares and was living in the house, then named Pride of India Cottage. An increase in the parish tax assessment suggests that Aubrey Fox's heirs added the larger hip roof section to the north about 1920. The present owners, the Dunkley family, bought the cottage in 1959.

The style of the chimney at Cocoa Bay Cottage suggests an 18th century cottage, as does the position of the windows under the eaves. However the roof must have been replaced, perhaps at the time when the attractive 19th century latticed porch was added.

The old brick steps at Dolly's Bay House contrast with a much more modern porch which is nevertheless in a style appropriate to the 18th century house. The modern chimney is solid but graceful, admirably suited to the house.

The west end of Dolly's Bay marks the border between the public land and the private land allotted to Hamilton Parish landowners. **Dolly's Bay House** is on the north side of the road. Norwood placed a marshy area in the vicinity of the house, suggesting that planter Thomas Sparks who worked the land lived elsewhere. In the 1750s it was still unoccupied, owned by Richard Somersall of St. George's.

A plan drawn in 1767 shows that Richard Somersall sold "near four acres" to Captain Benjamin Cooper. It was he who erected the house which stands today. The oldest part of Dolly's Bay House is the northeast hip and gable roof section—the massive rectangular chimney is typical of the 18th century. A similar but smaller chimney abuts the western end of the house, but it is actually a 20th century addition as shown by a 1923 photograph taken by architectural historian

John S. Humphreys. At that time the chimney was not there. To the northwest of the house is a very old chimney, now attached to a modern garage. This may once have been part of a kitchen built by Cooper.

In his 1786 will, Benjamin Cooper gave his dwelling house and land to his two children, John and Elizabeth. John subsequently moved to Warwick Parish and then to the Turks Islands, leaving his sister in sole possession of Dolly's Bay House. She married Benjamin Wright Hayward in 1810, and the house passed into the Hayward family for four generations. The Haywards were responsible for building the southeastern wing of the house, as well as the detached two storey hip roofed building to the north.

While joiner Thomas Seon Hayward was living there in 1868, an unusually bulky wooden raft was found floating in the open sea just off Bermuda and towed into St. George's Harbour. It was eventually beached on the western end of Dolly's Bay, where it still decays today. In 1872 a former US Navy captain identified the strange raft as a primitive minesweeping device intended for clearing the Confederate port of Charleston, South Carolina, in 1863. The captain had been towing the raft thither when it became detached in a storm, and for five years it drifted in the Atlantic before arriv-

This chimney, now attached to the side of a garage, seems to have been that of a separate kitchen, possibly originally with a shingled or thatched roof as it is separated from the roof by a masonry divide. Its simplicity also suggests a very early date. The kitchen would have been excavated from the hillside and the hearth actually cut out of the stone.

This immensely sturdy chimney at Dolly's Bay House betrays the rough nature of the stone with which it was built. The two storey cottage seems to be early 19th century.

Plain Victorian austerity, relieved only by the decorative gables and the crenellations on the tower, give the St. David's Chapel of Ease its distinction. Lancet windows and simple buttresses relieve the length of the building and a simple porch protects worshippers at the door.

rounded by an extensive graveyard. The chancel was built in late 1891, while the imposing tower is a recent addition, constructed in 1957. After the Mission House was demolished for base construction, a curate's house was acquired near the Chapel of Ease. At the same time a family graveyard near Carter House was relocated to the cemetery surrounding the chapel.

Narrows **House,** to the north of the Chapel of Ease and near the narrow channel between St. David's and Smith's Island, has had a house on the site since at least 1710, but has had many later additions. The land on which the house stands was farmed by Mary Mountaine (formerly Stowe) in the 1660s. Norwood's 1663 survey states that she held 25 acres in St. David's, linked with five Hamilton Parish shares. In 1662 she was presented to the annual assize and accused of being "a profane and very evill tonged woman" for calling Governor William Sayle a rogue and his wife a whore.

In 1710 her son, Thomas Stowe, sold a house and land to John Lightbourne for £51. This was probably the hall-and-parlour core of Narrows House, flanked at each gable end with a substantial chimney.

From John Lightbourne's initial purchase until Robert Hayward Lightbourne's heirs sold the property in 1955, Narrows House seems to have been home to at least eight consecutive generations of Lightbournes and their Skinner cousins. A 1795 advertisement for the land of Captain James Lightbourne may have referred to this property. It mentions a dwelling

ing in Bermuda. Dolly's Bay House now belongs to William Frith, whose father acquired it from the heirs of Thomas Seon Hayward in 1947.

The Chapel of Ease is St. David's oldest surviving place of worship. It was built in 1848 to replace Mission House, about a mile to the west. Throughout the 17th and 18th centuries, St. David's islanders had to cross St. George's Harbour every Sunday to attend services. In 1829 Archdeacon Spencer purchased Isaac Cox's early 19th century house, Mount Airy, and converted it into a mission church and school to serve St. David's. Author Suzette Lloyd taught there

briefly in 1830 and noted that there were "separate school rooms for whites and negroes" and a chapel and dwelling house for a catechist. Mission House, however, could not meet the increasing demands of the community, so the Chapel of Ease was built.

The chapel, built to seat 150, is situated on a hill, with a commanding view of the harbour. The land was acquired from the estate of Daniel Edward Lightbourn who owned the Narrows property to the north, and the building was consecrated by Bishop Feild on April 11, 1849, amidst much fanfare. The gable-ended church has an imported slate roof and is sur-

The plain but graceful chimney of Narrows House is flanked by an array of roofs. The original roof has been given a porch extension on the left. Beyond the chimney appears the gable of an addition of about 1900.

The Villa is a classic 18th century hillside house, hip roofed and stretching between substantial but refined chimneys which have the appearance of 19th century alteration or even construction. There is a separate kitchen building and buttery to the right. Heavy pilasters and buttresses have been added to stave off roof spread. The fenestration has undergone a certain amount of alteration and some of the windows have been replaced with metal.

house, store, buttery, cistern and kitchen on five acres, but failed to find a buyer, for it was advertised again in 1798 with eight acres. Daniel Edward Lightbourn was undoubtedly living there in the 1840s and E.A. McCallan mentioned that Martha Lightbourne taught sewing classes in St. George's about the 1880s and was one of the first women to work outside St. David's Island.

The house has been much added to, but the old chimneys clearly date from the 18th century and the detached buttery to the east of the main house, perhaps that mentioned in the 1795 advertisement, adjoins the old fashioned water catchment. Its placement, away from the house, emphasises the historical incorrectness of so many of today's buttery-type roofs gratuitously added to modern structures.

The **Villa**, once called **The Willows**, is the quintessential St. David's house, with tangible links to

The Villa comes close to being the 18th century Bermuda house which has it all. Here is the barrel vaulted tank cheek by jowl with the elegant chimney and the strong pilaster style buttresses with watershed capitals.

the islanders' many activities. In the 1660s the "evill tonged" Mary Mountaine lived in an earlier house on the site. Her son, Thomas Stowe, in

1691 gave a dwelling house to his youngest daughter Elizabeth, the wife of Christopher Smith. The Smiths in 1711 shared their various properties between their children, Samuel and Christopher Smith and Fridisweed Brownlow. It was probably Brownlow who built the rectangular core of The Villa soon after. She willed her house to her grandchildren, Benjamin and Fridisweed Brownlow, in 1776, but specified that if they died, her nephews Thomas and John Smith were to inherit the property. By 1789 Captain John Smith was living in the house, then worth £100 and standing on five acres of land. The next known owner is William, the Comptroller of Customs, who was living there with his five slaves in 1800.

William Smith was extremely well-to-do and either considerably expanded or replaced the earlier house. By the time he sold it to brothers Samuel Apoin and William Fox Hayward in 1819, it was worth £900. The

The once separate kitchen of The Villa has the usual solid chimney and asymmetrical shape to accommodate its oven. The low pitch of the roof suggests a later alteration, but it is possible that the entire kitchen building may be 19th century.

Hamilton Hayward caught about 25 turtles a year.

In the late 19th century, arrowroot was processed at The Villa, and it would have been a common sight to see trays of the ground pulp spread about the yard drying in the sun. The adjoining tanks, one of them domed, provided the water for the processing, while the cellar beneath the eastern section of the house was used to store the finished product. The house is still owned by the Hayward family, once again divided between two branches, and has survived with little alteration from the days when William Smith lived there.

Ambleside, on Emily's Bay Lane, dates back to at least 1789. In that year, Samuel Roberts was assessed £66 for a house and five acres of land, about the right value for this small, hip roof cottage built into the side of the hill. It is an exceptionally good and rare example of its type, lovingly cared for and one of the few which has not been extended. Nearby Roberts' Hill was part of the tract and was named for Samuel Roberts. Before he died in 1814 he left all his property to his wife, Rebecca, who sold it to Phillis Fox, perhaps her former slave. In her 1866 will, Fox left her "small dwelling house" and three and a half acres to Benjamin Minors "a youth now residing with me", but reserved lifetime use of the cellar under the house for Jane Dickinson. Fox died in 1872 at the age of 97.

Hayward brothers shared the house between them. Samuel and his descendants occupied the eastern half while William lived in the western. After several generations of living separately but side by side, one side of the family purchased the other's half and restored the house to a single unit.

The Haywards of The Villa included boatbuilders, fishermen, sailmakers, and schoolteachers. E.A. McCallan states that Joseph William Hayward's two daughters (granddaughters of Samuel Apoin Hayward) taught school in the eastern half of The Villa in the 1880s. The fishpond by the shore kept alive countless harvests from the reefs, while fishing and turtling nets were stored in the brick floored cellar, formerly used as a kitchen. As late as the 1950s Herbert

Not to be outdone by the impressive gateposts to be found across the harbour in St. George's, the walled garden at The Villa on the water side of the house has its own substantial, if simple pair.

Ambleside is one of the best surviving examples of the resolutely simple mid 18th century cottage. Without symmetry or adornment, even its chimney is unrelieved by stepping. Its windows are placed directly under the wall plate in the early style. The cottage nevertheless has an elegant balance of masses and fenestration, retained here by the use of top hung blinds, typical of our 18th century architecture.

Carter House on St. David's has been claimed as Bermuda's oldest house, but it probably dates from the early 18th century. Built in classic hillside style with a serviceable basement and two rooms on the living floor, it is of rural simplicity. The front steps are idiosyncratic, but provide sitting niches at the top. Windows are directly under the wooden wall plate. The section to the right is a later addition.

Benjamin Minors inherited the house and lived there until he sold it to blacksmith John Brownell Carris in 1890. Carris was a lighthouse keeper for a spell and lived at Stentaway to the west. After he was displaced from Longfield Farm in 1941, Howard E.D. Smith purchased Ambleside and Point House, a larger but now much altered house to the northwest.

One of the few west end houses spared when the US base was built, **Carter House** was named fairly recently for Christopher Carter, arguably the first Bermudian. Carter was among the *Sea Venture* castaways and remained on the island when the rest left for Virginia. When Sir George Somers returned in 1610, Carter again declined to leave the island. Between 1610 and the arrival of the first permanent settlers in 1612, he and two other men carved out a farm on

Smith's Island where they planted corn and tobacco. The three found an enormous lump of ambergris, a sperm whale by-product which was much sought after as a perfume fixative. They failed to smuggle it aboard the *Plough* because Carter told Governor Moore about it, and thus lost a fortune. Seven years later the Company gave Carter tenure of Cooper's Island in recognition of his valuable find. In 1623 Carter was aboard the magazine ship *Seaflower* in Castle Harbour when a careless tobacco smoker ignited the ship's gunpowder and the vessel exploded, cutting short his adventurous life.

The connection between Christopher Carter and the house which bears his name is tenuous at best. Tradition has it that the house was built by Carter's descendants. Although Carter did have several children, they either stayed on Cooper's

Island or had moved to Paget Parish by the mid 1620s. In 1663 the land on which the house now stands was owned with Hamilton Tribe shares 13, 14 and 15 and was farmed by Elizabeth Nailor. It should be remembered that in 1688, there were only 29 stone houses in the whole colony, and the likelihood that Carter House was one of them is slim.

Nevertheless, Carter House has all of the elements associated with late 17th and early 18th century vernacular structures. Originally it was a hall-and-parlour house with a cellar below, carved into the side of a hill. The large chimney on the north side was engulfed when a room was added, perhaps in the late 18th century, but the imposing southern one survives. The narrow welcoming arms steps are certainly original and are strikingly steep. They are among the few that retain the bench spaces on either side of the

The sturdy chimney at Carter House faces southwest as a bastion against storms and is girded by a good example of stone guttering.

When the US government bought the land, the "old fashioned stone house" was practically a ruin.

In this case the US takeover provides a bittersweet story. Smith was a farmer and cultivated lilies at Longfield Farm. About 1920, was created a hybrid early blooming lily which he named *Lilium longiflorum Howardii*. When he began to export in the late 1930s his lilies were much in demand, and his sales jumped from £120 in 1936 to £1,110 just three years later. The construction of the airfield demanded that he sacrifice the fields he had so painstakingly manured and cultivated for decades, and he was awarded less than half the value he claimed the land was worth. The 64-year-old Smith felt he was too old to begin from scratch with new fields, so the sale effectively forced the farmer to retire. He moved to Point House and continued to grow lilies on a more modest scale until his death in 1962.

On the other hand, Carter House almost certainly would have perished through neglect, so we have the US base to thank for its continued survival. Soon after the acquisition, army engineers moved those interred in the small family graveyard which adjoined Carter House to the Chapel of Ease. Once a part of the base lands, the old stone house was repaired and used as a beauty salon. In 1976 it was restored and converted into a small museum devoted to Bermudian and US military history. The fate of Carter House, like that of the rest of the former base, is currently undecided.

Longbird House (now demolished) bridged the distance between the ancient traditions of St. David's and the modern character of Tucker's Town. Built on Longbird Island, it was geographically situated between the two locales. In the 1650s the 62-acre island was used as a voluntary retirement home for Somers Island Company slaves, who, according to a dispatch from the Company to Governor fforster, "through age are growne past labour". Later it was settled by two weavers, and in the 18th and 19th centuries it was home to the Burch, Trott, Hayward, Musson and McCallan families. The Causeway, finished in 1872, used Longbird Island as a stepping

door, where visitors might wait to be received. Buttresses added to the exterior of the front help support the gracefully-sagging roof. Two small tanks are situated at the back, along with a small shed roof extension.

Carter House was probably built by John and Martha Hayward, who owned the land on which Carter House stands, in the 1720s. Martha, reputed to be a Carter descendant, died in 1791 at the incredible age of 114. In 1800 the heirs of Captain Joseph Hayward, Martha's grandson or great-grandson, offered to sell a "house below Capt. Sawyers, with three rooms and two capital cellars, with a kitchen and terras cistern", a description which fits Carter House.

A plan drawn in 1809 reveals that the house went unsold, and in 1819 Joseph Hayward Jr. of Jamaica mortgaged it to John James Tucker, who foreclosed upon it when Hayward

failed to pay his debt. John Tucker apparently transferred the property to his brother, Searcher of Customs Benjamin Tucker, who left it in his 1822 will to his daughter Sophia. The property was presumably rented by Territt and Sophia Tucker for much of the 19th century. Their son Henry C. Tucker had emigrated to Fiji by the time he sold it in 1894. Reeve and Howard Smith purchased the 19-acre tract in 1913 with Howard's brother-in-law, E.A. McCallan, to farm Easter lilies. Reeve Smith and McCallan eventually left the enterprise entirely to Howard.

By 1941 Carter House had fallen on hard times. Howard Smith abandoned the old cottage and built a fine nine-room house to the northwest in 1924, which he named Longfield. Carter House became a barn, to which Smith added a stone stable and wooden poultry and cattle sheds.

Longbird House, the residence of the commanding officers on the former United States Naval Base, was demolished in 1997 to conform to the international requirements for civil airports. It was an interesting example of mid 20th century Bermudian vernacular architecture.

stone for reaching St. George's.

In 1939 the eastern half of the island was purchased by William Marcus Greve, a millionaire who had been extensively involved with building the Empire State Building. The following summer he began constructing a house surrounded by a model dairy farm and citrus orchard. The house was designed by architect Robertson (Happy) Ward to rival Vincent Astor's nearby house to the north. Greve dug a million gallon tank to support his farming and built a massive greenhouse on the tank's roof. The work was still in progress when the property was requisitioned to build the US base in 1941. Greve's lawyers managed to extract nearly $300,000 from the arbitration commission.

Military personnel finished the house and erected Kindley Field's first air traffic control tower on its roof. The extensive stable complex was converted into quarters for bachelor officers called the Hotel de Gink. After 1944 the millionaire's house housed VIPs in transit, including General Eisenhower on his return trip from Europe, and was the home of the Base

Commander. Longbird House was demolished in April, 1997, to conform with international civil airport regulations which require a minimum distance between runways and residences.

Nowhere in Bermuda has experienced as many extremes in change as Tucker's Town. Following the "if you build it, they will come" line of logic, Daniel Tucker laid out a grid of streets and built a small chapel in his new town, only to utterly fail to attract settlers. Unlike St. David's, the Tucker's Town lands at least had a new, large road. Built between 1620 and 1623, a 12-foot wide road ran from Hamilton Tribe to Castle Point for quick travel to Castle Island in the event of an invasion. After the planned town failed, the land was allotted to the officers of the forts. Many commanders lived with their families on shore and travelled to work by boat. Likewise, off-duty Castle Island soldiers preferred Tucker's Town to their sentry post at the fort.

During the 18th century a small community eked out a living at Tuck-

er's Town. A small whaling station at Tucker's Town Bay was built to process whales harpooned off the South Shore. By mid century there were about 35 families living on the 350 acres of public land. In 1758 the shares were regranted by Governor Popple to a handful of rich landowners, a foreshadow of things to come. Unlike St. David's, none of these merchants actually chose to live on the land they had bought, so the old public tenants just acquired new landlords. There was a short lived boom in the late 1780s when the Bermuda government, in an effort to promote agricultural diversity, offered bounties for growing cotton. By 1790 one nine-acre tract at Tucker's Town had between 2,000 and 3,000 cotton trees, and another 40-acre expanse had more than 7,000. The cotton proved to be the short fibre variety which English textile merchants did not want.

The quality of land in Tucker's Town deteriorated steadily, especially those shares on the peninsula ending at Castle Point. When a hurricane approached Bermuda in 1856, massive waves actually broke over the finger

Lookout Cottage was the school house serving the residents of Tucker's Town before the Mid Ocean Club was built. It has the simple pilasters and cornice moulding of its period.

of land and dumped up to 20 feet of sand on the few fields and pastures in the area. The vicinity of Tucker's Town was also prone to waterspouts and tornadoes which wrecked many homes and cut paths of destruction across the land. In the early 20th century Tucker's Town was one of the most desperately poor and neglected locales in Bermuda.

About 1800 Benjamin Dickinson Harvey had assembled 12 lots totalling nearly 200 acres in the Tucker's Town area, between Tucker's Town Bay and Trott's Pond to the west. Harvey, a lawyer who lived nearby in Hamilton Parish, seems not to have built on the property. In 1862 his heirs sold 11 of the lots (103 or more acres) to James Talbot, then aged about 42. Talbot, a black man and son of Baker Talbot, also of Tucker's Town, is variously described in the records as fisherman, labourer, farmer and planter. He and his wife brought up a large family in the area. It was James Talbot who in 1882 sold for a nominal amount the

land for a school to serve the area. This school survives as **Lookout Cottage** on South Road, just before the entrance to the Mid Ocean Club. The eight trustees had the aim of erecting a building "suitable for a schoolroom and for the holding of meetings for the encouragement of temperance".

In 1885 James Talbot was assessed in the church records for a new house and it is probable that this is the original wing of **Earnscliffe.** Two wings to the south were soon added, and a large new domed tank built when the original small tank was enclosed by the wings. Fronting on South Road, near the junction with Paynter's Road, Earnscliffe is still remembered as Talbot's Store, run by one of the sons of James Talbot in the early years of this century. It had the first telephone in the area. The Bermuda Development Company later used it for offices, and when the wooden verandah, which at that time ran along the road, collapsed they proposed to de-

molish the whole house. In the 1970s Dr. William (Peter) Outerbridge (now of Clifton Vale in St. George's) persuaded them to allow him to restore the building, and it was he who created the present handsome residence. He moved the access to the eastern side of the house, stopped up the downstairs old shop doors, built a chimney on that side and enclosed part of the eastern verandah.

Tucker's Town changed dramatically in the 1920s. In response to the rise of tourism, led by an influx of American visitors seeking an escape from the urban jungles of the east coast, a group of Bermudians formed the Bermuda Development Company to create an exclusive and prestigious enclave in this neglected backwater of Bermuda. In a move similar to the base lands takeover, the corporation was empowered to force those living in Tucker's Town to sell their land. James Talbot's son, Benjamin Darrell (B.D.) Talbot, still owning 74 acres of his father's 103, and reputed to have

Earnscliffe on the Old Military Road in Tucker's Town is a classic example of mid 19th century architecture that retains a formal Georgian symmetry at a time when the Victorian taste was already in evidence. The verandah has been infilled at each end.

been butler in his younger days to Benjamin Dickinson Harvey's son Seth, was forced to sell well below his asking price. Many of the displaced resettled in the Devil's Hole area. After the golf course had been laid out and the Mid Ocean Club established, the wealthy visitors the corporation hoped to attract began to purchase house lots and improve the area. The wealth and innovations used in constructing Tucker's Town's early houses were considerable, and today the area has some of the most expensive and eclectic buildings in Bermuda.

At the outset, there was some urgency on the part of the Bermuda Development Company. The first sales of building lots included stipulations requiring houses to be put up within a specified time, a clause reminiscent of the early 18th century land grants in the Town of St. George. The aim of the company and of the Furness Bermuda Line, who then had a major interest in the development, was to provide a unique destination for the very richest of Americans.

The ships of the Furness Line would bring these wealthy visitors to the island for long stays at the Mid Ocean Club, the Castle Harbour Hotel, or in their private homes, all in close proximity to two magnificent new golf courses, tennis courts, five

gorgeous private beaches and almost unlimited protected waters for sailing and water-skiing, not to mention exotic fishponds in the rock fissures surrounding the local bays. There was even a plan to have a splendid tender

Two 19th century chimneys, one an oven chimney, set off the long, barrel vaulted tank at Earnscliffe. The decorative inset plates are not original.

to ferry the guests directly from Murray's Anchorage to the large new dock at the Castle Harbour Hotel, thus sparing them the long carriage drive in possibly inclement weather from the ship's final berth in Hamilton.

The period was one of transition, but for the most part this infusion of very wealthy Americans came to Bermuda to escape a more hurried, harried life. Thus they sought the island's small scale and simpler way of life as a balance to their more lavish life at

home; most of them built accordingly. One of the first, the almost reclusive and old fashioned Childs Frick, whose sister still lived in what we now know as the Frick Museum in New York City, built his small, plain house out of sight at the end of Castle Point, keeping even his guests at a safe distance in a small guest cottage.

Visitors usually stayed at least a month and those who owned or

The ornamentation on the gatepost at Earnscliffe betrays how late in the century the house must have been built.

The Jungle is an elegant Bermudian interpretation of the Beaux Arts style Newport Cottage in miniature. Its recently added verandah, while in keeping with the architecture, severely impinges on the original graceful balance of proportion achieved by Hutchings.

rented houses would often stay the entire summer. The spring and summer season had by then supplanted the old winter season of the pre-war days.

Other Americans who built in Tucker's Town in the early days were Ford Johnson and Morgan O'Brien. Ford Johnson was a colourful character who loved a party and gave many. Tradition has it that he gave the internationally famous Talbot Brothers their start when he found them as teenagers playing their homemade instruments at Harris' Bay. The irrepressible Johnson is said to have immediately hired them to follow him around the golf course and thus to provide entertainment for himself and his golfing cronies during their games. Certainly for years afterwards the Talbots always played at Mr. Johnson's lavish parties and wrote their song, "Good Morning Mr. Johnson" for him. His house, **The Jungle**, was de-

The entrance to The Jungle demonstrates the Beaux Arts style of the period as well as the reason for the house's name. The brick paving is new.

signed and built by N. T. Hutchings and is a handsome Bermudianised version of a small Newport "cottage", with a Beaux Arts balance in its proportions. It is sited with dignity above Cable Bay and unlike many other prewar Tucker's Town houses, it has not been buried under massive subsequent enlargements, but survives almost exactly as it was built. Ford

Johnson's co-owner, Morgan O'Brien, predeceased him and his share passed to the Johnsons. One of the Johnson granddaughters married locally, but the house has changed hands twice.

Round House, recently demolished, was not built by people living in the fast lane. Abby Rockefeller, however, was safely in the category of the super rich. She and her then husband David Milton bought the land in 1936 and immediately built their house and guest house on what must be one of Bermuda's most beautiful locations, overhanging a small private bay, accessible only to small boats of the shallowest of draught.

The house itself was perfectly round. One entered via a circular courtyard from which the reception rooms and a then small verandah looked out over the lagoon. The upper floor was reached from an open double staircase rising from the circular courtyard. The house was quite small and guests were accommodated

The shape demands the name of this unusual building. The Round House was perfectly circular. The verandah was added about 1960.

In this interesting juxtaposition of curved roofs, the one in foreground covered the open walkway around the circular entrance courtyard of Round House, while the rising shed roof beyond covered the stairway to the upper level and the further roof the main building.

in a separate guest house, itself forming part of a circle.

Mrs. Milton married twice more and did not use her house much after World War II. It was sold in 1954 to

Floyd and Marjorie Jefferson. Mrs. Jefferson was celebrated for her large picture hats and frequent lavish dinner dances. They spent every summer in the house for almost 20 years, gaining a wide circle of Bermuda friends. They considerably enlarged and built a roof over the verandah to have room for their entertaining. After Mr. Jefferson had a stroke at the age of 88 in the late 1960s, they added a wing on the southwest side of the house to spare him the stairs. It is built in a reverse curve to the main house to share the view over the lagoon and on to Castle Island. After her husband's death at the age of 96, Mrs. Jefferson sold the house, but continued to spend her summers in the island she loved for many more years before she died at the age of 100. Of the subsequent owners, the first, a dealer in gems, introduced an exotic garden of ancient African cycads while the second enclosed the steps in the courtyard in cedar and glass.

Edna Whitman, one of first women to attend Cambridge University, built **But 'n' Ben** in 1951. By Tucker's

Town standards it was small, but nevertheless exquisite. It was designed by Wil Onions and is a fine example of his genius for marrying modern living requirements with the spirit, proportion and beauty of 18th century Bermudian architecture.

Mrs. Whitman herself found it necessary eventually to enlarge the house. This was done with some care and respect for the beauty of the original. Recently a subsequent owner has made very substantial changes, very greatly expanding the house so that it is now typical of the Tucker's Town

Looking as if it had settled into its site over a period of centuries, But 'n' Ben was designed by Wil Onions in 1951. This is the original cottage which is softened with buttresses, windows directly under the wall plate, top hung blinds and a St. Georgian low set of welcoming arms steps.

Buttonwood is a small Wil Onions masterpiece. A chimney to chimney, gable to gable, two room cottage with windows set under the wooden wall plate, with only the crispness of its construction to betray its lack of age. The sideways door stoop is a St. Georgian characteristic that copes with its steep hillside siting.

scale. Fortunately this has been undertaken in a style as close to that of Wil Onions as a mortal architect can achieve with remarkably satisfactory results. And the original small house remains, completely undisturbed and close enough to the road to obscure almost all the later additions.

Round House's nearest neighbour, **Buttonwood**, is the antithesis of the usual Tucker's Town house. It was designed by Wil Onions in 1955 for Sir Eldon Trimingham and finished in 1966. It is a recreation of an early 18th century chimney to chimney, gable to gable, two room cottage with a tiny

kitchen and bathroom added to the less visible side. In its perfect simplicity and proportion, the house is undoubtedly a Wil Onions gem.

It was built for Sir Eldon to provide his son Andrew with a place to live, but also to avail himself of his son's car to chauffeur him to and from Ham-

The absolute simplicity and fine proportions of the verandah overlooking the beach at Vertigo accounts for its success as a modern interpretation of the vernacular style. Note the modern styling, but traditional proportions of the chimney and the balance of the single window in the extensive wall space of the gable.

houses which preceded them. Other Tucker's Town houses push the limit to which Bermudian building materials can be taken to create new original buildings that aim to impress.

St. George's Parish encompasses the full range of building types and periods to be found in Bermuda in microcosm. Domestic, commercial, public, ecclesiastical and military structures cluster together in the old capital or dot the landscape beyond the town boundaries. St. David's Island and Tucker's Town offer two distinctly different collections of buildings that contrast with those of St. George's Island in form and evolution. From once-thatched 17th century cottages like the Old Rectory to modern twists on older themes seen in houses like Vertigo, and from impressive mansions built by Astors and Rockefellers to humble cottages built by freed slaves, St. George's has it all.

We hope that this book has been a sufficient guide through the ages of Bermudian architecture and has introduced the reader to the people and events which shaped the town, parish and its buildings. One would be hard-pressed to find a richer and more varied architectural heritage elsewhere in Great Britain's present or former colonies.

ilton every day. That way his own car was available to his wife during day.

The cottage was recently meticulously restored by Sir Eldon's grandson Christopher Trimingham. The exterior remains unaltered.

Vertigo, currently owned by Ross Perot, is quite a different style of house. In 1975 Peter Brant commissioned the architectural firm Venturi, Rauch and Brown to design a modern house inspired by, but not limited by, the Bermudian vernacular style. It was built on land previously owned by Stavros Niarchos. The result was both interesting and successful. A long house of light, bright feel, it translates vernacular idiom into crisp, balanced geometric elements. Perhaps the most successful of these is the deeply incised interpretation of quoins, creating the suggestion of the positive from a shaded negative.

Mr. Perot bought the property in 1985 and added the rather heavy, but nevertheless much photographed, double Flemish gables topping the entrance.

The irony of Tucker's Town is that this once poor neglected corner

of Bermuda has now become one of its most exclusive and sought after enclaves. The few old vernacular stone cottages that survived into the 20th century have been replaced by modern copies inspired by the very

The much photographed sequence of Flemish gables at Vertigo are an addition to the original Robert Venturi house.

One of Venturi's most imaginative interpretations of the Bermuda vernacular style is this simple, incised suggestion of quoins at the corners of Vertigo.

Appendix I

A Note on Research

The approach to this project differs from that taken towards Devonshire, the first book in the Bermuda National Trust Architectural Heritage series. That study traced individually 52 buildings selected for their outstanding architectural integrity. The Town and Parish of St. George warranted a different strategy because of its urban nature. From the earliest years, the area was densely settled, with many families living side by side in houses on small town lots. At the outset, tracing the more than 120 individual properties meriting inclusion in this book promised to be a demanding task which might potentially get derailed at any point in the search through the centuries due to missing deeds and gaps in the historical record. To create a more complete picture, I chose instead to pursue a more comprehensive approach towards reconstructing the physical evolution of St. George's. With the help of a skilled and enthusiastic team of volunteer researchers, the Bermuda National Trust initiated a full-scale "record stripping" project to document <u>every</u> property in the town and parish, not just those selected for their high level of preservation. Relevant information from all the available deeds, wills, newspapers, maps, photographs, sketches, mortgages and other records from the late 17th century through the end of World War II was extracted and collated. The information gathered from the Public Records Office in London, the Bermuda Archives and Registry General was supplemented by documents generously supplied by a number of St. George's property owners.

What has emerged from this monumental database of more than 6,000 records is a "deed chain" for virtually the entire town and parish. Sorting the records was akin to putting together an enormous three-dimensional puzzle whose pieces fit spatially into 26 blocks within the town and seven larger neighbourhoods elsewhere in the parish, and temporally into the four centuries of the parish's history. We now know who owned or lived in virtually every house in St. George's after 1700. Further research has allowed us learn something of the lives of many of the town's residents, recovering their histories from the oblivion of the past. This vast undertaking has made this book comprehensive, if nothing else, and I hope it may increase appreciation of the old capital as the Town of St. George approaches its 400th anniversary. There is perhaps no community of British origin in the Western Hemisphere whose history is as well documented as this ancient location.

Following the precedent set by the Devonshire book, we initially intended to include all of the deed chain information as a lengthy appendix. It was not long, however, before the volume of raw research data became overwhelming. The 400 or so deed chains compiled for houses in St. George's, St. David's and Tucker's Town built before 1898 exceeded 220 closely typed pages—far too lengthy to include as a comparison volume. Appendix II summarises the dates determined for properties within the 1708 town limits. The raw research that informed this book is available to anyone interested in individual properties, especially those not addressed explicitly in the book; copies are on deposit at Waterville, the Bermuda National Trust headquarters.

Despite the vast body of information we now have relating to the buildings of St. George's, the story is by no means complete. Indeed, the collective deed chain represents little more than a skeleton which can be fleshed out through further research into the lives of the town's many inhabitants. I sincerely hope that future scholarship will correct where I have erred, shed light on those I have omitted, and more perfectly reveal the history of St. George's as new documents become available.

Michael Jarvis
Williamsburg, Virginia

Appendix II

Names and Dates of Buildings
in the Central Area of St. George's

All buildings on this list can be found on the front side of the foldout map.

Buildings marked (*) are referred to in the chapter text. Buildings marked (**) are those chosen for their continuing architectural merit to be discussed in the chapter text and to be illustrated by modern photographs or old drawings or paintings. Consult the index to find this information.

Where a date range is listed, the building is known to have been built within these years; where a "circa" date is given, construction occurred within a year or two of the year given. The year that is stated represents the earliest date of the present building on the site. In most cases this is based on documentary evidence, but in a few cases we have relied on physical evidence. Later additions or renovations may have changed the appearance of earlier structures, in some cases substantially. Multiple dates reflect a series of building episodes.

Names and Dates of Buildings in the Central Area of St. George's

Address	Building Name	Construction Date	Owner or occupant in 1997
1 Aunt Peggy's Lane	** Harbour View	1801-1808	Delaey Robinson
2 Aunt Peggy's Lane		18C/pre-1854	Lucille B. Foggo
4 Aunt Peggy's Lane	Aunt Peggy's House	pre-1821/post-1876	Whitehead/John E. Kelly
5 Aunt Peggy's Lane	James Darrell House	pre-1796, gutted 1992	Hermit's Court
3 Barrack Hill	* Kate's Cottage/ Keystone Cottage	pre-1820/1935 (possibly totally rebuilt)	Paul King
2 Blockade Alley	* Chandler's Cottage	1726-1729	Thomas Wadson
1 Bridge Street	** Bridge House	1707/E19C	BNT/Bridge House Gallery
2 Bridge Street		1854-1876	Watermelons
3 Bridge Street		1845	Sports A Wear
5 Bridge Street	* Block House	pre-1791/1854-76	Bda. Electric Light Co.
7 Bridge Street	** Old Market House	1832-1834	Public Restrooms/Corp. St. George's
1 Broad Alley	** Old Rectory	1699 or earlier	Bermuda National Trust
4 Broad Alley	** Broad Alley Cottages	1700?/pre-1821	Ronald Smith
3 Chapel Lane	Chapel Cottage	c. 1815	Lois Perinchief
4 Chapel Lane	Ivy Cottage	1854-1876	Juan A.G. Smith
1 Church Lane	Simla	c. 1864 (rebuilt)	Derek S. Weller
Church Lane	** Hearse House	1854-1876	Anglican Church
1 Duke of Clarence Street	Carter House (northwest part)	pre-1854	Gregory Smith
2 Clarence Street	Windsor Cottage	pre-1835	O. Dickinson
3 Clarence Street	Our Lady Star of the Sea Rectory (west part)	pre-1784	Roman Catholic Church
4 Clarence Street	Ann's Cottage	pre-1835(pre-1808?)	I.E. Steed
5 Clarence Street	Our Lady Star of the Sea Catholic Church	1943-1966	Roman Catholic Church
6 Clarence Street	Clarence Cottage	pre-1709/20C	Madelyn L. Fox
7 Clarence Street	Bedford Cottage	1764--1790	Ralph Jennings
8 Clarence Street		1815-1824	Marion Bascome
10 Clarence Street	** Whitehall Cottage	c. 1875	Leonard Furbert
11 Clarence Street	Mitchell House Cottage	1876-1898	Historical Society
12 Clarence Street	** Whitehall	1815	Erskine Simmons
13 Clarence Street		1880-1893	Kiki's Hair Cutting Salon
15 Clarence Street		pre-1819	Phyllis Steede
2 Featherbed Alley	(much changed)	pre-1784	H. Outerbridge
3 Featherbed Alley	** Mitchell House	c. 1731	Historical Society
3 Government Hill Rd.	** Unfinished Church	1874	Leased to Bda. National Trust
3 Government Hill Rd.	** Government House	1721 ? (little old left)	Rectory, Anglican Church

Names and Dates of Buildings in the Central Area of St. George's (continued)

Address	Building Name	Construction Date	Owner or occupant in 1997
1 Governor's Alley		pre-1854	Henry R. Dowling
2 Governor's Alley	Roslyn	1854-1872	Wesley Trott
3 Governor's Alley	Boyd's Cottage	1854-1879	Deborah Williams
4 Governor's Alley		1898-1943	Wesley Trott
6 Governor's Alley	** St. Paul's Church	c. 1879	Salvation Army
10 Governor's Alley	** Fanny Fox's Cottage	c. 1707	Bermuda National Trust
1 Duke of Kent Street	** Toddings House/Snow Plant Inn	1868	Janet Outerbridge
4 Kent Street	** Kent Lodge	1881	Irene Coram
5 Kent Street	** Davis Cottage	1713-1717/19C	Francis family
6 Kent Street	* Greig Hall	pre-1782/1854-1876	Janet Outerbridge
7 Kent Street	* Longford House Ruin	1709-1713	Irene Coram
8 Kent Street	Rosebank	1865	Herbert Siggins
9 Kent Street	Formerly St. George's Welfare Society	c. 1959	Grace B.V. Smith
11 Kent Street	Rossville	1864-1876	Wilfred Furbert
2 King Street	** Buckingham	1745-1768/19C	Bermuda National Trust
3 King Street	** Reeve Court	1706	Bermuda National Trust
1 King's Square	** Stiles House	1765-1766/19C	Bank of N.T. Butterfield
2 King's Square		Rebuilt 1972 Former building was pre-1823	Roberts' Paradise Gift Shop
3 King's Square		1826/1830-54	Freddie's Pub/Tourist Trap
4 King's Square		1924	Bank of Bermuda
5 King's Square	** Town Hall	1803-1809/ 20th c	Corporation of St. George's
6 King's Square	** Esten House	pre-1782	Guerlain/C. Holding Studio
7 King's Square		1898-1943	Visitors Service Bureau
8 King's Square	**White Horse Tavern	c. 1930	
1 Nea's Alley	** Hillcrest	pre-1786/20C	Delaey Robinson
1 Old Maids' Lane	** Pearson House	pre-1704	Frederick Dowling
2 Old Maids' Lane	* Brown House	pre-1783	Irene Coram
4 Old Maids' Lane	Cumberland Villa	c. 1795	Clair's Stitches
5 Old Maids' Lane		pre-1854/post 1876	Gladwin Hall
7 Old Maids' Lane	Doynton/Tranquil Bank	pre-1800/1810-1814/20C	Jean French
8 Old Maids' Lane		rebuilt 20C? 1854-76/ 1876-1898	Anna Govia
10 Old Maids' Lane	**Higgs Cottages	1866	Elizabeth Dowling
11 Old Maids' Lane	Palmcliff	1898-1943	Corlett Schuler
12 Old Maids' Lane	Hannibal Lodge	1898-1943	Hannibal Lodge
13 Old Maids' Lane	Wyncliff	1898-1943	Gregory Foggo
15 Old Maids' Lane	Hill View	1798-1814/20C	Kelly family
16 Old Maids' Lane	Gush House	1898-1943	Arthur B. Fox
17 Old Maids' Lane		c. 1945	Stanley O. Bean
18 Old Maids' Lane		1898-1943	Arthur B. Fox
3 One Gun Alley	** Foster House	1770-1780	Clyde Earlington Basden

Address	Building Name	Construction Date	Owner or occupant in 1997
3 Ordnance Island	Torpedo Workshop	core pre-1854 (or rebuilt)	Customs & Marine Police
5 Ordnance Island	** Storekeeper's House	pre-1816	Corporation of St. George's
9 Ordnance Island	** Customs Hall/Cruise Ship Terminal	1991	Bermuda Government
2 Penno's Drive	** Long House	c. 1794	W.E. Meyer and Co.
4 Penno's Drive	** Hunter Building	pre-1781	W.E. Meyer and Co.
6 Penno's Drive	* Coal Sheds	1854-1876	W.E. Meyer and Co.
19 Penno's Wharf	** Penno's Warehouse	1860	Corporation of St. George's
2/4 Pieces of Eight Lane	* California House	1762-1770/19C	Allan A. Powell
8 Pieces of Eight Lane	Swainson Cottage	1854-1876	Dorothy A. Trott
10 Pieces of Eight Lane	Herchalat	1947	Allan A. Powell
12 Pieces of Eight Lane	Annie Meech Cottage/ Noah's Ark Cottage	pre-1826	D. Hillier
4 Princess Street	** State House (reconstructed)	1620/1970	Corporation of St. George's
6 Princess Street	** Rendell House	c. 1729/post-1876	Clyde Earlington Basden
1 Printer's Alley	** Wainwright House	1865	Rita Rothwell
2 Printer's Alley	Palmetto Cottage	1876-1890	Jean L. Smith
3 Printer's Alley	** Stockdale	1706-1708	Gavin Shorto
4 Printer's Alley	*Lemon Grove (west part)	c. 1705/1780s/1863	Simba Trust
5 Printer's Alley	** Skerrett's Cottage	pre-1706	Arthur Ming
2 Queen Street		c. 1930	Friths Apartments
3 Queen Street	** Taylor House	pre-1704/ 19C	Clifford Rowe
5 Queen Street	** Stewart Hall	pre-1707/19C	Bermuda National Trust
7 Queen Street	Rosewood Cottage (formerly 6 Printer's Alley)	1830-1834	J.A. Houghton
9 Queen Street	Lemon Grove Estate	pre-1854 (looks c. 1800)	A. Arnfield/D. Edwards
10 Queen Street	** Poinciana House	1852	Irene Coram
11 Queen Street	Ruin	pre-1772	
12 Queen Street		20C	Carol Bennett
13 Queen Street	Probably totally rebuilt	1854-1876/20C	Betty Brown
15 Queen Street		1898-1943	Corp. of St. G.'s workshop
17 Queen Street	Rosedale	pre-1821	Leroy Burgess
18 Queen Street	Phineas Wright House/Nosa Casa	pre-1770	Carol Bennett
19 Queen Street	Parklyn Cottage	1943-1966	Paynter family
20 Queen Street	Croton Lodge	1859-1867	Frederick Dowling
21 Queen Street	Claude McCallan House	1828	Norma Durrant
22 Queen Street		1943-1952	H.R. Dowling
23 Queen Street	Richard Allen A.M.E. Church	1898-1943	A.M.E. Church
24 Queen Street	Stables on site of Hannah Bursley House		
25 Queen Street	La Delicia (replaced Bishop's Lodge)	1898-1943	Lois Perinchief

Names and Dates of Buildings in the Central Area of St. George's (continued)

Address	Building Name	Construction Date	Owner or occupant in 1997
26 Queen Street	* Park Villa	pre-1826	Venture Nursery
28 Queen Street		pre-1854	K. Brangman/ S.E Washington.
30 Queen Street	Cedar Lee	c. 1875	R. Richardson
4 Rose Hill Road	Long House	1854-1876	Fire Station
1 Shinbone Alley	** Banana Manor	c. 1742	Janet Outerbridge
1 Shinbone Alley	**`Banana Manor stables	c. 1880	Janet Outerbridge
3 Shinbone Alley	Pearl Cottage	1714-1725/ 20C	Janet Outerbridge
4 Shinbone Alley	** James Burch House	1903	Leon C. Williams
5 Shinbone Alley	Crooked Elbow	1714-1729/20C	Clifford Rowe
7 Shinbone Alley	** Hillside	1714-1717/19C/20C	Steven Masters
9 Shinbone Alley	** Good Templars Hall	1874-1884	Janet and Alan Outerbridge
11 Shinbone Alley	La Casa	1854-1876	G. Outerbridge
13 Shinbone Alley		1898-1943	Smith family
15 Shinbone Alley		1854-1864	Charles O'Brien
17 Shinbone Alley	Royal Arms Tavern	pre-1808/1854-76	Laundromat/Barber Shop
1 Silk Alley	** Lyncliffe	1795-1800	Irene Coram
2 Silk Alley	** Seven Gables	pre-1704	Lydia Waterman
3 Silk Alley	** Somerled	1702-1704	Dianne Mary Green
4 Silk Alley	Kate's House	pre-1798	Frederick Dowling
16 Slippery Hill	** Sandhurst	1781?(core)/1800-1805/1898	Bermuda Housing Authority
18 Slippery Hill	* Mount Pleasant	1825	Bermuda Housing Authority
23 Slippery Hill	** Arcadia	1898-1900	Bermuda Housing Authority
25 Slippery Hill	* Paradise Cottage	pre-1817 (core)	Physical Abuse Centre
35 Slippery Hill	Royal Lodge	1845	Constance Pascoe
1 Turkey Hill	Timothy Hall Cottage	1898-1943	Lois Perinchief
2 Turkey Hill	Lynton	pre-1790	Irene Coram
3 Turkey Hill		1768-1802	L. Packwood
4 Turkey Hill	Beyond	pre-1854	Irene Coram
5 Turkey Hill	Wainwright Cottage	1848	Monte Carmela
6 Turkey Hill	Windsor (much changed 1990s)	pre-1854	A.M.E. Rectory
7 Turkey Hill	Cherry Grove	(probably totally rebuilt) 1876-1898?/20C	M. Barnard
9 Turkey Hill	Homestead	pre-1854	Brangman family
10 Turkey Hill	Rabbit Hut	pre-1815, rebuilt	D.C. and M.C. Caisey
11 Turkey Hill	Adelaide Cottage	1815-1819	Brangman family
12 Turkey Hill	Florence Cottage	post-1943	Kyril Burrows
13 Turkey Hill		1898-1943	Hyacinth Stovell
15 Turkey Hill	Burleigh House (formerly a ruin)	1898-1943	M.P. Wales
16 Turkey Hill	Richard Wright House (old chimney remains)	L 18 C/20C	Blanche Roberts

Address	Building Name	Construction Date	Owner or occupant in 1997
18 Turkey Hill	Winleigh	1854-1876/20C	A.N. Bean
1 Turkey Lane	Beverley Cottage (west half)	pre-1854	N.J. Francis
2 Turkey Lane	Wainwright Cottage	1898-1943	Rita Rothwell
1 Water St.(west)	** The Armoury	1794-1796	Robert Trew Sr.
5 Water St.(west)	** Tucker House	c. 1753	Bermuda National Trust
9 Water St.(west)		c. 1836	Vera P. Card/Sinclairs
11 Water St.(west)	** Post Office (old gaol)	1760/1853	Bermuda Government
12 Water St.(west)		1957	Dowlings Service Station
13 Water St.(west)	Alder Lodge	1854-1876	Frangipani
14- Water St.(west)	Cox Wharf/ Musson Wharf, Criterion Bar	1854-1876	W.E. Meyer and Co.
16 Water St.(west)	14, 16 and 18 were all partly rebuilt 1962	20C	W.E. Meyer and Co.
18 Water St.(west)	Cox/Musson Wharf, Meyer's Machine Shop	1854-1876	W.E. Meyer and Co.
21 Water St.(east)	** Casino	1716	Kingdom Hall (Jehovah's Witnesses)
22 Water St.(west)	** Commissariat Wharf	1812-1837/20C	Carriage Museum & Restaurant
23 Water St.(east)	old building burned	c. 1923	Youth Centre, former Primary School
25 Water St.(east)	Site of Ruth Massey's house	c. 1930	Raymond Spurling
27 Water St.(east)	** Samaritans' Cottages	pre-1704/1719	B. N. Trust/Peter Dunne
29 Water St.(east)	** Samaritans' Lodge	c. 1843	B.N. Trust/Bermuda Heritage Association
30 Water St.(west)	* Smith House	pre-1759?/pre-1786	Taylors/TESS
32 Water St.(west)	** Perry Building (Higgs's Wharf)	1841	Bermuda Railway Co.
34 Water St.(west)	Paynter's Wharf	pre-1791, rebuilt	La Bouchee
36 Water St.(west)	W.S. Trott Wharf	c. 1835	Mello's Grocery
38 Water St.(west)	W.S. Trott Wharf	c. 1835	J.F. Burrows
40 Water St.(west)		c. 1961 (rebuilt)	W.J. Boyle
42 Water St.(west)		1964	Crisson's
50 Water St.(east)	Ordnance Arms Tavern	pre-1814	Chick's Bar and Grill
52 Water St.(east)	Ordnance Arms Tavern	pre-1814	Welch's Rooming House
54 Water St.(east)	Banks' Wharf	c. 1820	Warren D. Foggo
56 Water St.(east)	** Upper Davenport Warehouse	1833-1842	Ocean Sails/Janet Outerbridge
58 Water St.(east)	** Lower Davenport Warehouse	1833-1842	Norman Roberts
60 Water St.(east)	Shepherd's Lodge	1833-1842	Corbin's Plumbing
31 Wellington Street	** Melrose	1848-1854	Donna M. Bell
33 Wellington Street	Booker House	1940	Janet Outerbridge
36 Wellington Street	** Durnford	1792-1795	Janet Outerbridge
37 Wellington Street	* Somers Opera House	1898-1921	Odd Fellows
40 Wellington Street	Durnford Cot./Lucas Cottage (much altered)	1814-1821	Studio Cottage/R. Outerbridge

Address		Building Name	Construction Date	Owner or occupant in 1997
1	Duke of York Street	** Wellesley Lodge	c. 1865	Lily Ann's Bargain Boutique
2	York Street		1876-1898	Egmont Brown
3	York Street	* Crofton	c. 1865	Gladwin Hall
5	York Street	** Ex-Home Sunday School	c. 1875	Methodist Church
6	York Street	Armoury Cottage	1794-1796	Robert Trew Sr.
7	York Street	** Ebenezer Methodist Church	1840	Methodist Church
8	York Street		1966-1974	Music Box/St. George's Liquors/Georgio's
9	York Street	* Methodist Parsonage	1865	Methodist Church
11	York Street	Glanville	c. 1840/ 20C	Frederick Dowling
13	York Street		1943-1966	Gombey Trader
14	York Street		pre 1854 (north section)	Juliette
15	York Street		1898-1943	Cracker Box Gift Shop
16	York Street		pre-1854 (east section)?/20C	Pasta Pasta
17	York Street	** Tower House	c. 1882	Betty's Needlecrafts
18	York Street	York House	1828-1838	H.A. & E. Smith
19	York Street		1854-1876	York Street Men's Shop
20	York Street	** Stephen Judkin House	c. 1765/19C	Perinchief Apartments
21	York Street		1854-1876	Dowling's Cycles
22	York Street	** Police Station (replacing Provost Marshal's House	1911	Bermuda Government
24	York Street		1977	Robertson's Drugstore
25	York Street		pre-1800/ 20C	Gosling Bros.
26	York Street		c. 1880	Dowling's Cycles
27	York Street		pre-1854/20C	Frith's/Churchill's Cigar Store
28	York Street		post-1966	formerly Archie Brown's
29	York Street	** Ming House	c. 1715/pre-1854	Xpressions
31	York Street	Zuill House	c. 1830/1865	Temptations
32	York Street	** Globe Hotel	1700	Bda. National Trust Museum
33	York Street	** St. Peter's Church	1713/1815/1843	Anglican Church
35	York Street	** Sunday School	c. 1845/ 20C	Anglican Church
39	York/22 Clarence St.		1964	Tolaram Building
41	York Street	* Sail Loft/Storehouse	1814-1820	Somers Supermarket
41	York Street	** YMCA	1862	Somers Supermarket
43	York Street	** Old Homestead	1863	Irene Coram
43	York Street		c. 1876	Helen's Coffee Shop
44	York Street	** The Redan Hotel	1782 or earlier	Clyde's Cafe
47	York Street		L18C?/post 1892	Travel Connection/ N. Smith
48	York Street	Hall Building	1854-1876	Angeline's Coffee Shop
49	York Street		post 1878	Robinson family
51	York Street	Alpha Memorial Chapel	post-1878/pre 1898	7th Day Adventist Centre
53	York Street		1876-1898	Lillian E. Smith
55	York Street	Hall's Manor	1797	Marion Paynter

Appendix III

Names and Dates of Buildings on St. George's Island, Smith's Island and St. David's Island

All buildings on this list can be found on the reverse side of the foldout map.

This list only includes buildings of particular interest which have been discussed in the text. All buildings (or their sites if they are post 1898) have been marked on the map. Neither this Appendix nor the Savage map identify fortifications. For these, readers are recommended to refer to Dr. Edward Harris' *Bermuda Forts*.

Where a date range is listed, the building is known to have been built within these years; where a "circa" date is given, construction occurred within a year or two of the year given. The year that is stated represents the earliest case of the present building on the site; later additions or renovations may have changed the appearance of earlier structures, in some cases substantially. Multiple dates reflect a series of building episodes.

Names and Dates of Buildings on St. George's Island
(other than those in the central area listed in Appendix II),
Smith's Island and St. David's Island

Address	Building Name	Construction Date	Owner or occupant in 1997
St. George's Island			
23 Biological Station	Wright Hall	1911	Bermuda Biological Station
2 Cut Road	Boeotia	1899-1901	Thierry Cabot
4 Cut Road	The Palms	c.1845/c.1881/c.1903	Noela Haycock
1 Ferry Road	Echo Heights	1904	Dixon Spurling
69 Ferry Road	Ferry Reach/Astor House	1933-1934	H.O.P. Bierman
89 Ferry Road	Ferry Point Cottage	1781	Bermuda Government
2 Hidden Valley	Ocean View Cottage	1841-1847	Heman Richardson
12 Old Military Road	Barracks Block D	1854-1876	Bermuda Government
16 Old Military Road	Garrison Chapel	pre-1854	Ethopian Orthodox Church
11 Redcoat Lane	Military Hospital	1818-1854	Chelsea Apartments
2 Wellington Park	Wellington	1813	Baptist Church
71 Wellington Slip Road	Francis Cottage	1884-1898	Ethel Van Putten
6 Wellington Street	Glen Duror / Old Glenduror	1805-1807	Janet Outerbridge
12 Wellington Street	Clifton Vale	c. 1812	William (Peter) Outerbridge
14 Wellington Street	McCallan's Warehouse	c. 1861	Godet and Young Warehouse
16 Wellington Street	Edgewater	1867	David L. White
31 Wellington Street	Melrose	1848-1854	Donna Marie Bell
Smith's Island			
3 Smith's Island	The Forbes House	c. 1770	Rita Rothwell
St. David's Island			
20 Chapel of Ease Road	Chapel of Ease	1848	Anglican Church
Former US base	Carter House	E18C	Bermuda Government
3 Dolly's Bay Road	Cocoa Bay/Pride of India Cottage	1758-1789/20C	Dunkley family
7 Emily's Bay Road	Ambleside	pre-1789	Elystan Haycock
13 Lighthouse Hill	St. Luke's Church	1924-1928	A.M.E. Church
23 Lighthouse Hill	Hureka House	late 19C/ early 20C	Lucinda O'Brien
1 Mount Road	St. David's Lighthouse	1876-1879	Bermuda Government
5 Narrows Lane	Narrows House	c. 1710?/20C	Whayman family
49 St. David's Road	Dolly's Bay House	c.1767/E19C/20C	William Frith
Cashew City Road	St. David's Lodge/ Old Pilot Station	1758-1789/19C/20C	St. David's Primary School
14 Tranquillity Lane	The Villa	c. 1714/1800-1819	Edwin Hayward

APPENDIX IV
St. George's Buildings Built Before 1800

Note: Some of these buildings are considerably altered, some barely changed.
Later building dates are not always given.

St. George's Buildings Built Before 1800

Address	Building Name	Construction Date	Owner or occupant in 1997
2 Aunt Peggy's Lane		18C/ pre-1854	Lucille B. Foggo
5 Aunt Peggy's Lane	James Darrell House/ Hermit's Court	pre-1796, gutted 1992	Romano Ramirez
2 Blockade Alley	Chandler's Cottage	1726-1729	Thomas N. Wadson
1 Bridge Street	Bridge House	1707/E19C	B. N. Trust/Raine Art Gallery
5 Bridge Street	Block House	pre-1791/1854-76	BELCO
1 Broad Alley	Old Rectory	1699 or earlier	Bermuda National Trust
4 Broad Alley	Broad Alley Cottages	1700?/ pre-1821	Ronald Smith
3 Clarence Street	Stella Maris Rectory (west part)	pre-1784	Roman Catholic Church
6 Clarence Street	Clarence Cottage	pre-1709/20C	Madelyn L. Fox
7 Clarence Street	Bedford Cottage	1764-1790	Ralph Jennings
2 Featherbed Alley	(much changed)	pre-1784/20C	H. Outerbridge
3 Featherbed Alley	Mitchell House	c. 1731	St. G.'s Historical Society
3 Government Hill Rd.	Government House(little old remains)	1721 ? (core)	Rectory, Anglican Church
10 Governor's Alley	Fanny Fox's Cottage	c. 1707	Bermuda National Trust
5 Kent Street	Davis Cottage (south part)	1713-1717	Francis family
6 Kent Street	Greig Hall (mostly 19C- old part at rear)	pre-1782/1854-1876	Janet Outerbridge
7 Kent Street	Longford House Ruin	1709-1713	Irene Coram
2 King Street	Buckingham	1745-1768/19C	Bermuda National Trust
3 King Street	Reeve Court	1706/19C	Bermuda National Trust
1 King's Square	Stiles House (major 20C renovations)	1765-1766	Bank of Butterfield
6 King's Square	Esten House	pre-1782	Guerlain/ Carole Holding Studio
1 Nea's Alley	Hillcrest	pre-1786	Delaey Robinson
1 Old Maids' Lane	Pearson House	pre-1704	Frederick Dowling
2 Old Maids' Lane	Brown House	pre-1783	Irene Coram
4 Old Maids' Lane	Cumberland Villa	c. 1795	Clair's Stitches
7 Old Maids' Lane	north part Doynton/Tranquil Bank	pre-1800 (north part)	Jean French
3 One Gun Alley	Foster House	1770-1780	Clyde Earlington Basden
2 Penno's Drive	Long House	c. 1794	W.E. Meyer and Co.
4 Penno's Drive	Hunter Building	pre-1781	W.E. Meyer and Co.
2/4 Pieces of Eight Lane	California House	1762-1770	Allan A. Powell
4 Princess Street	State House (reconstructed)	1620/1970	Corporation of St. George's
6 Princess Street	Rendell House (much altered)	c. 1729/post-1876	Clyde Earlington Bsden
3 Printer's Alley	Stockdale	1706-1708	Gavin Shorto
4 Printer's Alley	Lemon Grove (southwest corner)	c. 1705/1780s/1863	Simba Trust
5 Printer's Alley	Skerritt's Cottage	pre-1706	Arthur Ming
3 Queen Street	Taylor House	pre-1704	Clifford Rowe
5 Queen Street	Stewart Hall	pre-1707	Bermuda National Trust
11 Queen Street	Ruin (part)	pre-1772	
18 Queen Street	Phineas Wright House	pre-1770	Carol Bennett
1 Shinbone Alley	Banana Manor	c. 1742	Janet Outerbridge
3 Shinbone Alley	Pearl Cottage (much changed)	1714-1725/20C	Janet Outerbridge

St. George's Buildings Built Before 1800 (continued)

Address		Building Name	Construction Date	Owner or occupant in 1997
5	Shinbone Alley	Crooked Elbow (altered)	1714-1729/20C	Clifford Rowe
7	Shinbone Alley	Hillside	1714-1717	Steven Masters
1	Silk Alley	Lyncliffe	1795-1800	Irene Coram
2	Silk Alley	Seven Gables	pre-1704	Lydia Waterman
3	Silk Alley	Somerled	1702-1704	Dianne M. Green
4	Silk Alley	Kate's House	pre-1798	Frederick Dowling
2	Turkey Hill	Lynton	pre-1790	Irene Coram
3	Turkey Hill	(much altered)	1768-1802	L. Packwood
16	Turkey Hill	Richard Wright House (only old chimney remains)	L 18 C/20C	Blanche Roberts
1	Water St.(west)	The Armoury	1794-1796	Robert Trew Sr.
5	Water St.(west)	Tucker House	c. 1753	Bermuda National Trust
10	Water St.(west)	Post Office (old gaol)	1760/1853	Bermuda Government
21	Water St.(east)	Casino	1716	Kingdom Hall (Jehovah's Witnesses)
27	Water St.(east)	Samaritans' Cottages	pre-1704/1719	Bda. Nat. Trust/Peter Dunne
30	Water St.(west)	Smith House	pre-1759?/pre-1786	Taylors/TESS
36	Wellington Street	Durnford	1792-1795	Janet Outerbridge
6	York Street.	Armoury Cottage	1794-1796	Robert Trew Sr.
20	York Street	Stephen Judkin House	c. 1765	Perinchief Apartments
25	York Street		pre-1800	Gosling Bros.
29	York Street	Ming House	c. 1715/pre-1854	Xpressions
32	York Street	Globe Hotel	1700	Bda. National Trust Museum
33	York Street	St. Peter's Church	1713/1815/1843	Anglican Church
44	York Street	The Redan Hotel	1782 or earlier	Clyde's Cafe
55	York Street	Hall's Manor	1797	Marion Paynter

Appendix V

St. George's Buildings Owned or Occupied by Blacks
Prior to 1850

Year denotes when a Black owner acquired the property, not when the house was built. Houses with * are included in chapter text. "Replaced" means that the original building was destroyed and a more recent one stands in its place.

St. George's Buildings Owned or Occupied by Blacks prior to 1850

Year	Building	Address	Owner/Occupier
1795	Hermit's Court	5 Aunt Peggy's Lane (gutted 1992)	James Darrell, pilot
c. 1806		19 Turkey Hill (replaced)	Leticia Mitchell
pre-1808/1826	lot and house	12 Pieces of Eight Lane	Tom Parker
pre-1808/1835	Ann's Cottage	4 Clarence Street	William Foot's slave Tom; David Richard
1815/1819	lot and cottage	11 Turkey Hill	James Stowe, butcher
1815	Hall's Manor	55 York Street	Jacob Tucker/Pitcairn, pilot
1815		10 Turkey Hill (replaced)	Mary Davis
pre-1819		17 York Street (replaced)	James Forbes, pilot
1819		13 Clarence Street	slave Bess, freed by Sarah Milbourne
1820		3 Barrack Hill (replaced)	slave Kate, freed by Sarah Wright
1824		8 Clarence Street	Thomas Bascome, carpenter
pre-1826		4 Shinbone Alley (replaced)	William A. Astwood
pre-1826		9 Shinbone Alley (replaced)	Diana Jones/Tucker/Bascome
1826	California House	2 Pieces of Eight Lane	Mary Catterall, tavern keeper [tenant]
1826		28 Queen Street	Daniel Mileroy [Mallory]
1826		not located	Sue Fisher, house of Capt. John Fisher
1826		not located	Ben Gilbert
1826		not located	Judy Rush
1826		not located	Richard Trott
1826		not located	Mary Tucker
1829		"northside"	Sarah Loan
1829		not located	George Allen
1831	Foster House (tavern)	3 One Gun Alley	William & Isabelle Archer
1833	The Redan Hotel (tavern)	44 York Street	Mary Catterall, tavern keeper [tenant]
1835		2 Clarence Street	John Fox, house joiner
1835		28 Wellington Street	James Athill, shipbuilder
1841		49 York Street	Robert J. Packwood
1841		1 Kent Street (replaced)	Bustern Bruce, carpenter
1841	Ocean View Cottage	2 Hidden Valley Road	Bustern Bruce, carpenter
1842	Sail Loft	41 Kent Street	Robert J. Packwood, trader
1842	Mitchell House	3 Featherbed Alley	William and Isabelle Archer
1843	Bedford Cottage	7 Clarence Street	John Smith, pilot
pre-1846		53 Cut Road	Peter Tucker, mason
1846	Underwood	49 Ferry Road	Robert James Packwood, planter
c. 1848	Ocean View Cottage	2 Hidden Valley Lane	Stephen B. Richardson, pilot
1849	lot only	11 Shinbone Alley	Rebecca Outerbridge

Appendix VI

A History of the Glebe Lots

A History of the St. George's Glebe Lots

The Glebe was originally two shares (50 acres) set aside by a Somers Island Company order of 6 February 1621/22 to support the minister based in St. George's; at that time he also received a salary from the Company (often in arrears), so the use of this land was his principal means of support. The land was to the west of the town and the twelve shares whose use was given to the colony's governor, and east of the colonial secretary's two shares and the sheriff's four shares. When Richard Norwood undertook his 1662/63 survey, the Glebe land was in the tenure of Mr. Samuel Smith, "ye present Minister." (Lefroy I:200; II:647).

Since most ministers were busy and learned men but indifferent planters, the Glebe shares were often leased to tenants. Throughout much of the 18th century, the hilly land was rarely farmed and provided a slight income. There was no incentive for tenants to build on or improve land that was not theirs, so the Glebe in St. George's was worth little - as was most of the other public lands set aside for the use of the governor, secretary, sheriff, and provost marshal. In 1758 Governor William Popple persuaded the Crown to auction the use of all public land except for the Glebe to willing buyers, who were then charged an annual quitrent of 3% of their winning bids. The arrangement was a vast improvement and brought in an annual income far greater than the previous system of renting to poor and often careless tenants. With a secure tenure on the land, the purchasers then built substantial houses, fenced in their grants and improved the land.

The main problem with the Glebe land (and the probable reason why it was not auctioned in 1758) was a line of shoals lying to the south of the foreshore of St. George's Harbour that made it difficult for all but the smallest boats to approach. In 1791, however, the minister of St. George's was willing to part with his Glebe upon the same conditions as those outlined in 1758, but with the two shares divided into smaller lots. On 25 May 1791, the Bermuda Assembly passed "An Act for the Sale of the GLEBE LOT, in the Town and Parish of St. George" so that the "present Rector . . . and his Successors may receive a greater and more certain Advantage" of the land. "At the same time, the Interest of the Public will be advanced by the Improvement of the said Lot, which at present lies in a manner waste and useless." The Assembly appointed the Hon. Francis Forbes, Bridger Goodrich and the Rector of St. George's [Alexander Richardson] to lay out and auction the lots in fee simple conditional on a quitrent of 7% the bidding price. The buyers were enjoined to build a "good and substantial smooth Wall of three Feet high within two Years from the Day of Purchase" or be fined £100. The act was approved by Council on 6 June 1791 and by Governor Henry Hamilton on 8 July 1791.

Two years were to pass before the actual auction was held. It took place on 29 June 1793. The overseers had laid out thirteen water lots to the south of the Ferry Road and three large lots to the north, as shown by a plan that was probably drawn by Major Andrew Durnford, R.E., a skilled surveyor. Two of the water lots (between 8 and 9) were reserved for the Rector's use. All but lot number 1 had 100' frontage on the Ferry Road to the north. The width of the lots (from the road to the coastline) varied considerably, and some lots were only 30 feet wide. In all cases the grants extended into the harbour to the line of shoals with the understanding that the owners could either erect wharves out to the rocks in order to make their properties commercially feasible or demolish (if possible) a section of the shoals in order to provide access for boats to reach wharves or docks built to the north of the rocks. Without this provision, it is doubtful whether the Rector would have found any buyers and the Glebe would have remained unimproved.

After the sale, the Glebe water lots developed relatively quickly. A house built by Francis Siddon around 1797 on lot number 11 was later used as a Royal Navy pilot's station and was James Athill's home and shipbuilding yard in the 1840s (since demolished). Glen Duror on lots numbered 1 and 2 was built in 1806-7 by John Stewart and required little extension to reach the line of shoals. Sunnybank and its associated wharf were built by Robert Tucker around 1810 on lots numbered 9 and 10 (demolished by the Corporation, post 1945). Antiguan merchant Richard Fisher built Clifton Vale and a wharf in 1812-14; from the configuration of the lower level, it is clear that Fisher was storing merchandise and longboats in his cellar. Naval Contractor Andrew Belcher had erected a house and wharf reaching to the shoals worth £3,000 by 1821 on the now vacant lot number 3. C.T. McCallan had built a wharf on lot number 5 by 1861 and during the American Civil War added the warehouse now used by Godet and Young. Profits from the war enabled McCallan to build Edgewater on lot number 6 in 1868. Lots numbered 7 and 8 and the Rector's Lot (finally sold in 1880) remained unimproved and were purchased by the Corporation of St. George's in 1881; these lots were extended to the line of shoals in 1971-72 to form the wharf at Tiger Bay. Today, lot number 6 (Edgewater) is the only grant that has not built out to the 18th century line of shoals. It nevertheless owns the water and sea floor to the south, as recognised by a compensatory payment made by the Corporation of St. George's in 1972 to then-owner Marian H. McCallan for encroaching on her water while building the Tiger Bay Wharf.

Michael Jarvis
College of William and Mary
June 1997

Appendix VII

Mayors of St. George's

Mayors of St. George's

1797-1798	Hon. Andrew Durnford, Major, R.E.
1798-1799	William Smith, Esq.
1799-1800	John Esten
1800-1818	John Van Norden
1818-1823	John Till
1823-1833	Augustus J. Musson
1833-1847	Dr. Joseph Stuart Hunter
1847-1849	Edwin Burch Todd
1849-1850	Dr. Joseph Stuart Hunter
1850-1851	Augustus J. Musson
1851-1855	Dr. Joseph Stuart Hunter
1855-1856	Robert W. Outerbridge
1856-1860	Dr. Joseph Stuart Hunter
1860-1861	Robert W. Outerbridge
1861-1862	James A. Atwood
1862-1880	James T. Thies
Feb.-Oct. 1880	Samuel Chapman
Oct. 1880-1892	William C.J. Hyland
1892-1906	Hon. Joseph Ming Hayward
1907-1913	Robert H. James
1914-1931	W.J. Boyle
1932-1942	William Eugen Meyer
1942-1954	Leon Davenport Fox
1954-1963	Harry G. Roberts
1963-1968	Leon D. Fox
1968-1989	Norman R. Roberts
1989-1997	J. Henry Hayward

Glossary

APSE A semicircular or polygonal ending to a building, usually used of the eastern extension of a church.

ARCADED One or more arches supported by columns or pillars that create a covered passageway.

ARCHITRAVE Ornamental moulding around doors and windows. Used more specifically in this volume as a rectangular projection above a door or window.

ARCHIVOLT Ornamental band of mouldings on the face of an arch.

ART DECO 1920-1940. An architectural style characterised by an overall linear, angular and vertical appearance.

BALUSTER One of a series of short pillars or other uprights that support a handrail or coping. The style of a baluster varies from period to period.

BALUSTRADE A series of balusters connected on top by a coping or handrail and sometimes on the bottom by a bottom rail.

BARREL VAULTED A vaulted roof, usually over an external water tank, taking the form of an elongated arch or half section of a barrel. Such tanks are commonly called DOMED TANKS in Bermuda.

BASTION A projection at the angle of a fortification, from which the garrison can see and fire shots.

BATTERY A number of guns placed in juxtaposition for combined action.

BAWN A fortified enclosure; the fortified court or outwork of a castle.

BAY A space protruding from the exterior wall that contains a BAY WINDOW. Usually there are three walls at angles making up a bay.

BEAM One of the principal horizontal timbers in a building. Its primary function is to carry transverse loads such as floor joists or rafters.

BEAUX ARTS The name originates from the school of that name in late 19th century France. The style is characterised by a monumental and imposing appearance, symmetrical façades, much embellished wall surfaces, and exterior walls quoins, pilasters and paired columns.

BLINDS Shutters; TOP HUNG blinds open out from hinges at the top rather than from side hinges.

BLOCKHOUSE A detached fort blocking a strategic point.

BULL'S EYE WINDOW a round panel or aperture that may be glazed, open, or louvred. It often is surrounded by a double arched frame.

BRIDGING BEAM Bridging is a brace, or series of braces, placed between other structural members of a building. A bridging beam is a beam used for this purpose.

BUTTERY In Bermuda, a small outbuilding used for a variety of purposes with characteristic steep pyramidal roof. The term originally meant a place for wine storage. Increasingly, but without historic justification, buttery-style roofs are being incorporated into the structure of larger houses.

BUTTRESS A stone support which gives additional strength to a wall and counteracts its outward thrust.

CAPITAL The upper decorated portion of a column or pilaster on which the entablature rests.

CASEMENT WINDOW A window containing two window sashes separated by a vertical dividing bar and opening sideways. In the early days in Bermuda the casements would have had many small diamond shaped panes of glass held together by lead strips.

CHANCEL The part of the east end of a church in which the main altar is placed; reserved for clergy and choir.

COPING The protective uppermost course of a wall or parapet or balustrade. It normally projects beyond the wall or railing below it to throw off rain.

COUNTER-WEIGHTS (FOR WINDOW) Lead weights hung inside the window frame of a sash window to balance the weight of the window so that it will stay in position when open.

CORBEL A projecting block or bracket, sometimes carved or moulded, that acts as a means of support for other structural members such as the beams of a verandah.

CORNICE A moulded ornamental projection at the top of a wall; the top course or moulding of a wall where it serves as crowning member.

COURSE A horizontal row of stones or other masonry units. Often extended to include any material arranged in a row (such as roof slates).

CRENELLATION A decorative element that simulates the squares and spaces of a defensive parapet.

CRUCIFORM HOUSE A house with four wings in the shape of a cross. Several of Bermuda's important early houses were cruciform. One wing normally contains an entrance chamber.

DENTIL MOULDING Projecting surface embellished with a series of small square blocks.

DORIC The earliest of the three classical orders of architecture. Doric was characterised by extreme simplicity; the second, IONIC, by capitals ornamented with volutes (spiral scrolls); the third, CORINTHIAN, by capitals ornamented by acanthus leaves.

EAVES That portion of the roof which projects beyond the walls.

EDWARDIAN The reign of King Edward VII (1901-1910), more often used to include the period from 1890-1914. The reaction to the excesses of the Victorians, resulting in a simpler style and a partial return to classical rather than Gothic decoration.

EMBRASURE An enlarged door or window opening bevelling inwards. Also used to describe a widening from within made in a parapet so that a gun can be fired through it.

ENCLOSED EAVES A style popular in Bermuda from about 1830-1930 whereby the rafter feet below the eaves were enclosed in concrete moulding. It has regained popularity in the 1990s.

ENTABLATURE A horizontal structure supported by columns. It may have any number of decorative elements.

EYEBROW A curved projection over a door or window, used in the early 18th century to deflect rain from windows and window frames built flush with the outer surface of the wall. Eyebrows became structurally obsolete when windows were recessed.

FAÇADE The principal face or front elevation of a building.

FANLIGHT A semicircular or fan-shaped window with radiating glazing bars, usually found over entrance doors.

FEDERAL Architectural style characterised by overall symmetry, semi-circular or elliptical fan lights over six-panel front doors, elaborate door trim including columns or pilasters, decorated cornices often denticulated, six-panel double hung windows arranged most often in five bays, and slender end chimneys.

FENESTRATION The arrangement of windows and other exterior openings on a building.

FIN DE SIECLE Literally "end of century", meaning the end of the 19th century. See also Edwardian.

FINIAL An ornament that caps a gable, hip, pinnacle or other architectural feature. In early Bermudian architecture most commonly a round masonry ball at the peak of a hip roof, said to have been placed there when the building was fully paid for, but occasionally covering the protruding ends of rafters.

FLEMISH GABLE Gable ends decoratively scalloped and raised slightly above the roof level. Thought to have been inspired by examples in the Dutch West Indies.

FLUSH MOUNTING (WINDOW AND DOOR FRAMES) The window or door frame mounted flush with the outer wall, rather than recessed as later. Flush mounting is a good indication of early age.

FRENCH DOOR A door characterised by having glass panes throughout, or nearly throughout, its entire length. Usually found in pairs.

GABLE ROOF A roof that slopes on two sides only. A sloping roof that terminates at one or both ends in a gable.

GABLE OR GABLE END The triangular end of an exterior wall in a building with a gable roof.

GEORGIAN Strictly 1714-1830, but in Bermuda the style arrived rather later. Architecture characterised by symmetry of floor plan and facade. In Bermuda associated with hip roofs, large symmetrical windows, side hung blinds and decoration round the main entrance.

GINGERBREAD Commonly used to describe the more ornate flat woodwork used in many Victorian verandahs.

GLAZING BAR (OR MUNTIN) Glazing is the technique of fitting glass into windows. A glazing bar is the piece of wood between panes of glass. Most traditional Bermuda windows have six panes of glass in each sash; therefore one horizontal and two vertical bars are necessary. At the end of the 19th century and well into the twentieth, when plate glass first became available, it was fashionable to use just one vertical glazing bar and, eventually, none at all.

GOTHIC Characterised by the pointed arch, the style originated in Europe and thrived from the late 12th to early 16th centuries. The Gothic Revival was a 19th century attempt to apply the designs and features of Gothic architecture. Very rare in Bermuda except in churches.

GREEK OR NEO-CLASSICAL REVIVAL A competitor to the Gothic Revival in the 19th century, it attempted to reproduce features found in classical Greek architecture. In Bermuda it is characterised by low pitched roofs, heavily moulded gables, parapets, keystones, transom and side lights of doors, and porches or porticos with columns.

HALF TIMBERING A method of construction, common in 16th and 17th century England, in which the spaces between the vertical structural timbers were filled with plaster or wattle and daub. Also called POST AND PLASTER.

HALL-AND-PARLOUR a two room house consisting of a large hall next to a smaller parlour which also was used as a bedroom. Sometimes constructed as a two storey building.

HIP ROOF A roof formed by four sloped roof surfaces (as against a GABLE ROOF which has two only).

IMPERIAL Pertaining to an empire, for example Edwardian architecture.

ITALIANATE Architectural style characterised by two or three storeys, low-pitched hip or gable roof with widely overhanging eaves supported by large brackets, a cupola or tower, visually balanced façades, decorative bracketed crowns or lintels over windows and doors, and narrow single pane double hung windows and double doors.

JACOBEAN Strictly, the style prevailing in the reign of the first Stuart monarch, James I (1603-1625), but still used in Bermuda a century later.

JOISTS Horizontal framing members that run parallel to each other from wall to wall.

KEYSTONE Wedge-shape stone found at the apex of an arch. Also the wedge-shape decoration placed above many 19th century Bermuda windows.

LATERAL STEPS (SIDE STEPS) Steps descending parallel to the side of a building rather than at right angles to it. Common in St. George's because of limited available space. DOUBLE LATERAL STEPS (or DOUBLE SIDE STEPS) a set of steps with two flights of steps at 180 degrees to each other, both parallel to the side of the building.

LATH-AND-PLASTER Thin wooden strips (laths) are attached to framing members and used as a supporting base for plaster (a mixture of lime, sand, and water) for walls, ceilings, etc.

LIME WASH White powder paint made from lime and used on roofs and often on both interior and exterior walls until the mid 20th century.

LOUVRE An arrangement of overlapping boards or glass slanted to admit air but exclude rain.

MORTISE A cavity cut into a member to receive a projecting part from another member, as a place cut to hold a vertical wooden joist.

MOULDING A continuous decorative band which serves as an ornamental device on the exterior of a building as well as sometimes fulfilling a practical purpose (such as enclosing rafter feet).

MUNTIN (see GLAZING BAR).

PALLADIAN WINDOW A central arched window flanked on either side by smaller side lights.

PALMETTO An indigenous palm, the leaves of which were widely used in 17th century Bermuda for roof thatching.

PARAPET A low wall or protective railing. In Bermuda frequently used in the 19th century to dignify shed roofed additions and outbuildings.

PEDIMENT A low triangle, framed by moulding, ornamenting the gable end of a building, or above a portico, door or window.

PILASTER A partial column raised beyond a wall surface or corner, quite frequently decoratively treated so as to represent an classical column. In Bermuda the term is often applied to a simple vertical element strengthening corners with none of the features of a classical column.

PITCH In the context of this book, the angle at which a roof rises.

POST AND PLASTER See HALF TIMBERED

QUEEN ANNE Last of the Stuart monarchs, the style of her reign (1702-14) was the precursor of the classic Georgian and far removed from the Jacobean style of the first of her dynasty.

QUITRENT a rent, usually of small amount. Originally the rent paid in lieu of feudal services.

QUOIN Large stones used to decorate (and sometimes reinforce) the corners of a building, laid in vertical series with, usually, alternately small and large blocks. Quoining is also used as

decoration around the outside of doorframes. Sometimes known as "long and short" work.

RAFTERS The sloping beams carrying the weight of a roof.

RAFTER FEET Sometimes known as FALSE RAFTERS. Short extensions of the rafters. In Bermuda they are fixed at a slightly different angle from the main rafter, causing the edge of the roof to be raised a little. The ends of rafter feet protrude below the eaves and are a useful dating tool.

RAVELINS An outwork consisting of two faces which form an angle, constructed beyond the main ditch of a moat.

REDOUBT An isolated enclosed structure built to define a prominent point.

REGENCY Strictly 1790-1820. A distinctive style, included in the late Georgian period and associated with the Greek Revival, represented by columns, cornices, bow windows, low pitched roofs.

RENAISSANCE Revival of arts and letters that began in Italy in the 14th century, or the style of art or architecture developed in, and characteristic of, this period.

RIDGE BEAM / RIDGE BOARD The topmost horizontal member of a roof frame into which rafters are connected. A ridge beam is a heavy timber, a ridge board is a plank or board. The oldest buildings in Bermuda had neither - the tops of the rafters were fixed directly to their opposite members.

ROSE WINDOW A circular window with ornamental intersections of leaf-shaped areas arranged like the spokes of a wheel.

RUSTICATION The decorating of a building to make it appear rustic, e.g., the scoring of lines on a stone building to resemble the outlines of building stones.

SASH WINDOW The "sash" is the framework into which panes of glass are set. A pair of sashes which slide up and down, passing each other, usually make up a window.

SHED ROOF A roof which slopes one way only.

SIDE LIGHT A small window or set of panes at the side of a door, usually in pairs.

STOOP An entrance platform, usually with several steps leading up to it; from STOEP, the Dutch term for a raised platform or verandah.

STRING COURSE A continuous horizontal band set in the surface of an exterior wall or projecting from it and usually moulded. Also called BELT COURSE.

STUART STYLE Characteristic of the Stuart dynasty in England (1603-1714). A period of rapid change from early renaissance classicism to the more refined Georgian classicism.

STUD PARTITION An interior wall that separates adjacent rooms, built with slender vertical members (commonly 2x4s) separating the two surfaces of the wall.

THATCH Roof with reeds, palm fronds or similar material tightly bound in overlapping vertical courses.

TIMBER FRAME A method of construction in which walls are built of interlocking vertical and horizontal timbers creating spaces which are filled in or covered over to create walls.

TRANSOM LIGHT or TRANSOM WINDOW A small window or series of panes above a door.

TRAY CEILING Overhead surface of a room which conceals the roof timbers and is constructed with panels that parallel the angle of the room's rafters for a foot or more before the horizontal overhead surface begins. The ceiling thus is recessed into the roof and resembles an upside down serving tray.

VERNACULAR REVIVAL The return to traditional Bermudian architecture in the 1920s and 1930s.

VICTORIAN Strictly 1837-1901, but the style persisted rather longer in Bermuda. An architecturally eclectic period characterised by numerous "revivals". In Bermuda it is a period in which traditional simplicity gave way to increased ornamentation and foreign imitations.

WALLPLATE In early Bermuda construction, a wooden beam on top of the walls to support the rafters.

WELCOMING ARMS STEPS An outside flight of steps at right angles to the building and usually leading up to an entrance on the main floor. They were a characteristic of the 18th century and usually wider at the base than the top.

Index

Gurr, Frank, 36, 76
Gwynn, Ann, See Pindar, Ann Gwynn
Gwynn, Benjamin, 80
Gwynn, Joseph, 45, 80
Gwynn, Jr., Joseph, 80

H

H.A. & E. Smith's Store, 94
Halifax, Canada, 9
Hall, Gladwin, Appendix
Hamilton, Governor Henry, 22, 45, 120
Hamilton Parish, 2, 4, 91, 143, 151
Hamilton, Town, 7, 9, 18, 21, 78, 80, 83, 96, 104,
    121, 136
    Trinity Church, 32
    Water port, 47
    See also *Bermuda Gazette*
Hamilton Tribe, 137, 147, 149
Handy, Martha Pearman, 66
Handy, Thomas, 47, 66
Hannibal Lodge 224, 37
Harbours, See Castle Harbour, St. George
    Harbour
Harbour View, 100
Harding, Honora, 66
Hare, Major Thomas, 116
Harlow, John, 95–97
Harlow, Rachel, 95
Harris Bay, 152
Harris, Dr. Edward, 6, 18
Harris, Francis, 61
Harris, Jr., Francis, 62
Harris, Moses, 62
Harris, Jr., Moses, 62
Harvey, Agatha, 105
Harvey, Althea, 91
Harvey, Benjamin Dickinson, 91, 149
Harvey, Lucy, 102
    See also Harvey, Seth
Harvey, Samuel, 20
Harvey, Seth, 102
    See also Harvey, Lucy
Hay, William, 32
Haycock, Senator Noela, 55
Hayward, Andrew Cochrane, 94
    See also Hayward, Jane Campbell
Hayward, Anthony B., 79
Hayward, Benjamin Wright, 143
    See also Hayward, Elizabeth Cooper
Hayward, Charles A., 55
Hayward, Elizabeth Cooper, 143
    See also Hayward, Benjamin Wright
Hayward family, 149
Hayward, Herbert Hamilton, 146
Hayward, Jane, See Ming, Jane Hayward
Hayward, Jane Campbell, 94
    See also Hayward, Andrew Cochrane
Hayward, John, 148
    See also Hayward, Martha
Hayward, Joseph, 88
    See also Hayward, Martha Wright
Hayward, Captain Joseph, 148
Hayward, Jr., Joseph, 148
Hayward, Mayor Joseph Ming, 23, 79, 141
    Wife, 141
Hayward, Joseph William, 146
Hayward, Lillian H., 79, 83
Hayward, Martha, 148
    See also Hayward, John
Hayward, Martha Wright, 88

See also Hayward, Joseph
Hayward, Mary Ming, 79
Hayward, John S., 110
Hayward, Samuel, 146
Hayward, Thomas Seon, 143
Hayward, William, 92, 146
Hearse House, 31
Hen Island, 131
Herron, Alexander, 69
    See also Herron, Martha Mitchell
Herron, Martha, Mitchell, 69
    See also Herron, Alexander
Higgs, Benjamin, 37
Higgs Cottages, 110
Higgs, Eleanor, 59
    See also Higgs, William
Higgs, Elizabeth, See Green, Elizabeth Higgs
Higgs, Elizabeth Rankin, 100
    See also Higgs, Samuel Adams
Higgs, Henry E., 41
Higgs, Howard Roy, 100
Higgs Island, 55
Higgs, Jeremiah, 108
Higgs, John Darrell, 111
Higgs, Joseph, 48
Higgs, Robert, 48
Higgs, Richard Minor, 111
Higgs, Samuel Adams, 100
    See also Higgs, Elizabeth Rankin
Higgs, Samuel Rankin, 100
Higgs, William, 59
    See also Higgs, Eleanor
Higgs' Wharf, 48
Higinbothom, Eliza Prudden, 98
    See also Higinbothom, William
Higinbothom, Elizabeth, See Tucker, Elizabeth
    Higinbothom
Higinbothom family, 71
    Brothers, 42
Higinbothom, Reginald H., 81
Higinbothom, Richard, 78
Higinbothom, William, 98
    See also Higinbothom, Eliza
Hillcrest, 98–99, 106, 111
Hillside Cottage, 78
Hilton, Charity Briggs, 82
Hilton, John, 42
Hinson, Ann Forbes, 86
    See also Hinson, John
Hinson, Francis Forbes, 86, 125
Hinson, George, 86, 101
    See also Hinson, Sarah
Hinson, Georgianana Forbes, See Fleming,
    Georgiana Forbes Hinson
Hinson, John, 86
Hinson, Lucy, 86
Hinson, Mary, See Lough, Mary Hinson
Hinson, Mary Augusta, See Ball, Mary
    Augusta Hinson
Hinson, Nicholas,
Hinson, Sarah, 86
    See also Hinson, George
Hinson, Sarah Tucker,
    See Hubbard, Sarah Tucker Hinson
    See also Hinson, Nicholas
Hinson, Hon. Tudor, 44
Holland, Elizabeth, 67
    See also Holland, Reverend Dr. Thomas
Holland, Reverend Dr. Thomas, 67
    See also Holland, Elizabeth
Hollis, Dr. Austin, 116

Wife, 116
Hollis, Henry Hillgrove, 116
Hollis, Malcolm J.G., 140
Holmes, Alexander, 96
Honeyborne, Edward B., 110
Hope, Charlotte, 21
    See also Hope, Governor John
Hope, Governor John, 20, 21
    See also Hope, Charlotte
Horse racing, 136
Hotels, See Castle Harbour Hotel; Commercial;
    The George; Globe; Kennelly's Hotel;
    Redan Hotel; St.   George Hotel; St.
    George's Club; Somers Inn on King
    Square, Sommers Inn Hotel
House of Assembly, 40, 55, 123, 129
    See also Bermuda Assembly
Hubbard, Daniel, 89
    See also Hubbard, Sarah Tucker Hinson
Hubbard, Sarah Tucker Hinson, 89
    Daughters
        Jane, 89
        Rebecca, 89
    See also Hinson, Nicholas; Hubbard,
        Daniel
Hulbert, George Redmond, 41
Humpreys, John S., 143
Hunter Building, See Meyer Building
Hunter, Dr. Frederick A.S., 61, 101, 106
Hunter, Dr. Joseph S., 44, 80, 107
Hunter's Wharf, 40, 44, 45, 52, 54
Hurd, Captain Thomas, 49, 92
    Lieutenant, 120
Hurd's Channel, 128
Hutchings, N.W., 117
Hutchings, N.T., 152
Hutchinson, Dr. John, 108
Hutchinson, Dr. Joseph, 44, 61, 127
Hyland, William C.J., 35, 36, 4-9

I

Independent Company, 77, 82, 119
Independent Order of Good Samaritans, 66
    Rechab Lodge 7, 39
    Samaritans' Lodge, 39
    See also Samaritans' Cottages
Inglewood House, 153
Inglis, Albert, 48
Inglis, Bishop, 30
Inglis, Ellen, 100
Ireland Cove, 108
Ireland Island, 7, 108,120,130

J

James II, 74
James, Edward, 54
James, Robert, 87
James,.Robert Harley, 61, 102
James Burch House, 115
Jamestown, Virginia, 1, 2
Jefferson, Floyd, 153
    See also Jefferson, Marjorie
Jefferson, Marjorie, 153
    See also Jefferson, Floyd
Jehovah's Witnesses, 81
    Kingdom Hall Church, 81
Jennings, Ralph,
Jensen, Ole Edward, 86
Jenour, Rebecca, See Auchinleck, Rebecca

Index

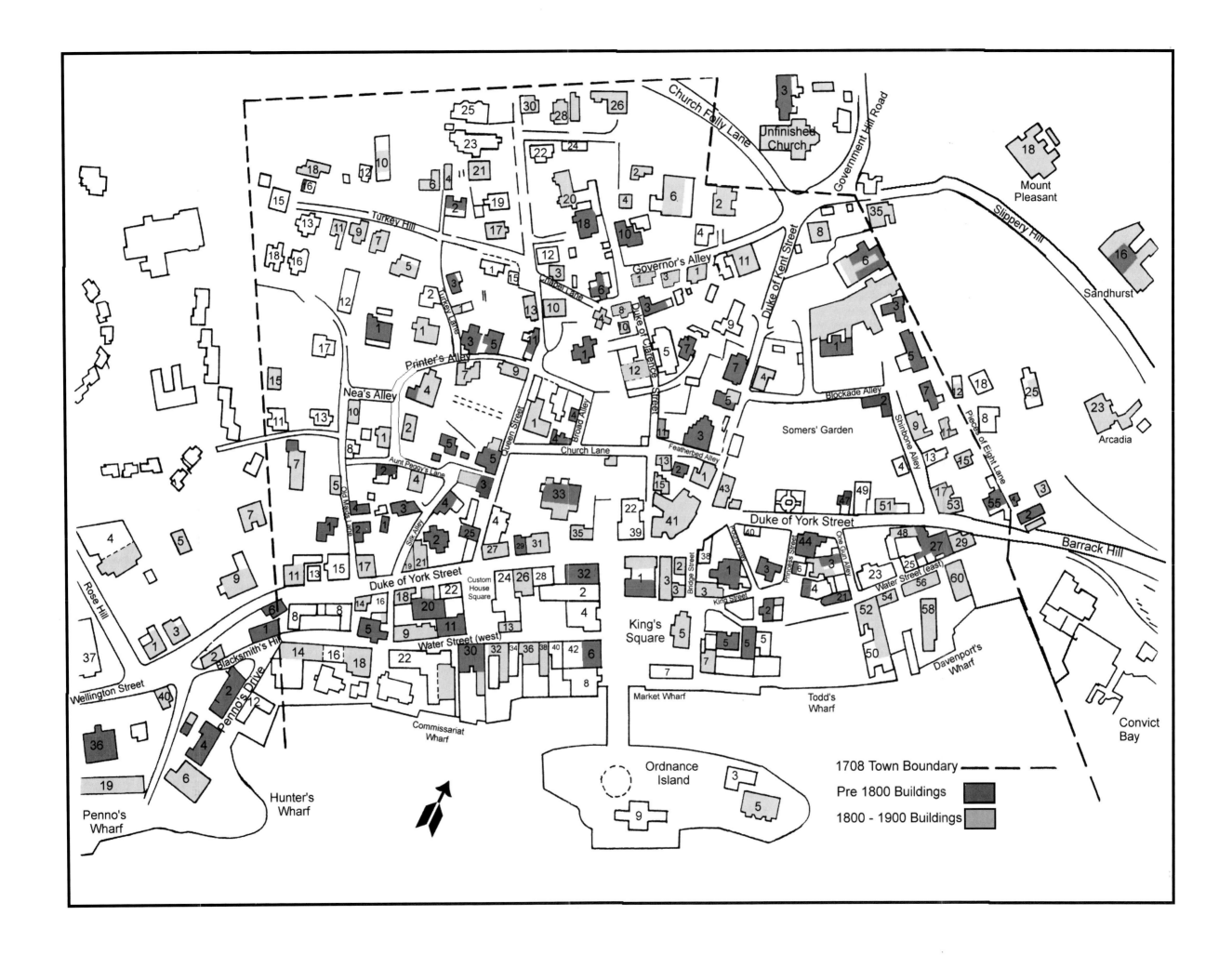

Church Folly Lane

Government Hill Road

Slippery Hill

Unfinished Church

Mount Pleasant

18

Sandhurst

16

Arcadia

23

Duke of Kent Street

Governor's Alley

Turkey Hill

Chapel Lane

Duke of Clarence Street

Printer's Alley

Nea's Alley

Blockade Alley

Somers' Garden

Shinbone Alley

Pieces of Eight Lane

Queen Street

Aunt Peggy's Lane

Featherbed Alley

Church Lane

Old Maid's Lane

Silk Alley

Barrack Hill

Duke of York Street

Rose Hill

Princess Street

One Gun Alley

Water Street (east)

Custom House Square

Bridge Street

King Street

Davenport's Wharf

Duke of York Street

Water Street (west)

King's Square

Blacksmith's Hill

Wellington Street

Penno's Drive

Commissariat Wharf

Market Wharf

Todd's Wharf

Convict Bay

Penno's Wharf

Hunter's Wharf

Ordnance Island

1708 Town Boundary ————

Pre 1800 Buildings ▪

1800 - 1900 Buildings ▪

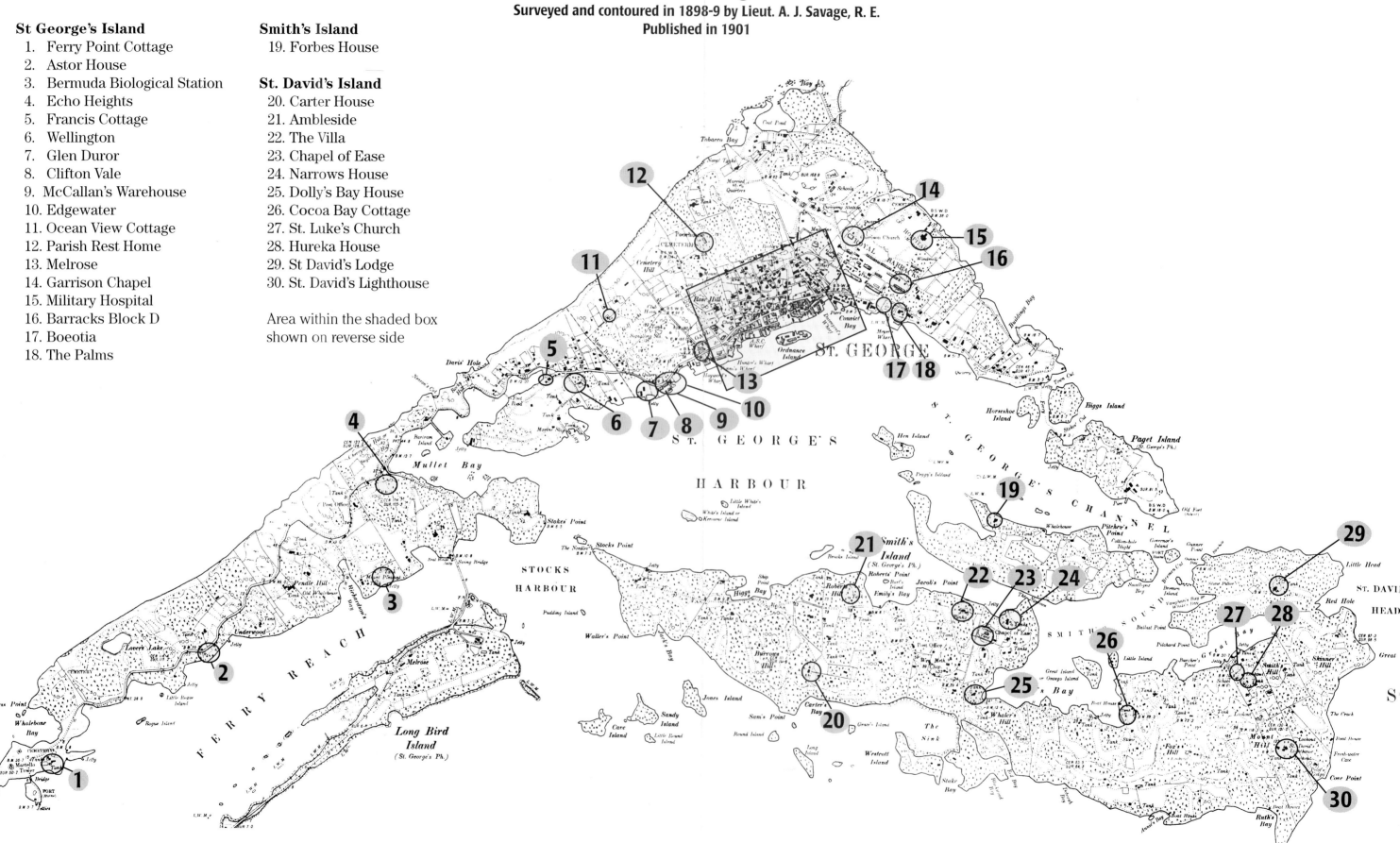

St. George's, St. David's and the Islands of St. George's Harbour

Surveyed and contoured in 1898-9 by Lieut. A. J. Savage, R. E.
Published in 1901

St George's Island
1. Ferry Point Cottage
2. Astor House
3. Bermuda Biological Station
4. Echo Heights
5. Francis Cottage
6. Wellington
7. Glen Duror
8. Clifton Vale
9. McCallan's Warehouse
10. Edgewater
11. Ocean View Cottage
12. Parish Rest Home
13. Melrose
14. Garrison Chapel
15. Military Hospital
16. Barracks Block D
17. Boeotia
18. The Palms

Smith's Island
19. Forbes House

St. David's Island
20. Carter House
21. Ambleside
22. The Villa
23. Chapel of Ease
24. Narrows House
25. Dolly's Bay House
26. Cocoa Bay Cottage
27. St. Luke's Church
28. Hureka House
29. St David's Lodge
30. St. David's Lighthouse

Area within the shaded box shown on reverse side